DRIVEN

I0337844

For Ali, who shared the journey

RICHARD BROINOWSKI
DRIVEN

A diplomat's auto-biography

ABC Books

The ABC 'Wave' device is a trademark of the Australian Broadcasting Corporation and is used under licence by HarperCollins*Publishers* Australia.

First published in Australia in 2009
by HarperCollins*Publishers* Australia Pty Limited
ABN 36 009 913 517
www.harpercollins.com.au

Copyright © Richard Broinowski 2009

The right of Richard Broinowski to be identified as the author of this work has been asserted by him in accordance with the *Copyright Amendment (Moral Rights) Act 2000*.

This work is copyright. Apart from any use as permitted under the *Copyright Act 1968*, no part may be reproduced, copied, scanned, stored in a retrieval system, recorded, or transmitted, in any form or by any means, without the prior written permission of the publisher.

HarperCollins*Publishers*
25 Ryde Road, Pymble, Sydney, NSW 2073, Australia
31 View Road, Glenfield, Auckland 0627, New Zealand
A 53, Sector 57 Noida, UP, India
77–85 Fulham Palace Road, London W6 8JB, United Kingdom
2 Bloor Street East, 20th floor, Toronto, Ontario M4W 1A8, Canada
10 East 53rd Street, New York NY 10022, USA

National Library of Australia Cataloguing-in-Publication data:

Broinowski, Richard P.
   Driven : an auto-biography / Richard Broinowski.
   1st ed.
   ISBN: 978 0 7333 2403 1 (pbk.)
   Includes index.
   Broinowski, Richard P.
   Diplomats – Australia – Biography.
   Ambassadors – Australia – Biography.
   Diplomatic and consular service, Australian – History.
   Automobiles – Anecdotes.
   Automobile driving – Anecdotes.
   Australia – Foreign relations – 20th century.
327.94092

Front cover photograph by Alison Broinowski
Back cover photograph by Jo Negrine-Aiello, JNP Studios
Cover design by Sarah Bull
Typeset in 11.5/18pt Berkeley by Kirby Jones

Contents

Introduction	1
An Obsession is Born	5
An Imp and a Prince in Japan	24
Into the Jaguar Jungle	47
Flashman Country	58
In an Antique Land	80
The Yellow Terror and a German Lemon	100
A Daimler and a Daihatsu in Canberra	119
Toyotas and Tanks	131
The Kimchi Olympics	155
Radio Static in Melbourne	177
Yank Tanks in Central America	197
Every Man Needs a Shed	219
Acknowledgements	241
References	242
Index	244

Introduction

My first motor car accident wasn't my fault. It was October 1972, and my wife Ali and I were driving our second-hand Beamer to a Halloween party in Tehran. The first snow of the season made the road slick. Round a blind corner came a Tehrani bus listing to one side with the weight of extra passengers hanging from doors and leaning suicidally into the sleet. It crabbed across the road towards me in sickening slow motion. We collided fairly gently, but the Beamer's bonnet crumpled. Ali seemed unhurt, and apart from a savage crack to my left knee hitting the dash, so did I. I staggered out and bargained with the driver over whose fault it was. My leverage was that I was foreign and dressed, for Halloween, as an Arab terrorist. But he had the moral authority of fifty indignant Tehrani passengers on his side. So I gave him a damp wad of rials, levered the Beamer's bonnet down, and on we went to the party. Later on that evening I blacked out on the dance floor from shock with a desert boot full of blood. I came to with a witch with chicken's feet dangling from her wrists binding up my torn knee.

That Beamer, a 1968 1800 four-door, was my first experience of German engineering — unimaginative, spartan but, thank God, built like a tank. It features in this story along with thirty-eight other cars that I have owned and loved, been frustrated by, or otherwise had access to during a 34-year career serving Australia as a diplomat in fourteen countries. The cars form the main narrative, but I have added to the story accounts of wildly varying road conditions, driving manners, standards of living, the engineering capacity of local mechanics, and the flavour of local politics.

Why focus a career memoir on motor cars? Well, the slow and subtle rhythms of diplomatic dialogues remembered over three decades are hardly page-turners to the reading public. Whereas motor cars have always been of universal interest — how fast they go, how well they handle, how beautiful or ugly they are. Since the advent of the horseless carriage at the beginning of the twentieth century in Europe and America, motor cars have become the most essential of household machines. But they are also capable of raising emotions of love, fascination, pride — or dread when they kill people. Some of my more effete colleagues would claim that motor cars are boring — simply means of transport. They usually own shabby, never-cleaned, anodyne conveyances and pretend not to care. Throughout automotive history, some motor cars have been specifically designed for them — from the mass-produced Model T Ford (you could have it in any colour so long as it was black), through to the average six-cylinder family sedans that increasingly choked Australian roads in the late twentieth century. But there is frequently an inverted snobbery about such

INTRODUCTION

people and their machines. In their own way, they are just as hooked on their cars as those who delight in style, grace and speed.

My own cars have been everything from anodyne to stylish. Early on they were selected strictly for economy — economy in purchase, economy in running. But as the years went on, car prices came down, technology improved and my personal budget expanded. So, after making sure that the children were clothed and fed, I could lash out a bit, especially where overseas diplomatic discounts kicked in. My cars have ranged from utilitarian to semi-luxurious, but always with a common thread: I never bought gas-guzzlers. Even my Jaguars had smallish engines and were tuned to extract the best possible mileage.

Cars supplied to me by the Commonwealth government during my career are a different story, and I'll come to those in due course.

1

An Obsession is Born

Like many other boys who grew up in Melbourne's Surrey Hills during the 1940s, my first cars were miniatures. I kept about 20 Dinky Toys neatly lined up on a shelf in my bedroom, together with a small mixed squadron of lead Spitfires, Hurricanes and Mustangs. I'd add to the collection when I'd saved up some pocket money, or received a Christmas windfall from an uncle. The cars were mainly British. Among them, I recall, were an Alvis, an Armstrong Siddeley, a Bristol, a Singer, a drop-head pre-war Jaguar and an assortment of Austins and Morrises. I was not aware of the money or class distinctions that might attach to the cars each model represented, and I valued them all equally. My mates had about the same number in their toy garages, and occasionally we might do a swap after a game of marbles. We'd push the cars around tracks carved out of the numerous sand heaps on building sites in the neighbourhood, or fly the planes over the ground, walking very slowly with a loud droning sound until in position for a strafing run over a German tank column.

You couldn't actually *drive* Dinky Toys of course, which was frustrating. But we did have custom-made billycarts and would race them down the steep Surrey Hills streets. My cart was a bright red engine my Dad had built. It had a brass funnel and a steering wheel with a system of pulleys and wires connecting it to the front axle. The wheels were cast iron with no traction on corners, so I'd often skid viciously into the concrete kerb when taking a corner sideways. I was fastidious about my engine and where to park it: none of the other kids had a carefully designated square of lawn over a metal grease pan in their front gardens marked as a 'garage'.

Cars were very important in our family, and, like other kids, I took vicarious pleasure in the cars my father, Philip, drove. My earliest memory is of him or my mother, Mary, driving a 1936 'New Ruby' Austin Seven two-door saloon. Mum was a rough driver who savagely worked the clutch during shopping forays to Camberwell Junction, causing the heads of three children to jerk backwards in unison. I don't recall other mothers driving, but Mum was a feminist before her time. Across the road, the Borden kids' father had a grey, pre-war 'peanut' model Willys with a squealing clutch that woke the birds up on winter mornings. The Addys down the road had one of the very first FJ Holden. Unlike these machines, our Austin was a light car, which would sway alarmingly when Dad hauled timber in a too-heavy trailer down Warrigal Road and the Nepean Highway to a house he was building at Frankston.

In 1950, when I was ten, Dad upgraded the family transport to a navy blue 1936 Light Six DY Twelve Vauxhall, with the characteristic fluted bonnet. It wasn't anything like the sporting Vauxhalls built in the early 1920s with their aluminium touring bodies, outside gear and brake levers, and it certainly didn't have the dash to set fearsome cross-country records for Indian maharajas and other members of the privileged international motoring cognoscenti. But it still had Vauxhall cachet and a distinctive exhaust note. I accompanied the family up the Hume Highway on its first big trip to Sydney in the summer of 1950. Though the weather was hot all the way, the car did not falter or overheat. I remember having the most deliciously cold lemon squash in the cool depths of a tiled country pub in Goulburn.

Dad had been working with Mum's four brothers at their lighting company, Kempthorne, in Collingwood. But he complained that their perpetual fighting gave him headaches, and in 1951 he joined an automotive paint company, Lusteroid, in South Melbourne. Among other customers, Lusteroid supplied a network of panel beaters and spray painters with lacquers and synthetic enamels throughout rural Victoria. Dad's sales area was Gippsland and he had a succession of company cars, which I thought made his job exceptionally glamorous. For a treat during school holidays, he'd take me or one of my two sisters on a 'country trip'. We'd drive east out of Melbourne along the Princes Highway, stopping to take orders from crash repairers in Pakenham, Warragul, Moe, Morwell, Traralgon, Rosedale, Sale, Stratford, Bairnsdale, Lakes Entrance, as far as Orbost. We'd stay in grand two-storey hotels with wide iron-filigreed balconies, where the common bathroom was at the end of the lino-floored hall. In the early mornings you could hear the heavy smokers coughing up their lungs: a sound that, to this day, takes me back to those hotels and the commercial travellers who frequented them.

Dad drove company-supplied Hillman Minxes on these trips. The Minx was a well-known and popular car in Australia at the time. After World War II the manufacturer of Humber, Hillman, Sunbeam and Singer cars, Sir Reginald Rootes, was under enormous pressure to export his cars to earn foreign currency in order to alleviate Britain's crippling war debt. Rootes did not export in volume until around 1948, and he then exported the full range of vehicles, from the small Hillman Minxes, through the Sunbeam Alpine sports cars to the substantial Humber Hawks and Super Snipe saloons. Australia was one of his target markets, although Britain's hopes were pinned on the much larger and more lucrative markets of North America.

Australian companies stocked their fleets with cars from the wide range of four-cylinder British cars pouring off the assembly lines in factories in the Midlands, including Austin A-40s and A-70s, Morris Oxfords and Minors, Standard Vanguards, and Hillman Minxes. Not that sentimentality or loyalty to the mother country played much of a part in their decisions — the British Commonwealth Preference system left them no choice.

I loved the first Hillman Minx Dad drove home — a metallic bronze 1948 Mark III model. Several country trips later, this was replaced by a re-styled Mark IV, and ultimately, a new 1953 Mark VI Minx smelling beautifully of fresh paint and plastic. All these Hillmans were squat, neat, square cars with monocoque bodies, said to be inspired by the postwar Studebaker body style, although I could never see the likeness. They were powered by four-cylinder side-valve engines of 1185 to 1265cc capacities, which propelled them from 0–50 miles per hour in the leisurely time of 24.2 seconds. They had column-mounted gear shifts, with top speeds of around 65 mph at an average fuel consumption of 35 miles per gallon. But, especially with the wind behind them, they hummed with little effort through the flat, golden-brown paddocks of Gippsland. Car radios were rare, as was air-conditioning, so on these trips I talked football or tennis with Dad, day-dreamed or sang songs with words adapted from the number plates of cars or trucks we passed.

The first major upheaval in our lives occurred in 1954, when Lusteroid's management moved Dad to Adelaide to start a new branch in South Australia. The family took its first ever flight, from Essendon Airport to Parafield, in a Trans Australia Airways Douglas DC3. I think we were in the air for the better part of three hours.

We bought a spacious and cool old Victorian double-fronted stone house on Goodwood Road, Redfern, in the southern suburbs. It had a galvanised iron roof, massive chimneys, fireplaces in the bedrooms, a wide hall straight down the middle, a wrap-around verandah, and stables and an orchard in the back. With my complete approval, Dad took out the fruit trees and built a lawn tennis court. This was bumpy, and sloped laterally to the western back fence next to our neighbour's chook farm. With an erratic bounce and a strong whiff of chicken shit in summer (depending which way the wind was blowing), concentrating on the game was difficult.

The next six years were the most agreeable of my short life so far. Not only did we have space and friends and a tennis court, but I did well enough at school to pass my Intermediate Certificate (at Prince Alfred College), gain a Commonwealth scholarship at the end of Leaving (at Unley High School), and begin to think about what to study at Adelaide University once I got there at seventeen.

I had also developed an audacious plan: aged fifteen, I intended to save enough money in twelve months to buy my own car. Every Saturday morning during 1955, I served petrol and oil to motorists at service stations, first at Day's Garage on Main North Road in Prospect, then at a Plume service station on Cross Road in Unley Park.

Serving petrol had its moments. The pumps were electrical, at least in urban areas, and did not require manual pumping into a glass reservoir before gravity drained the fluid into the petrol tank. But neither did they have automatic cut-off sensors when the tank was full, so the operator had to listen to the petrol gurgling up the inlet pipe and finely judge when to release the trigger. I used to dread the order from customers to 'Fill 'er up with a squirt of Redex, and check the battery, tyres and oil'. Many times I misjudged the crucial second and received an ear full of lead-infused petrol, before adding the upper cylinder lube and trudging around the car checking levels under the bonnet and tyre pressures. It's a wonder I didn't go deaf or develop cancer of the ear.

At the age of fifteen years and nine months, I had saved nearly £50. Only three months until I could get a licence, a very easy challenge in those days: answer a short questionnaire about the rules of the road. There were no driving tests, no P or L plates, or zero tolerance towards new drivers for drinking, no points lost for driving transgressions. The only sensitivity Adelaide police seemed to have towards me was about my age. I was pulled over in North Terrace one day shortly after getting my licence by police unconvinced that I was legally old enough to drive.

But I get ahead of myself. What car should I buy? I wanted something small and light, not too heavy on petrol or running costs. A Renault 750 or Fiat 1100 would have been cool, but these were too new and too expensive. I would have to choose between older second-hand British cars — perhaps a Morris 8 or a Singer, an Austin or a Ford Anglia.

Meanwhile, while making it clear that he wouldn't be helping me with finance, Dad helped by pointing me in the direction of his more reliable contacts in the used car trade who would not rip me off. And one of these happened along at the crucial moment to offer me what he and Dad both claimed was an ideal vehicle for a young bloke of my age and experience — a 1928 canvas-topped, two-door, four-seater Austin Seven 'Chummy'. It was a proper car in miniature. It had a straight-four, side-valve engine of 747 cc, a wheelbase of just under two metres, a Duplex roller timing chain, a Borg and Becker clutch, an 'H' gated gear movement with three forward speeds and reverse (no synchromesh), a gravity-fed updraft carburettor which hissed importantly as we bounced along the road, a six-volt electrical system, dynamo, and a cut-off regulator. It was light, rugged, and easy on the petrol and maintenance.

My Austin Seven had iconic status. The man it was named after, Herbert Austin, had been an engineer. He started his car company at Longbridge outside Birmingham in 1905, after having been a troubleshooter for the Wolseley Sheep Shearing Machine Company in Australia. Herbert's company logo was a winged wheel, symbolising freedom and style. Like all British motor manufacturers at the time, his factory had made artillery shells, lorries, ambulances, aircraft and tin hats during World War I, only returning to his nascent motor car assembly line in 1918. But the world economy slipped into recession, and his new model Twenty failed to attract sufficient sales to avoid receivership, which happened in 1921.

But the following year, against the judgment of the board of directors and a large proportion of the workforce, Herbert and his designers came up with their model Seven. As Henry Ford's Model T had done in America, this car revived the company and Britain's car industry. Austin Sevens began coming off the Longbridge production line in 1922, and, with variations, continued until 1939. They were licensed and copied the world over. In Germany, the first BMW model — the Dixi — was an Austin Seven, as was the original American Austin. In France, Austin Sevens were made and sold as Rosengarts. In Japan, Nissan copied the Seven design, without licence, as its first car. And in Britain itself, the founder of Jaguar cars, William Lyons, then making sidecars for motorbikes, began to buy Austin Seven chassis and engines and re-bodying them with sleek new shells. His Austin Seven Swallow was very popular among middle-class British punters.

I knew none of this when I bought my Austin. I loved it for what it was, for its neatness and the freedom it gave me to come and go as I wished. I drove it to Unley High School, where I met my first girlfriend, Elizabeth Butcher. Liz was very useful in giving me a push start when the battery was flat and there was no convenient hill to park it on. I allowed a mad speed freak friend of Dad's to take me on a racing circuit after he had conned me into believing the Austin Seven was a wonderful racing machine (as indeed, properly tweaked and adjusted, it could be, but not mine at that moment). I was mortified as he drove the car flat out around the back streets of Brompton, its little engine screaming in anguish.

But I should have known the car's pedigree, and given it the respect its heritage demanded by restoring it, as other Austin Seven enthusiasts have done before and since. Another petrol-head, Chris Conybeare — a colleague in Foreign Affairs and later secretary of immigration in Canberra — recently told me how in his youth he had lovingly given his Seven a bare metal re-spray in its original colours, which he had carefully researched, and restored its interior. I did neither. Dad and I did re-spray my car at the Lusteroid factory on Port Road, Adelaide, but we chose a light, unauthentic grey, and drove the car home before it was properly dry, causing the body surface to be slightly pitted by a light rain. I also committed the solecism of dressing up the wheels with fake chrome hubcaps, and allowing my little sister, Susie, the undignified licence to christen my Austin 'Elmo', for reasons known only to her.

I had Elmo for about a year. I sold it after a particularly messy episode when I had to replace the torn fabric universal joint disc connecting the drive shaft to the rear wheels before taking Liz to a school dance. I finished the job just as it was getting dark, and turned up to collect Liz still with grease on my hands and a spotty face — not an attractive sight.

I gradually fell out of love with Elmo because of its mechanical problems. But the relief I felt at selling it lasted a very short time, and I soon hankered for another car. My testosterone-addled brain had not yet grasped the fact that — despite Dad's prompting — I needed to be financially solvent to run a car. Up till then, I somehow got by on pocket money to fill the petrol tank.

In 1958, during my first year at Adelaide Law School, I bought a navy blue 1936 Austin Ten. Called the 'Sherbourne' saloon, it was the predecessor to the famous post-war Austin A40 Devon. It had a pressed steel body on a cross-braced chassis, an 1125 cc four-cylinder side-valve engine, four doors, a divided rear window, and it could, when the mood took it, reach a speed of 60 mph while consuming 34 mpg. It was a neat car, but my love affair with it was tepid and short-lived. For one thing, when it warmed up, the clutch would slip. It was not much fun driving up some hill in Adelaide with a girl I wanted to impress to find the speed diminish to a walking pace as the engine revs rose to shrieking point. Maintaining sangfroid, I discovered, was difficult under these conditions.

Besides, my imagination was now being captured by the possibilities of driving an altogether more splendid motor car — my father's 1952 FX Holden. Apart from the tennis court, the best thing about our new living arrangements was that Dad now had a powerful black beauty — a company-supplied 1952 six-cylinder FX Holden. First released to an eager Australian public in November 1948 as the 48/215, the FX was promoted by its parent company, General Motors-Holden's, as 'Australia's Own Car'.

Well, yes and no. Certainly, the car was named after James Alexander Holden, who had founded a booming leather and saddlery business in Adelaide in 1854. When in 1917 the federal government considered the German U-boat threat to Australian shipping so grave that it restricted auto imports to engines and chassis (mainly from the USA), James' son, Henry, started building motor car bodies in 1917 to bolt on to the imported chassis. In 1931, Holden's Motor Body Builders Limited, as it was now called, merged with General Motors to become General Motors-Holden's.

The Great Depression that began in the late 1920s nearly bankrupted GM-H, as well as its parent company in Detroit. But demand for motor cars in both countries picked up in 1935, and from then until war broke out again in 1939 GM-H expanded by acquiring a Melbourne plant at Fishermens Bend to add to its Woodville plant in Adelaide, a spare parts division called NASCO, and a Sydney facility at Marrickville.

The driving force behind this expansion was Laurence Hartnett, an English migrant who had become managing-director of GM-H in 1934. With only reluctant support from Detroit, Hartnett was determined to build a car in Australia specifically for Australian conditions — neither as ponderous as American imports nor as small and underpowered as the cars from Britain. As soon as the war ended, he sent a team of GM-H engineers to Detroit to learn about tooling, design and engineering. By October of 1946, they had produced three prototypes which were first road-tested at GM's Milford Proving Ground 65 kilometres east of Detroit.

In December 1946, Hartnett was relieved of the project by a GM Board suspicious of his independence, but the project continued. In great secrecy, the three prototypes and about 90 Australian and American engineers sailed to Australia on a chartered vessel, the *Wanganella*. It berthed in Sydney and on New Year's Day 1947 the cars were driven under cover of night down the Hume (not the busiest Australian highway at that time, especially at night) to Fishermens Bend. GM-H had no proving ground, so throughout 1947 and 1948, as GM-H factories were tooling up for mass production, the three prototypes, together with two more assembled in Australia, were thrashed along various road surfaces around outer eastern Melbourne as far as Ferntree Gully, Belgrave, Monbulk, Emerald and Selby. The press was sworn to secrecy, and the public, when curious enough to ask what the cars were, were told 'small Chevrolets'. Finally, on 29 November 1948, Australia's prime minister, J. B. Chifley, launched the car at a public display in Melbourne, and named it the Holden.

The Australian driving public, including my father and I, loved the car's power, ruggedness and manoeuvrability. It was suitable not only for newly elevated managers of paint companies, but their commercial travellers as well as taxi drivers, doctors, solicitors, dentists, their families, and farmers who used their Holdens for paddock work or sheep droving, especially when their British Small Arms (BSA) Bantam — a popular two-stroke British postwar motorbike always painted green — broke down.

When I was in final year at high school and during my first year at Adelaide Law School, Dad would let me drive the Holden under his supervision, usually on the leisurely country road south from Adelaide down to our seaside place at Sellicks Beach. One early morning not long afterwards, however, as I was hounding Dad to get up and drive me to my violin lesson in Colonel Light Gardens, he handed me the keys and grunted at me to drive myself. So, increasingly, I did — to violin lessons, to take my ailing grandmother, Dais, on outings when no one else in the family wanted to, and — best of all — to take girls out on dates.

My father died suddenly in December 1960, aged fifty-one, of cancer almost certainly caused by the asbestos cement sheets he used to build our beach house. Two years before his death, he traded the FX in on a new company car, a 1958 FC Holden. Lower, wider, with a more powerful engine than the FX, it was a nondescript light grey. Dad instructed the painters at the factory to paint the turret a brilliant yellow. The car then looked like a taxi, but it certainly advertised Lusteroid paints. He died, and we grieved, and my mother Mary never got over the loss of her soul partner.

Before her own premature death in 1968, Mary bought herself another Holden, a white 1961 EK model. In Melbourne she had trained as an interior designer, and during our happy days in Adelaide before Dad's death, had been hired to do the interiors for the new Queen Elizabeth Hospital. When Dad died, she was determined to keep herself busy, and was hired by the South Australian Agricultural Department as a Country Women's Extension Officer. She drove her EK all over the state, talking to womens' groups about interior design.

During my law studies I completed two years of articles with Genders Wilson and Bray of Weymouth Street, and was fortunate to be able to drive Mary's car whenever I needed it. My boss was Alexander Forbes Genders, but I did a lot of work for two of the other six other partners as well — John Jefferson Bray, QC, (later chief justice of South Australia), and Pamela Mary Cleland. Pam was one of Adelaide's more colourful divorce and criminal lawyers. A timelessly attractive ash blonde, she gained notoriety by appearing nude when she put out her garbage, and hosting some wild parties at her home in Burnside. I appeared for some of her clients at Adelaide police and local courts, and visited some of her less successful ones at Yatala labour prison north of Adelaide. So I could visit Yatala, Pam would lend me her 1960 Citroen Goddess DS, a sleek, black, futuristic French car with a white fibreglass roof, hydropneumatic suspension and a vertical six engine. It raised itself weirdly on its haunches when you turned on the ignition, and as I drove up Main Northeast Road to Yatala I could believe I was Charles de Gaulle en route to the presidential palace in Paris.

I graduated from law school in 1961, and after admission to the South Australian Supreme Court Bar in 1963, joined the Department of External Affairs in Canberra as a cadet diplomat. This was my second upheaval, even more dramatic than the move from Melbourne. I arrived in Canberra in March, two months after most of the other cadets in the intake had found accommodation. The delay was due to a trip I took to India in January and February as part of a National Union of Australian University Students (NUAUS) delegation. But Geoff Bentley and Malcolm Campbell were still at the Kurrajong, a national hostel close to the parliamentary triangle where Prime Minister Ben Chifley had had permanent lodgings. Both Bentley and Campbell were sick and tired of the control freaks, the moral guardians, who ran it. No guests, women or men, were allowed to remain overnight in the rooms, and there could be no drinking, let alone fun and games. The three of us decamped and found a cramped house on Banks Street, Yarralumla, and drew straws for the two rudimentary bedrooms and a sleepout at the back. I scored the sleepout.

Australia's capital city was a thoroughly unfinished place. Laid out on a vast windswept plain, it still had an air of emptiness, completely uncivilised by the rich tapestry of Australian city living. It was a grey, bureaucratic town, freezing in winter, remorselessly hot in summer. Lake Burley Griffin had not yet filled, and there was a temporary wooden bridge on Commonwealth Avenue over the Molonglo, leading from south Canberra where the bureaucrats worked into Civic, where the few shops and restaurants were. External Affairs shared accommodation in the Stalinesque administration building in Parkes with Defence, Trade, and a host of other fledgling Commonwealth departments.

When not working at various 'desks' or sections in the department, the twelve cadets in the 1963 intake attended language classes at the ANU (I studied Japanese with Professor Joyce Ackroyd), or lectures in the department on arcane matters such as diplomatic drafting. I worked at two desks, the first in the Legal and Treaties Branch where, under the department's always cheerful principal legal advisor Alf Body, I attempted to determine more precisely how the boundary between Australian and Dutch New Guinea could be defined along the Bensback River and the Fly River bulge. My second desk, in 1964, was in the SEATO Aid Branch, where we dispensed 'material assistance' — that is, barbed wire and galvanised roofing sheets — to the Republic of Vietnam for American 'Strategic Hamlets'; in truth concentration camps for peasants which allowed free-fire zones in the vacated areas that were spreading like a cancer across the green southland.

I was frankly disappointed at the tedium of these first two jobs, the first overburdened by finicky technical detail, the second associated with what I uneasily suspected at the time was a gross violation of Vietnamese human rights. The tedium was alleviated by perpetual speculation about who would be posted overseas, when and where. There were also Friday night booze-ups at the Wellington hotel in Kingston, the original Canberra Yacht Club (now under Lake Burley Griffin), and at the back bar of the Canberra Hotel (now the Hyatt) on Commonwealth Avenue. There was amateur theatre, skiing at Perisher and Thredbo, waterskiing on Lake George (amazing as it may seem today, in 1964 it was full of water), or escaping to Sydney on weekends.

Sometime in 1964 I was told that Charlie Nichol, a former commodore of the Canberra Yacht Club, had eaten a live spider for a dare. Without thinking, I said I'd do the same. Miraculously, a large glass jar of huntsman spiders obtained from the CSIRO materialised during the week on the club bar under a sign, 'Monster Spider Eating Contest'. The spiders fought and devoured each other during the week preceding the event, leaving one fat specimen with five legs still intact. On the Friday night of the contest the bar was crowded and a TV crew had come from Sydney. Nervous, queasy but defiant, I made my way to the bar. Several punters informed me that they had a syndicate that was betting I wouldn't go through with it. Another group told me that they had a lot of money riding on my eating the spider. I hoped that the practice I had done during the week of slamming peanuts against my teeth, biting and swallowing as fast as I could, would help. When the time came, to the accompaniment of much barracking, I shook the spider out on the bar, grasped it firmly, inserted it against my molars, crunched it and gulped it down. A gin and tonic quickly followed. The spider tasted juicy and musty, like a badly ventilated cellar. I received an ornate certificate stating in solemn prose that I had indeed eaten the spider — mandibles, poison sac, abdomen and all. Sadly the certificate was lost many years ago during one of my numerous house moves.

This interlude interrupted my search for a suitable car. I had now been in Canberra for six months without one. Public transport in Canberra was almost non-existent. Even getting into Civic from the department at lunchtime was impossible without a car or cadging a lift. And very importantly, I couldn't pursue an increasingly serious relationship with Alison Woodroffe, the only woman in the 1963 Foreign Service intake.

I had a meagre surplus of cash from my very junior grade public service salary but I wanted a quality British machine. Tony Bishop, a fellow student at Adelaide Law School, occasionally drove his 1937 Jaguar SS Tourer to lectures. I loved it and lusted after it. Blood red, it had leather bucket seats, a walnut fascia, sleek bodywork and a subdued but powerful exhaust note. But I knew I could not afford anything in that class: Jaguars were too rich for my budget. However, there was the Riley, with a pedigree almost as good. Reg Little from Melbourne, another cadet, already had a maroon 2.5 litre Riley. A health freak rather than a petrol-head, Reg kept a sack of oats on the rear seat, and would occasionally strain a handful through his beard for breakfast or lunch.

The Riley had a long and honourable history. William Riley, who started a bicycle-making company in Coventry in 1896, diversified into constant-mesh gearboxes and detachable wheels for Austro-Daimlers, Hispano Suizas, Mercedes, Napiers and Rolls Royces. Riley motor cars were then developed, and throughout the 1920s and 1930s they took vigorous part in European road races. In 1934, Rileys took second, third, fifth and sixth places for 1500 and 1100 cc classes at Le Mans. Rising from a war-damaged factory that made weapons and munitions, the company launched its new and vastly improved series in 1945. In 1948 Riley's owners, Nuffield, decided to move the company from Coventry to Abington to join MG — the idea being to put the two specialist sporting names together under the one roof.

I found my Riley at a used car yard in 'petrol alley', also known as Mort Street, in Braddon. It was a beauty — a black 1951 1.5 litre saloon, long and lithe, with four doors and a fabric-covered roof. The headlights were faired into the inner valances of the rounded wings. It had walnut-capped doors and a walnut instrument board, nicely balanced independent front suspension, and rack-and-pinion steering. I kept it clean and polished at Banks Street, Yarralumla, and visited Ali frequently at the house she shared with three other cadets in Wickham Crescent, Red Hill. We often went on romantic and racy drives out to the Cotter River or down to the coast to Batemans Bay.

I drove the Riley to Adelaide in December 1963 for my wedding to Alison. My groomsman, Graham Patterson, an education officer in Papua New Guinea, and Margaret Ochiltree, a public servant in Canberra, went with me. The generator mounting on top of the engine broke in Narrandera on the Sturt Highway in New South Wales, but we had it welded together and arrived in Adelaide in time for the nuptials. Sharing the driving, Ali and I then journeyed to an uncle's house in Sorrento in Victoria for our honeymoon, and then back to Adelaide to pick up surplus luggage, before heading back to Canberra along the Sturt. A fierce summer tailwind kept the engine near boiling, and we had to stop and refill the radiator at creeks along the highway to keep it from seizing up.

Before being posted to Tokyo in January 1965, I sold the Riley to a colleague, Tony Dingle. I was sad to hear that soon after he bought it, the engine blew up. It was no one's fault and could not have been predicted, but it was bad luck for Tony. He took the incident philosophically, and to his credit we remained on speaking terms throughout our careers.

2

An Imp and a Prince in Japan

Ali and I left the Canberra summer behind in December 1964, and flew to Japan via Hong Kong, where we had to stock up on tailor-made clothes, shoes and linen. We'd been married for twelve months and had few household goods. We'd been told that Japanese stores had no clothes big enough for *gaijin*, except those that stocked extra large sizes for sumo wrestlers. But these had no style and little choice, especially for women.

We arrived at Haneda (Feather Field) airport on a freezing winter's morning. Everything in sight was grey, and snow swirled across the tarmac. Kato san, an embassy driver, met us in a new, black EH Holden that had been chosen by the trade staff as a fleet car. It was rugged enough for driving conditions in Tokyo, and it was supposed to show off Australia's automobile technology to the Japanese. But since the war, they had already reverse-engineered most American cars, so all the Embassy Holdens demonstrated in Japan was that the Americans were making reasonably good cars in Australia.

Kato san drove us to the Azabu Prince Hotel, just behind the German Embassy. Originally the residence of a Meiji-era baron, it was about eighty years old. Low and rambling, it had a heavy pantile roof, sliding doors, polished floors, and tatami (rice straw) mats. There were tiny, enclosed courtyards, and outside, snow-laden pine trees were propped up with straw and bamboo poles. We felt we had stepped backwards in time to a less polluted era. Indeed, it was at first the only building that fitted our conceptions of Japan, which were fixed firmly in the pre-industrial Tokugawa period of the mid-nineteenth century. Everything else seemed monochrome, postwar and industrially ugly.

Above the double bed in our room were two admonitions: 'Leave your valuable article at the front desk!' and 'There will be earthquake drill. Guests should not evacuate themselves!' Their English, however, was better than our Japanese (I'd had a year of part-time study in Canberra, and Ali had had none). We both started Japanese lessons in our first week in Tokyo and kept on studying for years, determined not to perpetuate the monolingual Australian tradition. I attended a pressure-cooker school in the commercial complex of Shibuya near the embassy in Minato ward. I found it a difficult language, with everything back to front and the verb at the end. Meanwhile, since the 1964 Olympics young Japanese were trying hard to use their limited English, sometimes with bizarre results: a moonstruck Japanese youth followed Ali's pretty blonde cousin around for days when she visited, finally summoning the courage to tell her, 'You are so beautiful it makes my heart leap'. I later did exams run by the British Embassy on their squash court that smelled of stale sweat and jock straps. Not a pleasant experience.

Wide-eyed on that first morning in Tokyo, we went out walking around Azabu, a suburb in Minato ward south of the

Imperial Palace. We breathed the sharp, smoky air and tried to make sense of signs in *kanji* (Chinese-derived characters) and *kana* (phonetic script). Opposite the hotel we found a brown baseball diamond in a small stand of ancient trees. Down the hill were a shrine and a small temple, restaurants and shops in the Juban village street, and around the corner the little Azabu convenience store. In little back streets, twisted ceremonial straw ropes hung across the wooden doorways of small wooden houses. They had been left by Shinto priests in New Year purification ceremonies, with little piles of salt on either side of each doorway, and bright orange *mikan* (mandarins) as the fruit of the season. On Aoyama-dori, an upmarket Kinokuniya supermarket had just been opened, and it proudly advertised 'chemically grown' produce — reassuring shoppers that no organic fertilisers were involved — with prices to match this modern advance. But with an exchange rate at the time of 400 yen to the Australian dollar, most things in Tokyo were dirt cheap. (At the time of writing, the Australian dollar was worth about ninety yen.)

In the afternoon of the first day I set off to present myself at the Australian Embassy, an easy walk from the Azabu Prince down narrow streets, across two-lane Meguro-dori, over the stone bridge — Ninohashi — that crossed a noxious creek, and up a small hill into Mita ward. Mita had been a fishing village before land reclamation pushed it inland, and there were once water views from the hill where the Australian, Italian and French embassies stood, with Keio University just below. It was a beautiful area because the embassies had preserved the gardens of the original wealthy Japanese owners.

The embassy was opposite the Mita Buddhist temple in Tsunamachi. Behind a high, tiled wall was a new, modern, three-storeyed, 1960s chancery or office building. To one side were three square grey houses with lawns and small gardens for senior embassy officers. A block of flats for secretarial staff — 'the girls' — had been built beside a clay tennis court. The Ambassador's residence was a two-storeyed Victorian pile with an ivy-covered porte-cochère. The original Japanese owner had brought the design back from England, but to the dark wood-panelled reception rooms he had added stained-glass window panes depicting the animals of the Chinese and Japanese zodiac. Upstairs, there were some tatami rooms, one facing south-west with a Fuji-viewing window in the shape of the mountain. On the day after a typhoon, the air cleared enough to see it, an amazing and rare sight as it hovered, framed in the window, above the horizon.

The residence overlooked a lawn ringed with azaleas and ancient cherry trees that coloured the air a delicate pink a couple of months after I arrived. Below was a forest with winding paths, stone lanterns and engraved rocks. One commemorated the spring where Shinto priests in the Edo period (1600–1868) had given the baby son of the Lord of Mita his natal bath. In crowded, modernising Tokyo, the whole property, but particularly the garden, was a sanctuary that had survived the bombing, a priceless piece of Japanese heritage given to Australia as war reparations. Many Australians who had worked there, as well as the Japanese priests across the road to whom we had repeatedly assured its preservation, were disgusted thirty years later when the Keating government sold most of it as part of an effort to balance the Australian budget. (The budget surplus was later returned in the form of reduced taxes on beer and cigarettes.)

First Secretary Philip Peters took me around to meet some of the embassy staff. As Australian missions went, Tokyo was a large one, with around twenty Australians and maybe thirty locally engaged staff. I was introduced to the ambassador, Sir Lawrence McIntyre, a courtly and wise diplomat who had been in the service since its inception at the end of the war, and then Political Counsellor Jim Jamieson, a former naval intelligence officer and Japanese interpreter. I met the military attaché, senior trade commissioner, senior administrative officer, the vice-consul, and as many of the locally engaged Japanese staff as could be found. Three junior colleagues at my level were Reg Little, now a full-time language student, Jim Short, a junior trade commissioner, and another political officer, David Parker.

Quite soon after my arrival, Sir Lawrence retired and was replaced by Sir Allen Brown, former head of the Department of Prime Minister and Cabinet, and one of Sir Robert Menzies' main fixers. Sir Allen was shrewd, and he knew much more about the political dynamics of Canberra than any foreign service officer serving overseas. He called us together and explained in so many words that he had spent his time at the coalface, and regarded his new position as a reward for the hard yards he had done in Canberra. (This was not the general view in Canberra of a posting to Tokyo.) He was not a professional diplomat, nor did he speak Japanese. But the Japanese Foreign Ministry highly respected his former status and influence in Canberra, and, assisted by a good interpreter, he made some effective representations during his tenure. (Except for sophisticated types who had served in London, Japanese officials never really got the hang of British honours. They inevitably addressed Sir Allen as 'Sir Blown'.)

There was a great deal for Sir Allen and his staff to make representations about, especially on the economic front, where Australian traders and miners were just beginning to see massive commercial opportunities for mineral and agricultural exports to Japanese markets. Japan's astonishingly rapid economic recovery owed as much as anything to restoration of the *zaibatsu*, the commercial oligarchies like Mitsubishi, Mitsui and Sumitomo that had built Japan's war machine, and to the massive American orders that had flowed into Japan at the beginning of the 1950s for trucks and military hardware to equip US troops fighting in the Korean War. These led in turn to an explosive expansion of Japanese shipbuilding, construction and heavy machinery industries. As a consequence, by the early 1960s Japanese steel companies were hungry for iron ore and coking coal, for which Australian mines were increasingly seen as a likely and geographically proximate source.

By 1965 a major part of Japan's postwar reconstruction, at least in the big cities, was complete, and the rail infrastructure between them had already surpassed anything in Australia. Japanese traditionally built new capitals every few hundred years, and wars, fires and earthquakes had made the people accustomed to urban destruction and renewal. Rather than bemoaning this impermanence however, the Japanese accepted with resilience the destruction and replacement of old buildings, even those of great significance. Alongside modern office blocks, artisans clad in jodhpurs and split-toe canvas boots, would — precariously balanced on bamboo scaffolding — painstakingly build shrines and pagodas using exactly the same tools and materials and in exactly the same style as the structures that had stood before them.

My posting also occurred at a time of significant demographic change in Tokyo. During the Meiji period (1868–1912), three quarters of the Japanese population had been farmers and fishers, and the rest city-dwellers. That had changed somewhat under the Taisho Emperor (1912–1926), but in twenty frantic years after World War II, the balance was completely reversed. People rushed into the cities to fill new jobs in rapidly expanding new industries, packing into dormitories and jerry-built apartments in miles of dreary suburbs that spread out across the flat farmlands. The fingers of railways poked through forested mountains, beckoning country people to leave their villages and become commuters. In the cities, many worked day and night for what Gavan McCormack of the Australian National University later called 'the construction state', building overhead highways, underground railways, bridges and ports. By 1965, Tokyo had the most polluted air, and some of the most congested roads, in the world.

I began my posting to Tokyo in the middle of Japan's accelerating trajectory from destruction to prosperity, from international humiliation to economic miracle. The Tokyo Olympics of 1964 had shown the world what Japan could do, restored national pride, and transformed the city. Kenzo Tange's magnificent Olympic architecture included his soaring swimming stadium and gymnasium complex at Yoyogi, opposite the gardens and shrine that commemorate the modernising emperor, Meiji. A modern cultural centre, the Ueno Bunka Kaikan, had been built in the city's northeast, and the first of Tokyo's skyscrapers, daringly engineered with very deep piers and innovative aseismic structures to survive earthquakes, was built at Kasumigaseki in 1968. The building had a smooth face with nothing hanging off it that might fall onto pedestrians in the event of an earth tremor. Similar skyscrapers were planned for the large commercial sub-centres of Shinjuku and Shibuya. Meanwhile, on the city's outskirts, construction companies were paving over every available rice paddy they could find, 'correcting' rivers with concrete banks, redistributing hillsides, and building zigzag roads over mountains.

I was intrigued by the energy of it all, and my main job was to help keep tabs on what was happening. I researched and reported on the main doings of the Japanese political parties, trade unions and emerging religious parties. I was early on struck by the similarities between Japanese and Australian political parties. The conservative Liberal Democratic Party was similar in conviction (and political longevity) to Robert Menzies' Liberal–Country Party Coalition. The Japan Socialists had characteristics in common with the Australian Labor Party, and the Social Democrats to the Democratic Labor Party. Only Komeito, the political wing of the Nichiren Buddhist sect Sokka Gakai, had no Australian parallel. Where the Japanese parties differed, however, was in their factionalism, a system that went back to ancient tribal loyalty. If a Japanese prime minister was ignominiously dumped as leader of the LDP, he could still exercise considerable political power if he headed a major faction in the Diet, or Japanese parliament. And Diet members from backwoods prefectures, if they were members of powerful factions, could spout the most racist, sexist or xenophobic nonsense in public without fear of expulsion or censure.

I was also a kind of protocol officer — a meeter and greeter, a buffer at the embassy between my ambassador and the outside world. Otherwise engaged in my office, my response to a call from the front desk to greet one of the ambassador's visitors was hair-trigger: grab coat, scoot down stairs, skid sideways around corner to residence entry, take deep breath, slow down, meet guest with aplomb as he alights from his vehicle, escort with deference to the ambassador's study where Ambassador (and sometimes Lady) Brown await, retreat to office in dignified manner.

On New Year's Day in 1966 Ali and I joined Sir Allen and Lady Brown and other staff to greet the emperor and his family at the Imperial Palace. The occasion called for hats and gloves and long dresses for women, morning suits for men. The procedure was as formal as the dress: enter reception hall, respectfully follow diagonal carpet in measured stride to dais, bow to Imperial Family arranged woodenly on same, show silent respect without eye contact for five seconds, retreat backwards with downcast gaze on other carpet to exit, repair to buffet breakfast of rice cakes and sake, collect *kagami-mochi* (rice cakes imprinted with the imperial seal), wrap them in a *furoshiki* (cloth napkin), go home.

On the afternoon of that same New Year's Day, I set off to climb Mount Fuji with Adrian Hohler, a colleague from the British Embassy. Now empty after a crowded rubbish-strewn summer, the slopes were glazed with slippery blue ice from which a bitter wind had blown the covering snow. The climb required crampons, ice axe, and unrelenting concentration. A fall would have resulted in an unimpeded accelerating slide to an abrupt death on rocks hundreds of metres below. Sleepless and feeling nauseous from lack of oxygen, we camped in freezing conditions at the sixth station before making a pre-dawn foray to the top. We reached the crater just before the sun rose. It was a glorious winter morning with the Honshu seaboard spread out 3500 metres beneath us — one place in Japan, I exultantly thought, where one was alone. Then, just in front of us, a Japanese climber emerged from an orange tent inflated like a sausage with a kerosene blower at one end. '*Ohayo gozaimasu!*'(Good morning), said he cheerfully, as his female companion emerged simpering behind him.

When escorting the ambassador on provincial tours, I acted as a kind of food taster. Once, in the port city of Karatsu in Kyushu, Sir Allen and his wife were the mayor's guests at a dinner to pay tribute to the crew of the Australian destroyer *Voyager*, sunk in February 1964, shortly after a visit to Japan by the aircraft carrier *Melbourne* during manoeuvres off Sydney. After preliminary courses and several toasts in sake, the house speciality was wheeled in. From a wooden barrel emerged a large *live* lobster. Before the horrified guests, the chef held it down on a plate, and, as it emitted crustacean croaks, frantically scattering mushrooms with its claws, sliced its back open, and cut the flesh into bite-sized cubes. The chef returned the flesh neatly into the lobster's carapace, from which we were invited to eat it with chopsticks. Lady Brown nearly fainted. Sir Allen fixed me with a steely gaze and instructed me to eat enough for all of us. I had no choice, and did my best to look enthusiastic about it all. I should have asked for a salary increase on the spot.

The excitement of working in the embassy was one thing, but where in Tokyo were Ali and I to live? And (more important to me), what kind of wheels should I get? The first problem was solved, at least temporarily, when we took over the house of my predecessor, Chris Clark. Chris had made himself deeply unpopular with colleagues in the embassy by telling a visiting inspector from Canberra that our local allowances were too high. He proved the point by inhabiting a rundown, low-rent house in Hatanodai, a distant south-western suburb outside the Yamanotesen train loop within which we were, for various practical reasons like proximity to the embassy, supposed to live. Hatanodai was twenty minutes by branch line train to Gotanda, itself forty minutes to downtown Tokyo. During my first week at the embassy, I came home to find my bride in tears with a burnt face and no eyebrows. The antiquated gas oven had exploded as she was preparing dinner.

We quickly found a more modern house with a safer kitchen in Aoyama ni-chome, just off fashionable Aoyama-dori, close to Aoyama cemetery and not far from the embassy. Our landlord was Matsuki-san, who affected a black beret and had lived in occupied Paris, where, I suspected, he might have been a spy for the *kempeitai* (the Japanese wartime secret police). He was extremely urbane, had good French and many senior contacts in the Japanese Defence Agency. Narrower than a Paddington terrace, our house had two floors, two bedrooms, and a carport. We got a ginger cat we called Tetsuan (Iron Arm), after the popular

Japanese cartoon character with pointy cap and rockets coming out of his feet who was later known as Astro Boy on Australian children's television. The Matsuki family, our maid Sachiko-san, a neighbour Kenzo Tomotoshi who ran his father's fish restaurant in the inner Tokyo suburb of Shimbashi, and my language teacher, Fujino-san, were our courteous and patient guides to this new world. All but Sachiko-san spoke English, and all, if asked, were always willing to give advice about living in Tokyo.

Barely twenty years after the city had been utterly destroyed by American B-17 and B-29 fire-bombing raids, Tokyo's railway system had been resurrected and, pretty amazingly, was now one of the most reliable and efficient urban transport systems in the world. The spine of the system was the aforementioned Yamanote-sen, a surface line that looped around and delineated the inner city through six major sub-centres and twenty-nine stations. During rush hour, a train left each station on the loop every two or three minutes; outside rush hour, every three or four. It carried vast numbers of commuters packed into their carriages by special railway staff. If delays occurred, due to an earth tremor or a commuter throwing himself in front of a train, each station suddenly resembled a stadium that had just disgorged a capacity football crowd. Interconnected with the Yamanote-sen was an intricate filigree of subway lines, some private, others run by the Japan National Railway (JNR). Ali and I would hop on a subway from our house and shoot into the Ginza or Shinjuku or Shibuya or Maranouchi in about as much time as it now takes to go from Edgecliff to Martin Place in Sydney, that is, five kilometres or ten minutes. I believe every New South Wales railway employee and their union bosses should spend a compulsory month working in the Japanese system.

Superb public transport aside, I wanted the freedom of personal transport. For one thing, no train or subway connected Aoyama ni-chome to the embassy at Ninohashi. For another, in my youthful pride (I was twenty-five), travelling by train sometimes made me feel like an anonymous cog in a vast urban transport machine. Which indeed I was, just like everyone else. But for Japanese commuters, anonymity was not a problem. They did not mind being cogs, and a train was a place to meditate, to sleep (although with an uncanny ability to wake up at one's station), or to unzip one's trousers to allow ventilation in steamy Tokyo summers.

I also wanted a car for weekend escapes from the hectic pace of the city. Not that this was easy. The construction of the metropolitan elevated expressway system had begun in 1959 in preparation for the 1964 Olympics. Modelled on the first urban parkway constructed in Los Angeles in 1939, it was still being built during most of my posting. But unlike the Los Angeles expressways which were connected to a larger rural freeway system, Tokyo's freeway stopped at the limits of the downtown area, remaining unconnected to either suburban or country outlets until much later. This resulted in massive traffic jams, especially as growing numbers of car owners sought to escape the metropolis to the country on Sundays. (Saturday was a workday for most workers.)

Construction of the expressway despoliated every residential, commercial and shopping district in its path, slicing through small communities, throwing parts of Tokyo into permanent shade. It generated huge noise and dust. On wet days the washing we hung out on our tiny terrace developed holes from acid rain. On dry days it were spotted with soot.

I knew the traffic was hellish, but I still wanted a car. The question was: what kind? I wanted something nippy and small that could cope with Tokyo's narrow streets and fearsome traffic. And, prejudiced against Japan's lingering reputation for poor quality control, I wanted something foreign that would fetch a premium price on resale. Not a sports car — too impractical — but something unconventional with four on the floor and plenty of ergs.

Remembering my affection for Dad's Hillman cars, I decided on one of the company's newest products, a short, square Hillman Imp two-door hatch, a sporty sedan at the lower end of the Rootes Group price range. I placed my order for an electric-blue Imp through the Japanese Import/Export Company C. Itoh, and waited impatiently for the car to be shipped from Britain to Yokohama. It seemed to take many months (in truth about three) to arrive. After a pre-delivery service and clean-up at the Itoh garage, in Roppongi as I recall, I took delivery — my very first brand-new car — and proudly drove it home to an indifferent cat and a sceptical but tolerant wife.

The Imp had been designed specifically to rival the Mini Minor. A key difference between them, however, was the Imp's 875 cc all-aluminium engine, adapted from a Coventry Climax fire-pump engine, and which had enjoyed some success on European racing circuits. The engine was mounted behind the rear wheels, and slanted at 45 degrees to fit in the boot. Partly to counter oversteer caused by this metal lump, the Imp had a semi-trailing arm independent rear suspension — quite sophisticated for a small car at the time. Front suspension was by swinging arms. I had it fitted with a wide-mouthed exhaust pipe which gave a satisfying sporty burble.

I enjoyed the agility and novelty of the Imp during my first year in Tokyo. It was nimble in city traffic and it willingly took to the tortuous trip out of Tokyo to the south and west, cutting and weaving among the gigantic Hino and Isuzu trucks that congested the narrow roads, their many lights blazing. We would speed through Zama, Atsugi, Matsuda, and Yamakita, up to Gotemba and the slopes of Mount Fuji. Beyond Gotemba the road became relatively quiet, winding through picturesque rice fields and bamboo groves to the village of Yamanaka (literally: 'in the middle of the mountains') on the shores of a volcanic lake. There we shared a shoji-screened, tatami-floored summer cottage with Merrick and Crystal Baker Bates, colleagues in the British Embassy. Japanese friends would visit and much beer and sake were consumed as we learned each other's languages. We had a narrow little fibreglass yacht called a Sea Snark in which we would meander around the lake.

But after about a year, I was beginning to face the painful fact that my Imp was under-engineered for Japanese road conditions, and not particularly well made. Bits kept falling off. If I'd been shrewder, I'd have read more about its development before buying it: how it was built by a militant strike-prone work force in an entirely new plant at Linwood on the outskirts of Glasgow, from where its engine castings had to be sent 480 kilometres to another plant for machining and assembling before being returned to Linwood — a round trip of 970 kilometres and how in 1964, there had been thirty-one stoppages at Linwood and only a third of the planned number of units — 50,000 instead of 150,000 — had been completed. I was lucky to get my car when I did, or at all.

Was I prepared also to cut my losses, sell the Imp, and invest in a more robust car? Indeed, something that was still fun to drive, but a bit bigger, in order to accommodate all the trappings and paraphernalia of the child we were expecting in the third year of our posting?

I have to admit that while enjoying the Imp, I had been looking with envy at some of the cars beginning to emerge from Japanese factories and flooding Japanese roads. Many had pretty faces and bodies and were well engineered and technically advanced. They included Nissan Bluebirds, Isuzu Bellets, Mitsubishi 500s, Mazda Carols and Capellas, the Nissan Fairlady, the Silvia and its sexy cousin, the 240Z, a sleek sports job that was Sean Connery's vehicle of choice in his James Bond adventure *You Only Live Twice*. The film was shot in and around Tokyo in 1966, and Bond's companion was the delectable Japanese film star, Akiko Wakabayashi, in real life the girlfriend of our embassy's own language student, Reg Little — the very man who used to eat oats stored on the back seat of his maroon Riley during our cadet days in Canberra. Reg now had a Honda sports car and Akiko. He had come a long way.

I should note in passing the peculiar proclivity of Japanese car makers to choose names for their vehicles rich in the letter 'L', a letter which does not appear in the Japanese language and invariably comes out as 'R'. To appear Western and sophisticated, they created Toyota Starlets, Corollas and Celicas, the Subaru Leone, Nissan Laurel (a real tongue twister), the Mazda Luce and Mitsubishi Lancer. The story goes that a young foreign secretarial officer newly arrived in Tokyo took her car in for a service, to be sadly informed by the mechanic that she had a reeking crutch.

I was particularly impressed with the technical advances of one particular Japanese car during a holiday in Kyushu in 1966. Ali and I caught the new and wondrous electric Shinkansen bullet train from Tokyo to its brand-new terminus at Shin Osaka, transferring there to a local train to Shimonoseki at the southern tip of Honshu. We crossed the Shimonoseki Straits to Kita Kyushu, the second most polluted city in Japan (outside Kawasaki near Tokyo). Here we rented a tiny red Honda S 800 sports convertible from Honda Rent-a-Car, put down the hood and left the smog behind. It was like touring Tasmania — the further south we went, the greener it became. For seven days we drove the Honda anti-clockwise around Kyushu — south to Fukuoka and Sasebo as far as Nagasaki, and then east to Kumamoto, stopping to view the smoking 1592 metre crater of Mount Aso at Uchinomiya. We finished up at Beppu, a hot springs resort on the Inland Sea, where we relinquished the Honda at its Rent-a-Car depot and caught a ferry up the Inland Sea to Kobe and home to Tokyo.

On the narrow and mountainous roads of Kyushu, the Honda was a dream. As Jeremy Clarkson would say, it had *soul*. True to the company's motorcycle-making origins, it was chain-driven. It had a conical hypoid final drive, powered by an 800 cc engine with a cylinder block and head made entirely of light alloy with wet-liner cylinders. It had twin overhead camshafts with V-slanted valves. The fuel was fed by four horizontal carburettors. The particularly high rotational speed of the engine (8500 revolutions per minute) enabled a specific power of nearly 100 horse power per litre. At 7570 rpm it reached 75 mph, with a flat chat speed approaching 100 mph. At high revs (which was most of the time), it sounded like a Formula One racer. In Osaka we had a diverting night in a former brothel, now a ryokan, a traditional Japanese inn, but still with mirrors on the ceilings and erotic wood carvings in the passages.

The Honda underlined to me the fact that the Japanese auto industry was catching up and beginning to pass the rest of the industrialised world. I was determined to learn more. If Japan could do so well with motor cars, how would they go with missiles, nuclear power plants and electronics? They started tentatively in 1902, well behind the Europeans, when two engineers, Shintaro Yoshida and Kamonosuke Uchiyama, produced a trial car with a two-cylinder, 12 hp American engine. There was further experimentation but not much production because the Japanese could not compete with foreign imports. Indeed, following the Tokyo earthquake of 1923, the Japanese government had imported a large number of Model T Fords and converted them into buses which they called the Entaro, a new form of city transport. Through the 1920s and 1930s local endeavours continued to be swamped by imports, particularly from the giant American companies Ford and General Motors, which set up subsidiary assembly plants in Japan.

In the early 1930s, Toyota and Nissan began their own production lines. But their efforts at producing commercially attractive motor cars were frustrated by two factors. In the business of forging steel plates, and in casting, stamping, machining, electroplating and painting, they were technically inferior to American and European companies. And any incentive to improve was stultified by a mid-1930s government edict that Japanese auto production must be diverted almost entirely into the production of trucks for the army.

But after the war, Japanese engineers were beginning to learn through the technical affiliations their companies made with European companies: in the 1950s Nissan made Austin A-40s; Hino, Renault 4CVs; and Isuzu, Hillman Minxes. By the late 1950s, the Ministry of International Trade and Industry (MITI) started to support and protect domestic industry. By the early 1960s an unprecedented expansion in Japanese motor car production had begun, and Western prejudice against them, based mainly on racist prejudice, began to crumble. Impressive new car factories were built: a Toyota plant at Motomachi; a Nissan factory at Oppama; one by Isuzu at Fujisawa; Prince at Murayama and Hino at Hamura. Rationalisations were also officially encouraged. Toyota absorbed Hino and Daihatsu. Nissan absorbed Prince and tied in with Toyo Kogyo (Mazda).

The results of new efficiencies and rationalisations quickly became apparent. In 1962, Toyota and Nissan produced 82,000 and 97,000 cars respectively. This was still only about one-eighth of Fiat's output in the same year, but the numbers continued to rise at a tremendous rate. In 1967 Japan produced its millionth car, rising by 1970 to 3,178,700 units. By 2005, the twelve auto makers in Japan produced 10, 799,299 motor vehicles. In descending order of magnitude the makers were Toyota, Nissan, Honda, Suzuki, Mazda, Daihatsu, Mitsubishi, Fuji-Subaru, Isuzu, Daimler-Chrysler, Hino and Nissan-diesel.

Japanese vehicle exports followed the same upward trajectory. Restricted in the 1950s to such marginal markets as Taiwan, Okinawa (then administered by the United States), Thailand, Republic of Korea and Brazil, exports quickly flooded into Europe and America. Through relentless effort and promotion, by 1963 Japanese motor vehicle exports rose to 100,000 units, including 31,500 cars, to over 100 countries. With their comparatively small engines and compact build, Japanese cars benefited immensely in world markets from the 1973 oil shock. By 1974, Japan had passed the Federal Republic of Germany to become the largest motor vehicle exporter in the world. Vehicles now represented ten per cent of the country's total industrial output.

Not that this development occurred without human cost. A journalist, Satoshi Kamaki, took a job in early 1970 as a seasonal worker on an assembly line at a Toyota plant near Nagoya. The contrast with working values in Britain and America was stark.

In his book *Japan in the Passing Lane*, Kamaki describes how he lived in a claustrophobic, regimented company dormitory. Toyota had close connections with the Self Defence Agency, and preferred recruiting former soldiers and NCOs used to military discipline. After early morning calisthenics and singing the company song, Kamaki and his co-workers assembled gearboxes, initially in a time of one minute and forty seconds each. The pace of the production line sometimes increased without warning. He was frequently transferred at a moment's notice on to other parts of the plant. Toyota's mantra was the elimination of waste: in over-production, delays, defective parts, in inventories and the shipping process. Toyota was one of the first companies in the world to design high-sided, purpose-built, drive-on drive-off ships for the export trade. (Naturally these were made in Japanese shipyards.) The Toyota enterprise union supported management rather than the workers. Kamaki left after six months.

I was now determined to get my own Japanese car. After looking closely at what was available and in my budget range, I settled on a very sporty machine — a Skyline GT sedan built by Prince, and introduced in 1965, a year before the Prince company was absorbed by Nissan. I was initially attracted to the name Skyline, which I associated with the famous Skyline Driveway high on the slopes of Mount Fuji (no doubt a deliberate calculation by its makers). Beige with a black roof, it was a real sports machine. It had a high compression 1988 cc six-cylinder engine fed by triple Weber carburettors, generating 106 hp at 5400 rpm. The body shell was taken from an earlier Prince with a smaller engine designed by the Italian stylist Michelotti, now stretched by eight inches at the front to accommodate the new power plant. It had front disc brakes with twin-piston calipers, finned rear drums, a limited slip diff on an independent rear suspension, and a five-speed floor-mounted gear shift. The trimmings included a wooden steering wheel and gearstick knob.

For several months I drove the Prince around Tokyo and up to our weekender at Yamanaka, constantly on the lookout for empty straight roads to let it out. The opportunities were rare but satisfying. They were, however, abruptly circumscribed by the birth of our daughter, Anna Mariko, at Eisei Byoin, the Seventh Day Adventist Hospital in Ogikubo, on 5 June 1967.

That day the Six-Day war between Israel and several Arab states broke out in the Middle East, and I remember Ali in hospital, breastfeeding Anna while she searched furiously on her bedside radio for the best coverage of the war and the ensuing UN debates. Before too long the Skyline was full of baby and baby paraphernalia, and the cat, whenever we ventured out on to Tokyo's congested roads. Not that my Prince would have survived any of today's rigorous child-restraint rules. We had no airbags, no safety belts, no child restraints of any kind. No child seat securely bolted onto the back of the rear seat in which these days we haul Anna's own daughter, our beloved Ava, from Sydney to our south coast retreat at Termeil.

Indeed, until we left Tokyo when Anna was six months old, we carted her around in a wicker basket designed to store bed linen and placed with absolutely no restraint on the back seat of the Prince. She didn't seem to mind, and was at that age always a happy, uncritical, if not very articulate, passenger.

I reluctantly sold the Prince to a colleague when we left Tokyo in early 1968 for Canberra.

At the end of our posting, three events stand out in my mind. One was playing myself in a recruitment film made by the Commonwealth Film Unit for the Department of External Affairs entitled 'Third Secretary'. In black and white, it ran for nearly an hour and was shot both in Tokyo and Australia. The department continued to use it for recruiting purposes until audiences began to laugh at how old-fashioned it (and I, its star) had become.

Second was a farewell party friends and colleagues gave us in a tramcar they hired from Akasaka Mitsukei to the entertainment district in Asakusa. It was on the Ginza line, the last tramway services still operating in Tokyo before all the tracks were ripped up, to be replaced by buses. The tramway regulations prohibited intoxicating liquor on their trams, but we took many brown-paper bags.

Third was news of the world bantamweight title fight on 27 February 1969 between Japan's Masahiko 'Fighting' Harada, and Australia's own Lionel Rose at the Tokyo Budokan. Frank Devine, an Australian journalist stationed in Tokyo, had managed to insinuate himself into the ring as a towel-waving second for Rose. Not then the self-styled conservative curmudgeon he was later to become, Frank wrote a riveting account of Rose's victory over fifteen rounds for avid fans in Australia. The story appeared, I recall (but I may be wrong) in the Melbourne *Herald*. It was on a par with Dawn Fraser's exploits at the Tokyo Olympics, especially her unofficial swim in the Imperial Palace moat, which Frank might also have covered.

Diplomats often say their first posting was the best. For me it was certainly one of the most vivid. We returned many times to Japan, and still do. In 1994, Anna and her brother Adam made a documentary film about Japan, mainly the dark side, called *Hell Bento*. Adam later became involved with an avant-garde Japanese theatre company called *Gekidan Kaitaisha*, and, based in Tokyo, remained with the company for five years.

3

Into the Jaguar Jungle

Ali and I returned to Australia with baby Anna in early 1968. We flew via Taipei to Sydney at the front end of a Qantas 707, or 'V' jet as it was called, the baby's bassinet securely fastened to the bulkhead. Anna slept most of the way, only screeching when the pilot reversed the engines on landing because it hurt her little ears. At Mascot we took a TAA Boeing 727 'Trijet' to Adelaide to use up some of my accrued leave. Ali's parents, Jack and Mavis, and my mother, Mary, all lived there, and we were keen to show off the baby. We stayed with my mother at our old family home at Goodwood Road, Redfern.

On top of my list of things to do during that summer holiday was getting a new car. I was moderately cashed-up, and was in a position to buy a good second-hand one. Ever since Tony Bishop had driven his magnificent pre-war Jaguar SS Tourer to law school in 1958, I had harboured a craving for a Jaguar, a car that I felt would support my secret self-image of being a suave and worldly character. A rare car like Tony's would have been too expensive, but there was an affordable alternative — a smaller

Jaguar — and one morning I took a tram into the city along Goodwood Road to find one.

Bryson Industries were the original importers of Jaguar motor cars into Australia. In Adelaide, they occupied a building near the centre of the city, in a showroom worthy of its product. It had wood-panelled walls, art deco plaster mouldings and cut-glass mirrors, and an agreeably strong smell of engines, leather, and auto wax rose from the oil-impregnated floor. Set amongst vases of gladioli, advertisements for Castrol motor oil and posters flaunting Jaguar wins at Le Mans were several gleaming Jaguars, all artfully displayed. I explained that I wanted a second-hand Mark 2 with not too many miles on the clock. Yes, they said, they had one, a 2.4 litre model in white with red leather upholstery. They drove it slowly out from the back of the shop for my inspection. It looked and sounded absolutely tremendous, and I lusted after it.

Why a Mark 2? Well, it was the last word in Jaguar saloon excellence, a splendid successor to the compact Mark 1 saloon, the first 'baby' Jaguar developed at enormous expense and commercial risk at Brown's Lane in 1955. This earlier Mark had a revolutionary monocoque body shell with beautifully proportioned front and rear ends. It was powered by a finely balanced, twin-overhead cam, six-cylinder XK engine, and had a Burman recirculating ball steering box, new suspension and servo-assisted front and rear brakes.

The Mark 2 of 1961 had the same dimensions and look as the Mark 1, but with a big increase in glass area: bigger windscreen, rear window, and side windows separated by thin chrome pillars. It had a wider rear axle for better stability and modified suspension. It also boasted a redesigned leather and wood-veneer interior, a new instrument panel with tacho and speedo grouped on the walnut fascia in front of the driver, and an array of dials and toggle switches in the centre of the dash neatly labelled by an internally illuminated strip beneath. Driving it was like flying a Spitfire.

There was also a lockable glove box, and small fold-out picnic tables behind the front seats for rear passengers to park their drinks at the football or country race meetings. (Not that I ever went to a country race meeting, but it was satisfying to know that I'd be set if I did.) The British police used the 3.8 litre model as a pursuit car — very effective, unless the crooks were driving one too.

My car had an automatic transmission and power steering. It also had better fuel economy but less grunt than its larger-engined 3.4 and 3.8 litre brothers. For that reason it was never exported to the United States, where the strong preference was for cars with bigger engines. But it was no slouch, and very popular in Australia. It could do nearly 100 mph on the flat at 4550 rpm, and would give a mean maximum average of 96.3 mph.

Two problems affected Jaguars at the time. One was the wind noise generated at speed. It didn't matter what kind of sound system the car was equipped with: above sixty miles an hour there was a roar from the wind as it eddied around the recessed windows. Not until the 1970s did car-makers seem to grasp the need for flat, aerodynamic side surfaces to reduce the problem. The other was a tendency for the cars to overheat in hot weather. The Brits didn't seem able to provide sufficient radiator capacity for their cars, especially for stop-start traffic in

Australian cities in summer. And the crowded engine bays hardly had space for air conditioners. But with all my Jaguar's faults — indeed, probably because of them — I loved it. They signified character.

After a couple of weeks of driving around Adelaide, to the beach and tennis and into the summer-browned hills for hikes, Ali and I packed Anna's bassinet in the boot and the three of us drove my mother across the Western Highway to stay with her brothers in Melbourne. On the sinuous drive up and over the Adelaide Hills the Jag conducted itself like a Le Mans thoroughbred, and cruised without fuss along the Western Highway through Murray Bridge, Tailem Bend, Keith and Bordertown into Victoria, thence across the Wimmera, past the Grampians, and on to Melbourne. We had the usual raucous extended family dinner in one of the Coffey houses, during which there were many compliments about our new daughter though few about the Jaguar. (Except for my maverick Uncle Selwyn, who had a red 1967 Chevrolet, all the Coffey brothers drove Rovers).

On a Melbourne morning in late summer, Ali and I then drove our little daughter up the Hume Highway to her new home in Canberra. After our first posting, it was now time to take a breather — a 'home stay', which the department prescribed as often as it could in order to re-ground its diplomats in Australian culture.

Our small house was on a corner block facing the bush in Bradfield Street, Downer, on the northern fringes of Canberra. We and the bank had bought it in 1964, just before Ali and I left for Tokyo. It was a basic Canberra model of the times — brick veneer, cement-tile roof, three bedrooms, single oil heater, wooden floors, a small L-shaped living-dining room separated from the kitchen by a breakfast bar, one bathroom/toilet, and no garage. It was perfectly adequate for our needs, and we were very proud of it.

But we lived a long way from Civic Centre, the department or anywhere civilised. If I didn't leave Ali with the car, she had nowhere to take the baby except for long walks in her pusher around the flat, treeless northern suburbs. I didn't leave her the car as often as I should have, and it was all a bit of a trial for her. Nevertheless, as well as looking after Anna, Ali managed to continue her Japanese language lessons at the ANU, and then to work as a journalist for the *Canberra Times*, first covering education issues, then writing editorials.

I had returned to Australia and to the Department at a very interesting time. John Grey Gorton had become the new Australian Liberal prime minister in January 1968, replacing Harold Holt who had drowned off Cheviot Beach in Victoria the preceding December. The Cold War had quickened in January with two major international events — a nationwide uprising of Vietcong guerrillas and North Vietnam Army regulars in South (Vietnam dubbed the 'Tet Offensive' because it coincided with the Vietnamese New Year), and the capture of the American spy ship, the *Pueblo*, by the Pyongyang government off the North Korean coast. Young people were demonstrating across Europe, supporting a wide array of left-wing causes. In the United States, Martin Luther King was assassinated in April, and Bobby Kennedy in June. Russian tanks rolled into Prague in August — the 'Prague Spring' — to crush an anti-Soviet uprising. East-West suspicions were running high, and the Cold War was now at its peak.

Professionally, none of these events concerned me at first. I was assigned to the Japan Section of the North Asian Branch, and was thus removed from the dramas in Eastern Europe, the United States and South East Asia. However, I was able to watch the bilateral Japan–Australian relationship develop from the Australian end. It had looked exciting and full of potential from the perspective of Tokyo, but two things now struck me. The first was that too much paperwork was coming out of the embassy in Tokyo for me and my two colleagues in the desk to absorb or analyse properly. The other was that no department in Canberra seemed charged with the responsibility of co-ordinating the burgeoning bilateral trade relationship very well.

At the time, the main departments with trade interests were Trade, Industry and Commerce, Primary Industry, Minerals and Energy, Treasury, Prime Minister and Cabinet, and External Affairs. But whenever we had an inter-departmental committee meeting (IDC) to discuss Japan, those who came were often uncommunicative and guarded to the point of truculence. They were narrowly concerned about 'their' patch, 'their' responsibilities, rather than Australian interests, and as a result not much was done or agreed on. A wise friend, a senior officer in Trade, advised me to keep in mind the two fixed objectives of those attending IDCs: to preserve both their power and overseas trips for the boys.

Meanwhile, among the other 'line' departments, External Affairs counted for very little. We were widely seen as dilettantes, adept at cocktail party chatter but hopeless at dealing with 'practical' issues, such as negotiating trade deals. This view was inaccurate and superficial, but our position was not helped by the fact that External Affairs officers usually stayed in Canberra only a year or two before being posted abroad again — barely enough time to build networks with colleagues in other departments who were permanently based there.

In contrast, the Japanese bureaucracy worked as a well-oiled team. Japanese intelligence about Australian political and economic conditions was usually timely and penetrating. The ministries in Tokyo and their business colleagues in the *zaibatsu* had an agreed agenda and goals. Negotiators could trade off one state against another, one mining company against the rest. And the Japanese Foreign Ministry had more prestige than did External Affairs in Canberra, and could co-ordinate and enforce its views where necessary.

Not until the end of the 1970s were we able to create machinery for developing agreed views between the private sector, the states and Commonwealth departments about our approach to Japan. The Myer Report recommended that three committees on Japan be set up — one to co-ordinate views between the permanent heads of seven selected Commonwealth departments, another between them and the private sector, a third between the Commonwealth and the states. Committee members were under strict instructions not to delegate to subordinates. Meetings were often fiery, but they sometimes brought results. I ran the Secretariat, about which more later.

In 1969 I was moved out of the Japan Section and into the department's Information and Public Relations Branch. Among other things, I replaced C. R. (Kim) Jones as Radio Australia Liaison Officer, and my job was to brief Radio Australia commentators in Melbourne each fortnight on current issues of the day. It was a delicate job with a controversial history. Radio

Australia had been conceived during the war as Australia's overseas propaganda arm, run by the government. After the war it was reluctantly handed over to the ABC, which saw its role as giving listeners in Asia the same impartial news as provided to the Australian listeners of ABC bulletins. International coups or corruption or scandals were to be reported accurately, without spin or gloss. But many Australian ambassadors in the Asian region took strong exception whenever an RA broadcast item embarrassed the government to which they were accredited. Sometimes they would be hauled in by the Foreign Ministry and given a dressing down. Most Asian officials, they argued, could not believe that RA was no longer an arm of the Australian government. Anyway, why should Australian diplomatic efforts be compromised by a service that was paid for by taxpayers' money?

External Affairs lost the battle to massage the news, but carried out a rearguard action on news commentaries. As the secretary of the department, Sir Arthur Tange, asserted in a letter he wrote to Chairman of the ABC, Sir Charles Moses, in 1956, 'an Asian audience is quite unlike the average Australian audience. Its standard of education is much lower, it is lacking in political discernment, and it is exposed continuously to Soviet and Chinese Communist propagandistic themes.' But at the same time, the writer and academic Macmahon Ball observed, 'In the last weeks I have been stunned by the news commentaries I have heard. They follow a fixed official pattern ... designed to persuade Indians, Indonesians and the others that Britain and France know what is best for East Asia, and that Australia knows they know what is best.' (He was referring at the time to the Suez crisis.)

Earlier Radio Australia commentators had included such luminaries as H. D. Black, later chancellor of Sydney University, Creighton Burns, founding chancellor of the Victorian University of Technology, and Zelman Cowan, later governor-general of Australia. All would listen with only grudging attention to whichever officer from External Affairs had flown down from Canberra that week to give them the latest government thinking on foreign events. An equally impressive panel existed during my time as Radio Australia Liaison Officer, but they were invariably lukewarm to my advice. In any event, their time in writing and broadcasting commentaries, and mine in influencing them, was fast coming to an end. As former senior ABC journalist Errol Hodge observed, by this time the very idea of a news commentary, in which a 'high credibility' figure gave a more or less authoritative interpretation of issues and events, had become an anachronism. In the ABC's domestic broadcasts, such commentaries had already been replaced by current affairs interviews in which a wide range of interpretations was presented.

Two events now shook my well-ordered universe. One was my decision, during a subsequent holiday to Adelaide, to trade in the Jaguar on a less expensive car. The other was news of another posting overseas, to the Australian Embassy in Rangoon.

The two events were unrelated. In Adelaide I hadn't known what the department had in store for me. Nor, despite a thorough search of my memory, can I be precisely sure why I wanted to trade in the Jag, a car I was so happy with. Maybe it was to find a more economical car for the increasing amount of family transport we had to conduct in Canberra — ferrying me to the department, Anna to her play school, Ali to the *Canberra Times*. Or perhaps I had an attack of the guilts at driving such a car. After all, Ali's parents, good Baptists as they were, had very down-to-earth views about what was important. Flashy cars were so low among their priorities as to be invisible. As my father-in-law Jack used to tell us, money and possessions never brought happiness. Certainly, I was under no pressure from Ali (or Anna) to trade down.

Whatever the reason, I can recall sitting glumly in the showroom of a used car yard in West Terrace opposite Adelaide Boys' High School while a salesman, hardly believing his luck, was busy calculating how much he would give me for the Jag, and how much he would charge me for the white 1967 Vauxhall Victor 101 sedan parked out the front. Immaculate the Vauxhall may have been, undoubtedly newer than the Jag it was, with many fewer miles on the clock, but it lacked all the refinements, the road feel, drivability and finesse of my Jaguar, and silently I grieved. It had a red vinyl bench seat in the front and ditto in the back and a tinny feel. To make matters even worse, I got back far less money in the exchange than I should have.

Feeling bad about the deal, I left Adelaide with Ali and Anna and set off once again for home across the Hay Plain. At least the Vauxhall did not once let us down, and proved to be a reliable car for the rest of our time in Canberra.

But I had little time to brood about being short-changed, or to mourn the loss of my beloved car. When I reported to personnel on my first day back at the department I discovered I was to be posted as first secretary to the Australian Embassy in Rangoon. I wasn't so much unhappy about this as shocked at the prospect of going to a country that was so different from Japan. But in those days you went where you were sent, and it was not unusual to be offered a posting in the Third World after one in the First. And, as the Monty Python team advised in *The Life of Brian*, always look on the bright side of life. So, gritting our collective teeth, Ali and I read the post report about Rangoon, the long colonial period of British rule in Burma, how the country had been virtually destroyed during the war and made an uncertain recovery since, and how Burma fitted into Australia's geostrategic interests.

We had to acquire this knowledge in a very short time because we were scheduled to leave for Rangoon in January 1970.

4

Flashman Country

It is hard to imagine a greater contrast between two peoples than the Japanese and Burmese.

In their crowded islands, the Japanese were rebuilding their country and their national self-esteem. They were seemingly homogeneous, industrious and technologically literate, introverted, but amiable and generally tolerant of strange *gaijin*. Our first impression of the Burmese, on the other hand, was of exotic and heterogeneous groups of people inhabiting wildly different regions of a vast country: the Burmans in the plains and river deltas, the Mons, Shans and Kachins in the jungly hills, Karens along the eastern border lands with Thailand, Chinese and Indians in the Irrawady Delta. Like Japan, the country had been ravaged by war, but unlike Japan, little had been done to repair the damage.

Driven by the conviction that one cannot understand a country without knowing its history, Ali and I plundered the Foreign Affairs library for information about this new posting. My starting point was the Tibeto-Burmans who invaded the country in the seventh century. In complex confusion, local kingdoms rose and fell from then until the Burmese kings of the Toungoo dynasty unified the country in the sixteenth century from their capital, Pegu, 100 kilometres north-east of Yangon. But it was the rise of a new Burmese dynasty led by an obscure local chief from Shwebo in Upper Burma in the eighteenth century that captured my imagination. King Alaungpaya, 'The Victorious', or 'The Embryo Buddha', founded the Kongbaung dynasty, and reduced the inhabitants of outlying provinces in India, Laos and Siam (including its capital Ayuthia), to the status of vassals.

Alaungpaya unified and strengthened Burma, and negotiated a treaty of trade and friendship with the British in 1757 (the first with any European power). But insular and confident in their military prowess, the Burmese kings were arrogant, and did not appreciate the technical strength and equal arrogance of the British. The Marquess Wellesley, governor-general of India between 1798 and 1805, declared that 'the British must be the one paramount in India, and ... the native princes could only retain the personal insignia of sovereignty by surrendering their political independence'. Unaware of this dictum, the Burmese launched a succession of military encroachments along their western frontier between 1784 and 1823, directly impinging on British India. Early in 1824, the governor-general warned the East India Company's Court of Directors in Leadenhall that war was inevitable, 'to humble the overweening pride and arrogance of the Burmese monarch', now King Bagyidaw, great-grandson of Alaungpaya. Three Anglo-Burmese wars were fought between 1824 and 1886, resulting in the British seizure of the whole of Burma.

I often thought Burma was made for Harry Paget Flashman, the antihero of George McDonald Fraser's pastiche Victorian novels. Flashman was the caddish bully in *Tom Brown's Schooldays* by Thomas Hughes, expelled in drunken disgrace from Rugby School in the late 1830s, and who, despite a craven streak, had a brilliant military career. Among his many decorations was the San Serafino Order of Purity and Truth, 4th class. He even won the Victoria Cross when he was found wrapped in a Union Jack, the last man standing at an outpost on the Khyber Pass during one of the Afghan Wars. Flashman was the honorary president of the Mission for Reclamation of Reduced Women, director of the British Opium Trading Co and author of *The Case Against Army Reform*.

Fraser missed a golden opportunity to include this bounder in the Burmese wars, for they were full of the improbable and desperate adventures in which Flashman inevitably became involved, and survival would have needed all his skills in languages and horsemanship. He would have been quite at home avoiding military danger while tupping some absent major's wife, or loafing and gaming among other cads in the British lines.

The British forces were commanded by such bewhiskered and rather dim characters as Commodore Charles Grant, General Joseph Wanton Morrison, the explosive Commodore Lambert, Sir Archibald Campbell, and the celebrated Major General Sir Harry North Dalrymple Prendergast. The British infantry in their red woollen uniforms were hopelessly ill-dressed for jungle warfare, and many more succumbed to the anopheles mosquito, dysentery and heat exhaustion than to the spears and muskets of the wily Burman.

But the British had superior numbers, training, tactics, as well as the world's first practical machine gun. As Hilaire Belloc wrote of Britain's African wars in an observation equally applicable to Burma:

Whatever happens we have got
The Maxim gun and they have not.

And in the end the East India Company prevailed.

A century of British colonial rule followed, and then an immensely destructive Japanese invasion and occupation. At the end of it all, worn out by the war, the British were compelled to grant independence to the Burmese in 1948. The conquered people had some advantages: a skilled civil service, an abundance of fertile land, and although most draft animals had been wiped out in the war, there were still farmers who could feed, clothe and house themselves. A newly elected Constituent Assembly chaired by the national wartime hero, General Aung San, was making progress towards unity and national reconstruction. But there was a dysfunctional element in Burmese politics. Dr Ba Maw, wartime leader of the Burmese nationalists had remarked cynically but prophetically at the time:

> The Burmese learned two things from the Japanese: the technique of leadership based on mass organisation; and the glamour and power of armed men. It is not elections that are going to decide the future of Burma, but the gun. All you want in Burmese politics is to start on the winning side and to have plenty of guns.

In July 1947, Aung San and six of his cabinet ministers were assassinated at a cabinet meeting in Rangoon. The assassin was a disaffected politician, U Saw, who was later tried and hanged with his henchmen for the crime. Aung San was an inspirational leader who might possibly have unified the country. His lieutenant and successor, U Nu, did not have Aung San's charisma, but he made a courageous go of things, with some success at first. He presided over a country with educated public servants, a strong Burmese middle class, and an animated and unrestrained media. He attended the Bandung Conference of non-aligned countries in Indonesia in April 1955 on equal terms with Nehru of India, Sukarno of Indonesia, Nkrumah of Ghana, Nasser of Egypt, and Chou En-lai of China. Neutral in Cold War terms, Burma was held in high esteem, and U Nu and his colleague U Thant (later secretary-general of the United Nations) travelled the world stage cultivating friendships with the leaders of many countries. Australia, being aligned with Britain and the US, was absent from all these activities, although as Alan Renouf, a senior Australian diplomat later observed in *The Frightened Country*, 'we could have got an invitation if we'd tried'.

In Burma however, the main political party, the Anti-Fascist Peoples' Freedom League (AFPRL), had become a confusion of alliances, suspicions and conflicting interests. A formal split occurred with a vote of no confidence in the government in June 1958. Murderous antagonisms escalated, not simply within the AFPFL, but between the Burmans and hill tribes such as the Shans, Mons, Karens, Kachins, Kayas and with Red and White Flag Communists and many heavily armed apolitical thugs called dacoits, bad hats and road devils living in their jungle fastnesses.

In October 1958, U Nu appealed to the head of the army, General Ne Win, to take power and re-establish order in the country. As Thant Myint U described him in his personal history of modern Burma, *The River of Lost Footsteps*, Ne Win had been a playboy, truant, tyrant and numerologist. But he had trained in Japan to become a competent general, and scrupulously honoured the terms of his appointment. With efficiency and occasional brutality he suppressed insurgency, restored communications, railways, roads and waterways, and lowered the cost of living. He ordered houses in Rangoon to be repainted, rubbish removed, pariah dogs destroyed, and — a bit like Clean Up Australia Day — ordered 100,000 people to remove rubbish from Rangoon's streets and parks every Sunday. After two years, he handed government back to civilians and U Nu won a sweeping victory in elections held in February 1960.

But the same vicious brawling and factionalism that had occurred before Ne Win's caretaker government erupted again. U Nu seemed unwilling or unable to re-establish control, and spent more time in Buddhist retreats than wrestling with temporal problems.

Early in the morning of 2 March 1962 the armed forces staged a *coup d'état*. This time, General Ne Win didn't promise return to civilian rule. He introduced two ideological manifestos — 'The Burmese Way to Socialism' and 'The System of Correlation of Man and His Environment' — a fusion of Buddhism and Socialism that disguised the consolidation of uncontested power by the military. He sacked all the competent senior civilian technocrats and sent packing Western aid agencies, including the Ford Foundation and the Asia Foundation. He nationalised Burmese and foreign banks, and stopped international airlines from landing at Mingaladon, until then one of the busiest international airports in Asia. Business and commerce fell away, and the country retreated into truculent isolation.

So why did Australia continue to maintain an embassy in such a hopeless country? The answer is simple: it was because we feared a takeover of a very substantial piece of real estate to our near north by the Chinese Communists, and wanted to keep a close watch. We also hoped that one day the country would settle down and become a constructive neighbour to Thailand, Bangladesh, India, Laos and Cambodia. We had a regional aid program with an idealistic streak, and wanted to spend some of it in Burma. And we knew that, under the good offices of Henry Byroade, the US ambassador in Rangoon, Ne Win had visited Washington in 1966 and established an easy-going relationship with President Lyndon Baines Johnson, who saw Burmese neutrality in America's best interests at the time. Lastly, inspired by Robert Menzies' foreign minister, Richard Casey, who had written *Friends and Neighbours* in 1955 as a blueprint outlining how Australia could get on with its neighbours, we saw ourselves as a Commonwealth country and a regional player with an interest in all the countries of Asia, including Burma.

Ali and Anna and I came to Burma by way of Bangkok eight years after Ne Win's coup. Not much had changed except for the imposition of tighter military surveillance of civilians and greater suspicion of foreigners. Despite our preparatory reading, arriving in Rangoon didn't ease the initial shock of entering the country. Mingaladon did not have the neutrality of most international airports. We were immediately subject to the essence of the Burmese military bureaucracy — about thirty minutes of dreary interrogations by a series of officials under pallid fluorescent lighting strips, dragging ourselves from official to official, bureau to bureau. Our status as diplomats didn't count for much.

Most passengers then piled into buses converted from wartime army trucks to take them to the city. At least we had separate transport. A secretary from the embassy met us with an embassy Holden (recommended to me before leaving Canberra as the most reliable car to have in Burma). 'What do you play?' she asked brightly. 'Maybe a bit of tennis,' Ali replied cautiously. 'No, no,' the secretary said, 'mahjong or bridge?' 'Neither,' Ali tersely replied.

She accompanied us to the Soviet-built Inya Lake Hotel and left us to our own devices. Our hearts sank. Built along the lines of a Moscow Metro station, the hotel had miles of soulless corridors lined with empty glass cabinets, an empty swimming pool, a few solitary guests — mainly Japanese businessmen — and a vast dining room serviced by not particularly attentive staff. A colleague arrived with his family shortly after us and decided on the veal cordon bleu for dinner. 'OK,' said the waiter, 'but we have no veal. Would chicken do?' 'Fine,' said my colleague. 'We also have no cheese,' said the waiter. So they had *cordon bleu chicken à la maison d'Inya Lake.*

After a few days we moved into a two-storey house in a treeless compound in Golden Valley, about twenty minutes from the city centre. It had dark, teak-lined rooms with red velvet curtains — a breeding ground for mosquitoes and a store of tropical heat. We quickly found another house, which became our permanent accommodation in Rangoon: a single-storey pukka (brick) bungalow in a large compound on Dubern Road, backing onto Inya Lake, just across from the house of General Ne Win. The house was laid out symmetrically, with a large entry hall leading out to a fly-screened verandah at the back and two rooms off each side, which we could aircondition individually. It had cool, red-waxed concrete floors. Its water-stained exterior walls were whitewashed by the *mali* (gardener) at the end of every rainy season. We shared the compound with Jean François Nougarede from the French Embassy and his bride Anique. They kept a pet mongoose and ducks, and would languidly come up for air from their incense-laden house for occasional strolls around the compound.

During my first week at the embassy, I came home to find Ali in the kitchen, busily killing a green snake with a steak hammer. It might have been harmless, but Ali took no chances around Anna, now nearly three. A more challenging situation confronted the Italian ambassador, who lived in a nearby compound and discovered a nest of cobras under his house. He offered five kyats to his *mali* for each snake caught. The word spread among every sweeper and gardener in the district, and every evening for a week he was rewarded with a seething mass of snakes.

Gradually our household took shape. According to Peter Smart, head of chancery at the British Embassy, we needed to hire a racially mixed set of servants. 'That way they will be too busy being suspicious of each other to gang up on you,' he said. It was a tried and true British tactic in administering their colonies, to which Burma was an abiding testament. So we employed Mary, a Kareni Christian nanny, and Maung Gyi, a gruff male Burmese cook. Forceful male cooks were best because they could negotiate crowded local markets for quality produce, including the best cuts of meat in the noisome and unrefrigerated butcher's section. Nonetheless, we frequently ate legs of lamb that appeared still to have goat's hair on them. We also employed a *mali* and a *durwan* (night watchman) from the Mon and Shan tribes respectively.

I delayed finding a driver until our 1969 Holden HT Kingswood sedan arrived from Australia. I had chosen the Holden with much thought. Apart from advice from colleagues about its reliability, it scored well on looks, price, robustness, ability to handle tropical conditions and ease of maintenance. Besides, all the cars in the mission were General Motors products — a massive, boat-like black 1969 Buick for the ambassador, and Holdens for staff duties. My car filled me with satisfaction. Ducoed white to reflect the heat, with a golden vinyl fabric covering its bench seats, it was a step up from the superseded HK, the 'new generation' Holden that had been released in January 1968. The Kingswood had a 161 cc six-cylinder engine, three forward gears with the shift mounted on the steering column, a synchromesh transmission, new-style tail-lights and grille. It was the first Australian model that the celebrated American engineer George Roberts (from Pontiac) had been involved in designing. He made it quieter and smoother-riding than its predecessor, with more extensive use of soft rubber bushes in the suspension and a small y-shaped sub-frame at the front end. Its name 'Kingswood', which replaced the old Holden 'Special', was lifted from the Chevrolet Division of General Motors, as was the name of the basic model Holden, the

'Belmont'. Our car in Rangoon became the 'Kingswoo' because the 'd' on its boot had been knocked off in transit from Australia.

But who was to drive and clean the Kingswoo, and get it serviced? After interviewing several candidates I hired Anthony, a soft-spoken, single Indian who seemed to have gentle manners and a careful driving style. He settled down in his room in the servants' quarters. After several months however, it emerged that Anthony was not entirely without fault. His foible came to light in a letter delivered to us one evening by a professional letter-writer hired by Mary, whose room was adjacent to Anthony's. At irregular intervals Anthony would get on the local piss, and in a state of lustful inebriation thrust his erect penis through a knothole in the wall between his and Mary's room. Some firm counselling followed, Anthony took his lust elsewhere, and he continued to be our exemplary and trusted driver for the rest of the posting. But we never again came back from a journey out of Rangoon without a premonition of domestic trouble.

The workday routine involved Anthony driving Anna to pre-school and me down Prome Road and University Avenue, past the gorgeous golden stupa of the Shwedagon Pagoda on Singuttara Hill, and the lesser prominent Sule Pagoda, into the network of downtown streets along the river front, to the Australian Embassy. There I would join a small embassy team — Ambassador Roy Fernandez, Military Attache Colonel Newton, Second Secretary Ken Laughlan, Third Secretary Allan Gyngell, and sundry administrative and local staff. Pretty soon after my arrival, Roy moved on to become ambassador to Yugoslavia, and was replaced by Wally Handmer. I remember Wally being deeply impressed by

General Ne Win when he paid his introductory call, but he never really told me why. Colonel Newton moved among the other military attaches, and, to a lesser extent, among the Burmese military. Ken Laughlan spent much time monitoring Chinese military incursions along the north-east frontier adjacent to the Salween River in the Shan State.

The most junior officer, Allan Gyngell, spent his days devising different ways of telling Canberra that not much had happened politically for the weekly Savingram, a cable-like document sent for economy reasons by bag. He also processed visas for Anglo-Burmans wanting to escape to Australia, and gave consular assistance to distressed Australians (at the time, tourists were given visas for three days, so there were few tourists, distressed or otherwise). Allan recalls that the claim of the Liberal Party that it abolished the White Australia Policy when Billy McMahon was prime minister before Gough Whitlam's election in 1972 was simply not true. After leaving his post in Burma Allan kept what he called his 'Dulux paint chart' used to measure the shades of whiteness in the complexion of Anglo-Burmese aspirants to see whether they qualified for a visa.

My job was to draft political and economic reports for the ambassador's consideration. Finding out what was happening was difficult because Burmese officials didn't talk frankly to foreign diplomats, and the two daily newspapers — the *Guardian* and *Working People's Daily* — were full of bombastic propaganda about great constitutional reforms being engineered by the Burmese Socialist Program Party, or civic projects occurring against 'the ever-changing skyline of Rangoon'. The only time the Rangoon skyline ever changed was when a building fell down.

There were also tedious and sometimes risible press headlines. Allan recalls two standouts: in the *Guardian* one day appeared 'CLEAN UP RANGOON SEWERAGE WITH A MASS MOVEMENT'. Another story asserted that 'ENGLISH WILL BE TAUGHT DIFFERENT FROM NOW ON'.

It also fell to me to oversee Australia's aid program to Burma. This consisted of bringing in Australian-bred Droughtmaster cattle to improve local animal genetics, and draughthorses for Burma's anti-snakebite serum stocks. The horses were injected with snake venom to build up antibodies and were then bled to make the serum. I have no statistics, but I like to think our serum saved the lives of thousands of farmers bitten by snakes during their twice-a-year rice harvesting. During my watch, we also constructed a workshop to fabricate rolling stock for Burmese railways. The Australian foreman from Snowy Mountains Engineering Corporation (SMEC) frequently complained to me that he tried to motivate the workers, but 'they were always sittin' down'.

Filling our weekends proved challenging. Rangoon's amenities were limited, and we had to call on our Canberra skills to escape the tedium. There was the inevitable mahjong and bridge among the diplomats (which we usually avoided), and golf at two courses — Rangoon and Burma (which I joined). The military had their own course, and, inspired by their leader General Ne Win who played off a handicap of six, spent much time playing golf. We brought Peter Thompson, five-time winner of the British Open, to Rangoon, where he played exhibition matches with the Burmese champion Mya Aye. He also gave me a couple of lessons, but although I hit a long ball, it came with an unpredictably ferocious slice, and I never reduced my handicap below sixteen. During the monsoon, one could extract one's ball without penalty if one's nine iron or wedge shot buried itself in the liquefied fairway — a wet-season gimme.

Rangoon had had some splendid clubs dating from the British Raj such as the Pegu Club, Rangoon Gymkhana and Rangoon Boat Club. But these were defunct or falling apart. There was also the British Council library, which smelled of the mildew of many monsoons. More lively was the American Club across from our bungalow at the end of Dubern Road, a haven to which we had occasional access, and where we could play tennis, buy Anna an ice-cream or have a swim in the pool. For weekend trips out of Rangoon, all foreigners had to apply for and receive a permit. We frequently went before the permit, inevitably late, was given. Ali and Anna and I would often join Peter and Joan Smart on a permitless jaunt to a *nat pwe* — a performance of a long traditional narrative, or to the Syriam glass factory where Chinese Burmese made tumblers and vases out of melted-down brown beer bottles. It was always a pleasure to come back from these events, hot and dirty, to sit down in airconditioned comfort in the Smart house clutching an industrial-strength gin and tonic.

Sometimes I went on hunting trips with diplomatic colleagues with my beautifully balanced Lee Enfield 303 jungle rifle. This was deadly and accurate, as proved when I once aimed at a duck swimming innocently in a local lake. I not only hit it with one shot, but literally blew it apart, an appallingly destructive and wanton act. I had recurrent attacks of conscience for a week, and comforted myself that the bird instantly went to duck heaven feeling no pain. The American ambassador, Arthur Hummel, also indulged in hunting, but for more serious game. Some of his bearers left a couple of tiger cubs at his front gate, the orphans of a mother tiger killed in one of his forays. One of our cherished photographs is of Anna aged three, cautiously patting the cubs on Arthur's lawn. The ambassador had a bamboo stockade built in the residence garden to contain the animals. This worked well for a while, but at an Independence Day party in his gardens on 4 July 1971, a pretty young thing waved her hankie provocatively at the cubs, now fit young beasts each weighing 100 kilograms. With delighted growls, they vaulted over their stockade, loped around the grounds and rounded up the guests. There were a few scratches, no-one was killed, and the indignant animals completed their adolescence in sterner surroundings at the Rangoon zoo.

I have to record that in all these activities, my faithful Anthony and our Kingswoo (to which he now had a fierce proprietorial lien) accompanied us in comfort and style. The car ran and ran. It was serviced regularly. It went through two sets of tyres. On narrow, pot-holed roads it went to Mandalay and Maymyo and back, and on several other safaris, during which Anna would chant monotonously from her baby-seat fixed in the back 'Rice, more rice, more rice'. Many times we were stuck behind a military convoy, but the trucks never deviated from the centre of the road, and we could not pass until they chose to stop. The Kingswoo never boiled or broke down. And it stood out nobly in the Rangoon traffic of rickshaws, horse- and oxen-drawn carts and gharries, and 1950s British cars — Austin A-40s and A-70s, Standard Vanguards, Hillmans and Humbers, Morris

Oxfords and Minors, Triumph Mayflowers, and the occasional Armstrong Siddeley, Bristol or Rover. These early postwar British machines may have been rusting out, their engines and suspensions enfeebled, their differentials whining, their tyres bald and patched. But with locally fabricated spare parts and ancient rubber vulcanising kits, their owners kept them wheezing and staggering on through the hot and dusty or hot and wet streets of Rangoon — much as the Cubans kept their American automobiles of much the same vintage going in Havana. Every car on Rangoon's roads was triumphant proof of the adage that if you keep your car serviced, it will run forever.

In 1971, General Ne Win decreed that vehicles throughout Burma would henceforth drive on the right-hand side of the road. The decree was couched in terms of freeing the country from remnants of British colonialism. But all it really did was compound Burma's isolation from its main neighbours Thailand, India and Bangladesh, which all drove on the left. Only China and Laos drove on the right, but there were no passable roads into those countries at the time. The decree also made driving extremely dangerous. Burmese drivers inevitably forgot from time to time which side of the road they were meant to be driving on and there were some horrific head-on accidents. Bus proprietors simply welded up the doors on the left of their vehicles — mainly wartime Chevrolet and Ford army trucks adapted to carry passengers — and cut more doors in the other side.

The decree also contributed to the failure to build an Asian Highway from London to Singapore. This has been a vision of travellers by road ever since the invention of the motor car, but it is unlikely to happen while the military control Burma.

We didn't have to fabricate spares for the Kingswoo, which, along with other necessities, could be imported under diplomatic exemption. But in other areas of daily life we were deprived, and had to make do. In 1971, we were trying to have another child. Ali's doctor at the Rangoon General Hospital was an Edinburgh-trained gynaecologist, but she had no access to drugs or equipment. Armed with a prescription for a thermometer, Ali went to the People's Pharmacy and joined a long queue of locals. At the head of the queue was an Indian assistant chanting monotonously to each customer '*Manaim-bu*' — we don't have it. Without even looking at her script, he repeated the same mantra to Ali. Sharply, she told him he did, and to fetch it. Startled, the assistant went off and found the thermometer. It was the same at the diplomatic store, almost always empty of stock. Ali remembers buying a tube of toothpaste, only to find that someone had inserted a syringe through the cap and withdrawn the paste, replacing it with water.

One of the worst aspects of living in Rangoon in the early 1970s was the sense of being cut off from outside events, particularly what was happening in Australia, including, for Ali, the ferment over women's rights and, for me, the growing unpopularity of the Vietnam War. Listening to the World Service of the BBC and Radio Australia helped. So did receiving Australian newspapers in the weekly diplomatic bag, but these were a week old when they came, and had to pass hierarchically down through the staff for another week before Ali and I could get to see them. Six months into my posting, however, I received a dose of reality, at least about what was happening in the neighbourhood. I was instructed to escort an Australian parliamentary delegation about to visit Thailand, Vietnam, Laos and Cambodia in June/July 1970. Led by John Grey Gorton's Minister for Repatriation, Mac Holten (Country Party), the delegation included Senator Reg Bishop (Labor), Senator Harold Young (Liberal), Gordon Bryant (Labor), Geoff Giles (Liberal) and Dr Malcolm Mackay (Liberal).

It couldn't have been a more politically diverse crowd. Mac Holten and his Liberal colleagues fiercely supported Australia's commitment to the Vietnam War, the Labor members opposed it and wanted the troops home. Their views reflected the polarisation of opinion in Australia: those who supported the war because they saw it as saving South East Asia (and Australia) from Communism, and a growing number — now the majority — who recognised the fraudulence of this claim and called for withdrawal. More and more people, particularly students, were protesting vehemently about B-52 bombings along the Ho Chi Minh trail in Laos and Cambodia, the massacre of Vietnamese civilians at My Lai by US Lieutenant William Calley and his company in March 1968, napalm strikes and tiger cages and strategic hamlets. Following the Tet Offensive in January 1968, Australia's resolve to stay the course had (like America's) gradually weakened. There were mass rallies of protesters in all Australian cities, an especially large one in Melbourne addressed by Jim Cairns attracted 70,000 protesters, but was scorned by the Victorian premier, Sir Henry Bolte, as being composed of 'Communist dupes'. While this was going on, Prime Minister Gorton quietly decided in April 1970 to withdraw 900 troops by November of the same year.

At the beginning of our tour in South Vietnam, the parliamentarians busily tried to score political points. Dr Mackay in particular was constantly on the lookout for proof that the NVA and Vietcong were agents of a world-wide Communist conspiracy as proven (to him) by the Chinese and Russian markings on captured weapons. He photographed a lot of weapons. But as we travelled by Iroquois helicopters and a twin-engined World War II RAAF Dakota to US and ARVN bases in I Corps in the north, II Corps, III Corps and IV Corps — sufficiently high to avoid sniper fire from the ground — the delegates became quieter and more reflective as they saw first-hand the poverty and misery, and the damage that bombs, artillery fire and napalm could do. And neither the fluent and uniformly optimistic briefings at every whistlestop by English-speaking ARVN officers in cravats and jungle fatigues, nor those of public relations officers at US bases, allayed the impression. Indeed, the sheer mass of weaponry at US bases, much of it dirty and ill-used, and the smell of cannabis occasionally wafting from the tent lines, added to the feeling that the Americans were having morale problems as they tried, against opposition at home, to win an unwinnable war.

I witnessed this at a time when some of our colleagues in Canberra, especially those who had served in the Australian Embassy in Saigon, were telling us with great certainty that they could see 'the light at the end of the tunnel'.

Things were better at the Australian bases at Vung Tau and Nui Dat, and at the small army base, 'Australia House', in Danang. Vehicles and equipment were clean and well cared for, and the soldiers were smartly dressed and optimistic. They had some good stories about the success of their civic action programs. So did the staff at the Australian Embassy in Saigon, and the doctors and nurses at an Australian surgical hospital we visited. But in reality, the total Australian influence on the course of the war was negligible, and our participation would make no difference to the outcome. It was the same in Cambodia and Laos. We met local leaders and US area commanders and Australian Embassy staff, and aid workers. All were determinedly upbeat, and none were prepared to state the obvious: that once the Americans went home, the Communist forces in all three countries would simply take over from corrupt local governments in their own time. What was not foreseen was the horrific situation developing in Cambodia — the rise of Pol Pot and his malignant and insane strain of Marxist theory that would result in two million deaths in that country between 1975 and 1979.

Re-energised by the reality check of this regional visit, I returned to Rangoon's time-warp with some fresh perspectives. One was that General Ne Win was quite shrewd in maintaining a policy of regional neutrality and isolation from both the Cold War and the war in Indochina. In any event, Ne Win had his hands full fighting Chinese forces that were encroaching into the Shan State from Yunan.

At the end of my two-year posting to Rangoon, I was not senior enough to send my thoughts to Canberra about what might happen in Burma, and how Australia might relate to it in the years ahead. That was for the ambassador to think about in his valedictory despatch. But if I had written anything, it would be something like the observations that the experienced journalist Hamish McDonald made to a gathering of the Sydney branch of the Australian Institute of International Affairs on 8 April 2008.

Hamish emphasised two phenomena: the absolute power of the military government, and economic rivalry between China and India for Burmese resources. He had entered Burma (now called Myanmar) from China disguised as an art dealer in the aftermath of the uprising by Buddhist monks and civilians in September 2007. He found the army was surprisingly invisible to a casual visitor, but its internal surveillance was sharp and pervasive. Locals were fearful of arrest and strongly disinclined to speak to foreigners. Despite trying to keep an invisible profile, Hamish and his photographer were shadowed and interrogated by intelligence officers for filming something as innocent as the rehearsal by an army brass band. Diplomats in Rangoon confirmed to him that the army was very strong and in control. Unlike the civilian community, it had good rations, a ferocious sense of *esprit de corps*, and a capacity to fight and prevail over Karen and Shan insurgency to the east.

Meanwhile Indian, Korean and Chinese companies were competing for oil and gas contracts on the Arakan coast. Their focus was the port of Sittwe, but also on building a network of roads connecting Maymyo, Bhamo, Mandalay and other towns. China wanted to build an oil and gas pipeline from Sittwe across country into Yunan. The Indians (and Koreans) were trying to convince the Burmese that China wanted to take over, and to divert these resources to them. Thailand, Malaysia and Singapore had strong commercial interests in Myanmar too.

Internally, the generals were working in harmony, and the number three general was well-positioned to take over from the number one, Than Shwe. Time and again, their cynical internal politicking displaced any concern for the Burmese people. The latest example was their indifference to the suffering of rural communities in the wake of Cyclone Nargis which struck the Irrawaddy Delta on 2 May 2008. They also showed remarkably little compassion towards Ne Win, who had died in 1993, and whose daughter was still in jail. Aung San Su Chi was effectively barred from running in elections for having married a foreigner. To provide a semblance of reform, the press continually blathered on about a referendum on a new constitution, but that sort of talk had been going on for fourteen years.

At the time of writing the Burmese generals remain unthreatened by their neighbours, who are competing fiercely for Burma's mineral and energy resources. In this context Western countries have no influence, and economic sanctions do not work. There are no opportunities to cultivate alternative power centres, and the country's isolation will probably deepen. I predict that a generation will grow up with little or no knowledge about the outside world, and the generals will grow richer and more corrupt — altogether a perfect recipe for another failed state in the Third World.

If this is a true picture, there seems to be little opportunity for Australia, even if it had the will, to do anything effective to change things. All we can do is continue as before to monitor the situation from the Australian Embassy in Rangoon, and work hard to bring pressure to bear at the United Nations.

After selling the Kingswoo to the Embassy of the Republic of Korea, Ali and Anna and I returned to Australia in November 1971. At the Adelaide Women's Hospital on 25th of that month Ali gave birth to our second child, Adam Richard Gracius. As the American doctor in Rangoon, who had guided Ali through a difficult pregnancy said, Adam was a 'high premium' baby. We were lucky to have him.

5

In an Antique Land

I met a traveller from an antique land
Who said: 'Two vast and trunkless legs of stone
Stand in the desert. Near them on the sand,
Half sunk, a shattered visage lies, whose frown
And wrinkled lip and sneer of cold command
Tell that its sculptor well those passions read
Which yet survive, stamped on these lifeless things,
The hand that mocked them and the heart that fed.
And on the pedestal these words appear:
'My name is Ozymandias, King of Kings:
Look on my works, ye mighty, and despair!'
Nothing beside remains. Round the decay
Of that colossal wreck, boundless and bare,
The lone and level sands stretch far away.

PERCY BYSSHE SHELLEY, *Ozymandias*

The airconditioned tents rose like a mirage in the desert. Arranged in the shape of a star, they had French silk draperies, caviar and Chivas Regal in every stateroom. In the bathrooms of tents assigned to kings and heads of state were gold taps, in those for heads of governments, silver ones. The extravaganza was organised by Mohammad Reza Shah Pahlavi, the Persian monarch, to celebrate 2500 years of imperial reign. Kings, presidents, sheiks and prime ministers all came to pay homage and enjoy the celebrations. The year was 1971.

Not known for his sense of irony, the Shah had the tents laid out beside the ancient ruins of Persepolis in southern Iran, on whose fire-blackened marble columns could still be found graffiti carved by the troops of Alexander the Great in 331 BCE. If someone had been reckless enough to suggest to the Shah that he was tempting fate by holding his celebrations at a place of such defeat, he would have said that Alexander's invasion had merely interrupted the glorious continuity of Persia's kings. These began 600 years BCE with the Achaemenid dynasty established by Cyrus I, and were amplified by his son, Cyrus the Great, into the world's first empire.

But the celebrations at Persepolis were designed to overlook the fact that along with growing weakness and corruption of the shahs, Persia's empire had shrunk through the centuries. By the time the Qajahs began their reign in the last quarter of the eighteenth century, their writ hardly extended beyond Tehran. The rest of the country was ruled by tribal leaders, regional chieftains and religious authorities. Humiliatingly, the Russians exercised territorial influence in the north through their Cossack brigade, and the British in the south with their Persian light rifles.

In his father, Reza, however, the Shah did have something to celebrate. Reza Khan was a fit and strong-willed soldier, an officer in the Cossacks. When the Russians went home during the revolution of 1917, he rose unimpeded through the ranks, came to Tehran and in a series of astute political manoeuvres forced the corrupt Qajars to abdicate. He wanted a secular republic like Turkey's under Kemal Ataturk, but the clergy preferred to retain the monarchy with Shi'a Islam as the state religion. So in 1925, Reza Khan proclaimed himself Reza Shah and began the Pahlavi dynasty.

At the Persepolis celebrations the fact was also obscured that the Pahlavi dynasty had itself been briefly interrupted. In 1953, Mohammad Reza Shah was forced to flee the country until Prime Minister Mohammad Mossadegh, who wanted to nationalise the oil industry, had been deposed in a coup urged by the British and engineered by the CIA.

The Iranian capital Tehran climbs from a vast high desert plain to the slopes of the Elburz Mountains. The cantilevered plain rises from 2000 metres in the south to 4000 metres in the north. Beyond the Elburz to the north is a watershed where rain is abundant and rice terraces lead down to the Caspian Sea. To the south are rugged deserts, underground rivers and mountain ranges as far as the Persian Gulf. Tehran is fiercely hot in summer, and cold and snowy in winter. Among its five million inhabitants, the rich live in the high north, with first access to the reservoirs and mountain-fed streams. The numerous poor live below the bazaar in the south and get what remains of the water after it has percolated through the city. Most southerners are conservative Shi'a Muslims, the women in chadors, despite earlier attempts by Reza Shah to ban them. Each evening and at designated times during the day comes the wail of the mullahs from the mosques, calling the devout to prayer through their loudspeakers. The plangent sound echoes through the dusty streets and infuses the city.

Our little family arrived at Tehran's Mehrabad airport late on a winter night in January 1972. Adam was two months old. There was no traffic in the broad boulevards, and under the illumination of the street lights, the city looked modern and clean, with occasional snowdrifts filling the deep concrete *jubes* (gutters) at the sides of the roads. In one of the embassy's two new Mercedes 220 compacts, our driver Mahmoud proceeded rapidly through the empty streets to the Intercontinental Hotel. There we spent several days getting our bearings before moving into the bachelor flat of my predecessor, David Reese. For reasons known only to himself, David had left behind a supply of canned chestnuts, which became the basic ingredient for Ali's chestnut mousse, served at parties throughout our posting. In the street outside the flat camel trains swayed past, bearing Persian rugs to the Tehran bazaar. The apartment was a resting place to acclimatise ourselves to the local environment, arrange kindergarten for Anna, and find a house suitable to the needs of a family of four. We also had to get some wheels.

The flat was also close to the Australian Embassy. This was in a tall, narrow building ten minutes' walk from the apartment, near the corner of Roosevelt Avenue and Takt-e-Jamshid Boulevard. When I arrived in Tehran the Ambassador was Barry Hall, a congenial and experienced officer near the end of his posting. Towards the end of 1972 he was replaced by H. D. (Doug) White, an ex-air force officer for whom I had worked in the first year of my career in the SEATO Aid branch of the department. We also had a couple of political officers, a trade commissioner and various Australian and locally engaged administrative and consular staff. The doorman was Mr Eboullion, who could always find us a 200-gram tin of Beluga caviar at a special price — a wonderful occasional supper treat with blinis, sour cream, chopped onion and hard-boiled egg, washed down with a bottle of vodka in a sleeve of ice.

Iran was important to Australia in three respects. It was a growing market for live sheep, sheep meat and grains. It was a major world supplier of oil. And it was becoming a powerful player in the politics of the Middle East. My job was to follow the oil industry, keep track of the Shah's ambitious military expenditure and monitor the political situation. I also took it on myself to find out what I could about the Shah's fledgling nuclear facilities.

The oil industry was complex. In 1972, Iran was exporting between six and eight million barrels a day, the second largest Middle Eastern supplier after Saudi Arabia. During my time, a conjunction of events dramatically changed global oil pricing and supply. One was a simultaneous surge in industrial growth in Europe, Japan and the United States. Another was competition between the 'majors' (Exxon, Mobil, California Standard, Texaco, Gulf, BP, Shell and Compagnie Française des Pétroles) and a growing band of independent oil companies for what was suddenly seen as a finite global resource. A third was the new power of the Organisation of Petroleum Exporting Countries (OPEC), including Iran, to set oil prices. The Arab–Israeli war of October 1973 triggered the so-called 'Oil Shock', driving up oil prices to the then unheard-of level of US $10 per barrel. I also covered the oil industry in the United Arab Emirates and Oman, on the southern shore of the Gulf, and occasionally travelled to Dubai, Abu Dhabi and Muscat to see what was going on.

The Shah's military plans were ambitious. Driven by fear of Soviet military encirclement through Yemen in the west and Afghanistan to the east, he was radically re-equipping his army, navy and air force. Using funds from his enormous oil revenue, he was buying British Chieftain tanks and hovercraft for the world's first hovercraft squadron; American frigates, missiles, F-4 Phantom and F-5 Freedom Fighters and helicopters; and bits and pieces from France, Germany, even the Soviet Union. As if all this was not enough, the Shah wanted more ambitious weapons systems from the United States, including Spruance-class destroyers and cutting-edge fighters such as the new F-14 Tomcat and F-16 Falcon. Iran had its own small-arms factories, and traded knowledge and weapons with Israel and South Africa. At the time 35,000 American military technicians were in Iran training the Iranian military in operating and servicing all this new equipment.

Advised by the World Bank and particularly Australia's Sir John Crawford about Iran's resources, the Shah believed oil was a finite resource that should be used for petrochemicals, not for generating electricity. He had established the CENTO Institute of Nuclear Science at Tehran University in 1959, equipped by Britain and staffed by British, Turkish, Pakistani and Iranian scientists. He had ordered four large nuclear power reactors along the Persian Gulf to come on line sequentially in 1981, 1982, 1983 and 1984. The first two — pressurised light water reactors (PWRs) of 1200 mW each — were to be built by

Kraftwerk Union of West Germany. Framatome of France was building the second two — PWRs each of 900 mW. Iran was also negotiating for a further eight more PWRs from Westinghouse. I have no doubt that the Shah wanted also to develop a uranium enrichment facility. He might also have toyed with the idea of developing nuclear weapons, but this remains uncertain.

It is worth noting that the Shah's nuclear ambitions are seldom recalled by observers when condemning those of President Ahmadinejad in the first decade of the 2000s. These were seen by the Bush Administration as malevolent, the sole purpose being to develop nuclear weapons. But all we know for certain is that, like the Shah, Ahmadinejad wants to enrich uranium, as well as develop nuclear power. Both are legal options under the terms of the Nuclear Non-Proliferation Treaty, of which Iran continues to be a signatory.

As for politics in the 1970s, the Shah was a constitutional monarch. He worked with an executive which he appointed, and a *majlis* (national assembly) chosen by the people. He drove himself and his officials hard to modernise Iran after centuries of backwardness. He wanted industries, agriculture, hydropower, modern schools and universities, and emancipation for women, and he wanted them all at once. Iran was rich in cash but poor in skilled labour. The country was seething with skilled foreign technicians, mainly Americans, especially in the arms industries. There were also French, Italians, Germans, British, Israelis and Scandinavians. The few Australian experts were mainly agricultural technologists.

Initially, it seemed to me that the Shah was safe and secure, and adored by his people. Every merchant in every bazaar had a framed photo of the Shah and the Shahbanou (Farah Diba) in their window. Some wealthy and articulate Tehranis (not those associated with the former Qajar dynasty) would enthusiastically affirm that the Shah was wonderful.

He certainly did have a great sense of theatre, as I discovered when I accompanied Doug White to the summer palace in northern Tehran in early 1973 to present his credentials. We made our way between two ranks of court officials in braided gold uniforms, before walking into a vast assembly hall. At the end of a long Persian carpet runner stood a refulgent Shah in full court regalia. He was backlit by a ray of sunshine streaming in from a high window.

They say the embassy is the diplomat's security blanket: he or she escapes every day and becomes immersed in important matters while the spouse remains at home trying to negotiate a worthwhile existence. Because of highly sexist and discriminatory public service rules that applied when we married in December 1963, Ali was disqualified from remaining in the Commonwealth Public Service. But with her work ethic, intellectual curiosity about Iran, socialising and looking after two infant children, she was fully engaged.

And I was anxious to get us all into a living environment more spacious than David's flat.

We soon found what we wanted in Farmanieh, a suburb on the high, northern fringe of the city near the Shah's Niavaran Palace. The two-storey, flat-roofed house was made of the usual rough brick, like most houses at the time. But the brickwork was disguised with marble cladding, and we had sunny terraces and a spacious garden behind high mud-brick walls. Again, like many other Tehrani houses, its roof was made of straw and camel dung, sealed with a waterproof bitumen membrane. This insulated the house during the dry summers, but when the winter snows melted, moisture found its way through cracks in the ceiling. At one spring dinner party, a section of camel dung and straw suddenly detached itself from the ceiling and landed with a wet thud on our dining table as I was about to carve the roast.

Servants cost much more in Tehran than in Rangoon. We had a dishwasher, a gas stove, and Ali did the shopping and cooking. Our single servant was Fatima, a short, wide Turkoman of indefinite age who helped look after the children. Fatima (Fats for short) was devoted to Adam, chanting monotonously '*boko, boko*' (eat, eat) as she stuffed food into him. Fatima was illiterate, but she communicated well enough in Farsi, which Ali and I were studying. If we did not at first understand, Fatima would raise her voice and enunciate slowly as if to idiots. Her idea of a good day out was to attend the funeral of one of her many cousins, aunts, brothers or sisters, who seemed to die fairly regularly. In her black chador, she could weep and wail and beat her breast with the best of them. She always came home from these occasions thoroughly envigorated.

It was now time to find some transport. After much agonising, I had decided that we could just afford to buy a 2.8 litre Jaguar XJ6. I fantasised that it would eat up the miles as it loped across the Persian deserts. Ali, who fancied herself driving such a car in an elegant straw hat, needed little persuasion. We decided we would take delivery of the car in London, and drive it back across Europe to Iran. I had read in the literature that the XJ6, which first appeared at Brown's Lane in Coventry in 1968, was a comprehensive upgrade from previous Jaguar saloons. With a new body and radical new suspension system, it squatted widely on fat Dunlop radials. In the brochures it always seemed to be going very fast, even when standing still.

But the car I had ordered wouldn't be ready for several months. Meanwhile, we needed something cheap to get around Tehran in. A colleague in the American Embassy suggested I visit Tehran Customs, where foreigners frequently abandoned their cars rather than pay the exorbitant excise required to bring them in or out of Iran. So early one Saturday I took a cab to the bleak Customs lot in the southern reaches of the city and gazed at a motley collection of cars huddling under mounds of dirty snow. Nothing looked inspiring until a BMW radiator badge caught my attention. I smoothed the snow off the bonnet and found an unbent, white, four-door sedan. I asked the attendant to get some jumper leads. The engine coughed into an uneven beat, and I gingerly drove it round the yard. Brakes, clutch and steering all worked. So did the lights, indicators, instruments, radio and heater. It had 20,000 kays on the clock. I couldn't take it for a run without paying the tax, so without even checking for rust, I took a punt and bought it on the spot. It cost me about $US500.

It was a brilliant punt. I had purchased a 1966 BMW 1800 Neue Klasse, a car celebrated for its performance and keen handling, the 1500 cc version of which had allowed a failing company at the start of the decade to avoid being swallowed up by Daimler-Benz. BMW had been famous for its fast coupes and roadsters in the late 1930s, but its postwar recovery had been hampered by inappropriate model choices — tiny bubble cars and overweight luxury sedans. The Neue Klasse, with four-cylinder engines ranging from 1500 to 1800 ccs, appealed strongly to 'Aufsteigers', the growing number of German buyers suddenly affluent on the strength of the Wirtschaftswunder economic boom, and who craved something more youthful and dynamic than a Mercedes.

We drove the Beamer all over Tehran. It was dependable and solid. This was the car in which we hit a bus head-on and survived with minor injuries during the late autumn of 1973 on our way to a Halloween party.

When the Jag was ready the Beamer became Ali's car, in which every morning she would ferry Anna to the British School for kindergarten, then drive with Adam to the Tajrish bazaar to do the shopping. The roads were frequently crowded, and Iranians (almost all men), drove recklessly and fast. They had no patience for queuing at traffic lights, even mounting the footpath as they jockeyed for position like Formula One racing cars waiting for the flag to fall. In such conditions the Beamer's acceleration, quick handling and ruggedness were essential safety factors. As for the Jaguar, we finally got a telegram saying it was ready to collect. In April 1972 I took ten days leave and Ali and I flew off to London, leaving Anna with an Australian family whose younger daughter, Emma, was her close friend and whose dad was an aeronautical engineer with IranAir. At eight months, Adam had no say in the matter, and he remained contentedly at home in Farmanieh with Fatima.

In Britain we stayed with the Smarts, our British friends from Rangoon, near High Wycombe. A couple of days later, breathless with anticipation, I went into London to collect the Jaguar. Like the Kingswood, it was ducoed white to deflect the Iranian sun, with a sandy-coloured interior of Connolly hide to match the Iranian desert. It was crouching on the delivery floor, freshly washed, tyres blacked, with large British number plates and a round Jaguar decal with running-in instructions on the windscreen. I opened the bonnet and inspected the beautiful XK 2.8 litre engine with its polished cam covers, twin SU HS8 carburetters and gleaming black exhaust manifold. The car's interior lit up when I opened the door and I breathed in the perfume of new leather and polished woodwork. The car started with a soft purr, with only one thing slightly puncturing my mood: almost no fuel in the dual tanks. A cost-saver by the company, but such a miserable one.

After a couple of days driving around country lanes with our friends, enjoying picnics at county cricket matches and an air show, Ali and I were ready for the trip back to Tehran. We had to get there fast because I had promised Barry Hall we'd be back in time for some dinner he wanted me to help him host (something I later regretted: the trip would have been far more enjoyable if taken slowly). We went across the Channel in a ferry to Oostende then drove through Belgium to Germany; from there to Vienna, Budapest, and down to Belgrade. Five days on the road and all going well. Thence to Greece — from Thessaloníki, keeping the Aegean Sea on our right, and across the border into Turkey.

So far, so good. The Jaguar was performing beautifully. But on the long stretch from the Turkish border to the Bosphorus, I noticed a squeaking noise in the front end. It had to be the power steering. In Istanbul we found the authorised Jaguar dealer was housed in a reassuringly solid building with mechanics running around in clean white overalls with 'Jaguar' emblazoned on their biro-filled breast pockets. Several quickly came over to inspect the car.

'I'm glad we made it to here before we try crossing the Anatolian plateau into Iran,' I said. 'I'm sure you blokes can fix the problem.'

'Fix it?' exclaimed the foreman. 'We've never seen one of these before!'

So, with a large can of power steering fluid and a good night's sleep, we proceeded on our way into Asia Minor. We drove from Istanbul to Ankara, then north to the Black Sea, passing along a spectacular coast through Samsun, Ordu and Trabzon, from where we climbed steeply inland to Erzurum. The locals were not very happy to see us and we were occasionally pelted with small stones. Aagh! The duco! But on, on we went, like hash-house harriers, across rugged mountain ranges and through small villages to the Iranian–Turkish border at Maku. After an overnight wait in a parking area full of overloaded Mercedes trucks and buses with myriad coloured lights like Christmas trees, we proceeded through Customs into Iran. Then we went southeast, the road deep in valleys running parallel to high mountain ranges, through Khvoy, Marand and Tabriz in Azarbayjan. And, on what was becoming an increasingly good bitumen road that lifted the spirit, through Mianen, Mehrabad, Zanjan, Qazvin and Karaj into Tehran. We were finally home.

Anna and Adam were delighted to see us. So was Fatima. And we made the ambassador's dinner party. I sent a telegram to Jaguar in London about the steering rack, and they promptly air-freighted out a new one. But it was for a left-hand drive, so back it went and a couple of weeks later a right-hand one arrived, to be fitted by the local agents.

There were no more mechanical problems until the following winter, when the Jaguar developed a temperamental personality. Sitting in its snow-covered garage at Fermanieh, it was reluctant to start. The automatic choke would stick and flood the engine. So we established a routine: open the bonnet, remove the air cleaner, lift the pistons of the carburettors and allow the engine to breathe while activating the starter motor. Ali usually did the lifting, until one day the engine blew back and she and the car caught fire. I knew instantly which one to put out first, but I still got to Ali before any serious damage had been done. The problem could not be fixed in Iran, teaching me a basic lesson: never take a sophisticated car into a country which did not have an established modern auto service industry. The Iranians were assembling Hillman Minxes and re-badging them as Peykans, but that hardly counted.

During weekends and when I was on leave, we drove the Jaguar to the snow, to the desert, and to as many towns as we could. The Iranian roads were generally excellent, and although Iranian drivers were aggressive and sometimes dangerous, there weren't many about outside Tehran. We drove north-east over the Elburz mountains to the rainy shores of the Caspian Sea, stopping to sample chello kebab and caviar and local salted pistachios at resort towns like Gorgan, Amol, Babol, Lahijan, Bandar Anzali and Rasht. Each town had its own peculiarities and traditions. At Rasht, for example, the men are reputedly not the sharpest knives in the drawer. The story goes that a Rashti businessman comes home unexpectedly for lunch with a colleague to show him his new house. He shows his guest the garden, the entrance foyer respendent with tribal rugs from Tabriz, and the living room. They ascend the broad staircase to the upper level. 'And this is the main bedroom,' says the Rashti, 'and that is our bed. And there is my wife. And that must be me.'

We drove up to the northern ski resorts at Dezful and Shemshak, and west across the Zagros Mountains to Hamadan and Bakhtaran as far as Khorramabad. Also south through Qom and Isfahan, through the deserts as far as Shiraz, where we could smell the roses, lilac, narcissus and jasmine — their original Persian botanical names — and hear the nightingales sing in the pure night air of the desert. During these forays, we would stop at carpet dealers to look at their wares, and occasionally buy a particularly attractive piece. Always these exceptionally courteous merchants would beg us to just take the rug we fancied back to Tehran free of charge or obligation, and 'try it out'. They well knew the seductive quality of their rugs, and that only rarely would a carpet be returned.

I met Richard Nixon and his National Security Adviser Henry Kissinger at Mehrebad airport in early 1973 en route to Washington after a visit to Europe. Doug White was out of Iran at the time. As a junior chargé, I was placed at the end of the receiving line and when I was introduced, Nixon drew me aside to tell me at length how much he had appreciated the support of Australian Prime Minister William McMahon in his 'difficult decision' to bomb Hanoi and mine Haiphong harbour with repeated B-52 strikes in Exercise Linebacker in December 1972.

I wanted to tell Nixon that Mr McMahon might have supported Nixon's decision, but the new prime minister, Gough Whitlam, would not, and nor did I. But I wasn't paid to express my own feelings. I merely thanked him and sent a priority cable to Canberra the next day recording the event.

At the time, we only occasionally glimpsed the heavy hand of the Iranian State Intelligence and Security Organisation (SAVAK), or heard rumours of state-sponsored torture. The Shah was certainly well guarded. I remember taking Ali and Anna to a masters' tennis tournament in a Tehran stadium. John Newcombe was playing the Mexican Raoul Ramirez in the men's singles final. The gallery, players, ballboys and umpires all had to wait for the arrival of the Shah and Shahbanou in a helicopter. As the players warmed up, I glanced around and found every second seat in that crowded place occupied by a man in sunglasses with his hand inside his jacket. One could occasionally catch the dull glint of gunmetal. No one present could have guessed the pathetic fate that awaited the seemingly all-powerful Shah barely seven years later.

Our posting ended after two years, in December 1973. All too soon our household goods had to be packed and shipped home. I sold the BMW to a colleague in the embassy. As for the Jaguar, I had decided to drive it down to the Shatt al-Arab for shipping back to Sydney. So I set off south through the cold winter desert, through Qom, Arak, once more traversing the Zagros Mountains to Khorramabad, then through the southern Iranian oil fields, their gas flares perpetually lighting the sky, through Dezful and Shush and Ahvaz, and down to Khorramshah near the giant former British oil refinery at Abadan. At Khorramshah the car was to be carefully prepared for the long sea voyage to Sydney. I reluctantly left it to its portside handlers amid many assurances that it would survive the voyage unscathed. On collecting it in Sydney months later, I found that on the voyage someone had broken into the car and used it as sleeping quarters. We eventually got rid of the dirt and smell of cheap cigars and liquor, but it took some effort.

In Tehran, I had heard rumours of regular piston failures in the Jaguar's 2.8 litre engine. The fault was said to be due to residual carbon deposits that built up in the combustion chamber, valve and piston surfaces, causing detonations which could burn through a piston. I was assured that if my car had been driven hard with wide throttle openings, the problem would not appear. But throughout its young life, I had treated it gently. I didn't want to be faced with a major engine reconstruction, so without getting to enjoy it on Australian roads, I reluctantly sold the car to a Sydney Jaguar dealer in mid 1974. Owning and driving the XJ6 had been one of the more disastrous experiences of my life so far.

Two events occurred which kept Iran in my mind. The first was a state visit to Australia by the Shah in 1974. I was head of the department's South Asian Section at the time, but I nevertheless put in a lengthy submission to the divisional head, Michael Cook, about the Shah, and what we might consider aiming to achieve during his visit. But a peculiarity in the department at the time (it probably still exists), was that an officer's previous experiences are seldom exploited. Cook barely acknowledged my analysis of the Shah and Iran, let alone suggesting that I should be involved in the visit. I suppose it went well enough without my input, but my non-involvement was frustrating.

The other event was the resurgence of fundamental Shia Islam in Iran during the late 1970s, culminating in the ignominious flight of the Shah and his family in 1979, and Ayatollah Khomeini's triumphant return from France, where he had been living in exile. Having lived in Iran, why could I not have predicted this? More to the point, perhaps, how did the Americans, the French and the British with their large embassies, their intelligence operations, and their trading networks, fail to see what was coming?

Two factors were at play here. The first was something many Western embassies in Tehran, especially the British and American, preferred to forget: the overthrow of Prime Minister Mohammad Mossadegh in 1953 by the CIA. Mossadegh was the first (and only) democratically elected leader in Iran, or for that matter, anywhere else in the Middle East except for Israel. He was a European-educated Iranian aristocrat who believed passionately in nationalism and democracy. He wanted to nationalise the Anglo-Iranian Oil Company and use the money to develop Iran. The British were not powerful or wealthy enough to engineer a coup themselves, so they enlisted the Americans, falsely claiming that Mossadegh was a secret member of the communist Tudeh Party. This was a red rag to Secretary of State John Foster Dulles and his brother Allen, director of the CIA. They inserted a talented CIA agent in Tehran, Kermit Roosevelt, grandson of President Theodore Roosevelt, who organised the de-stabilising Operation Ajax using substantial agency funds for bribing local thugs to stage 'popular' demonstrations against Mossadegh. The beleaguered prime minister and his loyal followers held out for some months, but he was eventually overthrown and imprisoned. The Shah gratefully returned from Rome to regain his Peacock Throne.

The second factor was that many Western embassies fooled themselves into believing the propaganda about the popularity of the Shah and his reforms. Their locally engaged staff — mainly Armenian Christians, hardly ever Shi'a Arab who were reluctant to work for Westerners — were no help. Meanwhile, adulation in the government-controlled press and ubiquitous photographs of the royal family in every shop window concealed the fact that most Iranians hated the Shah and his modernisation efforts. The Shahbanou was also deeply unpopular for advancing the rights of women. Throughout 1979, the American Ambassador, Bill Sullivan, had repeatedly tried to tell Secretary of State Cyrus Vance and National Security Adviser Zbigniew Brzezinski of the Shah's unpopularity, and recommended that the US cut its losses, withdraw support from him and start dealing with moderate elements in the Shi'a revolutionary movement. His advice was rejected by President Jimmy Carter and he was told to get on with his job. He remained in Tehran until his embassy was machine-gunned and overrun by Islamic revolutionary guards. When he was repatriated to Washington, Bill promptly resigned from the Foreign Service and retired to Mexico. (A full account of Bill's misadventure is in his book — see References.)

Thus Iran denounced materialism, modernity, democratic pluralism, and embraced theocracy and sharia law. But I believe it is a mistake to brand the country a rogue state as President

George W. Bush did, or to rush to judgement about its nuclear ambitions or its perceived wish to destroy Israel. The best course for an American administration of whatever persuasion would be to establish lines of communication, *talk* to the Iranians and understand their thinking. A bombing strike, either conventional or nuclear, against their nuclear facilities, or an invasion, would be a catastrophic mistake that would further destabilise the whole Middle East.

I hope to go back one day and drive another car across Iran's spectacular southern deserts, through Shiraz and Persepolis and Isfahan up to the high plain of Tehran, and from there over the Alborz Mountains to the rain shadow which hovers over the Caspian Sea. And I hope when I do, the country will not be contaminated by nuclear fallout.

6

The Yellow Terror and a German Lemon

Ali and I managed to work together as diplomats in the same overseas mission only once in our careers, in Manila from 1975 to 1977. Progress towards this goal was agonisingly slow. The Public Service Act had been amended in 1966 to permit married women to be permanent officers in the Commonwealth Public Service. And in 1969 and 1972, the Conciliation and Arbitration Commission had established the principle of equal pay for equal work for all Australian women.

The Department of Foreign Affairs had been forced to accept both amendments, though some traditionalists had been unhappy. But management had not considered the next logical step: joint postings for married couples. They claimed that the department had always been progressive in recognising women's rights, but this was not the case. A prevailing but unspoken conviction in top management was that diplomacy was a man's world in which married women backed up their diplomatic husbands and single ones were secretaries who served the tea. Overseas, women married to diplomats were hostesses and social arrangers, with a bit of part-time charity work on the side in poorer countries where it did not offend the host government. Someone like Ali was resented by management and some of the more conservative senior wives, many of whom had sacrificed their own careers. Why should a woman have it all — a husband, children and the right to work as a diplomat? One or two single women diplomats in the department harboured similar resentment.

In 1973, Gough Whitlam rattled these prejudices when he recalled Alan Renouf, the liberal-minded ambassador to Paris, and appointed him secretary of Foreign Affairs. Joint postings were hardly at the top of Renouf's agenda, but Ali forced the issue when she was invited to rejoin the department in mid 1974. 'Could I expect an overseas posting with Richard,' she asked, 'or would I be penalised if I refused to accept a posting without him?' Personnel hadn't considered this, but after consultations with the Public Service Board, senior management came back and agreed to a joint posting. Two married couples were given the nod. Geoffrey and Rosemary Forrester were sent to the Australian Permanent Mission to the United Nations in New York and Ali and I were posted to the Philippines, where two positions at our levels were available.

During pre-posting consultations in Canberra, we had arranged to meet our new ambassador, Gerry Nutter, then in the middle of his own pre-departure briefings. Whatever his private reservations, Gerry was outwardly enthusiastic about our joining him, and said he looked forward to our arrival in Manila. And so in January 1975, full of optimism about living and working together in a tropical paradise with the family, we packed our goods for storage, let the house, and sold the car.

This had been a well-travelled and most useful 1973 Renault 16 TL, the first European hatchback, European Car of the Year when it first appeared in 1966, and still very popular at the end of its production run in 1980.

We had mental images of the Philippines: 7100 islands with white sand, coral lagoons, coconut trees and nipa huts. If my reservation was that the 7100 islands were without a decent highway for serious driving, I kept it to myself. I didn't want to rain on Anna or Adam's parade.

As it was designed to, the departmental post report dashed some of these expectations — it emphasised the negative to ensure that Manila was designated a hardship post to attract better living allowances. The report portrayed the Philippines as the odd man out in Asia: a hybrid society consisting mainly of Chinese, Indian and Malay émigrés with a Third World economy. The report painted Manila as an overcrowded and dirty city with institutional corruption, a high crime rate, primitive medical facilities, inadequate public transport, frequent electricity cuts, and annual typhoons that brought flooding and chaos.

All this was true, but colleagues who had been posted there offered an alternative perspective. At all levels, they agreed, Filipinos were informal and friendly, even in government. A political counsellor like me could easily make friends with a cabinet minister. The people were also hospitable, and the poorer they were the more unstinting their generosity. Forty years of American colonialism overlay three centuries of Spanish Catholicism. The Americans had left a presidential system of government, well-organised courts, a remarkably good education system, widespread literacy, and a press so free it bordered on irresponsibility. But like their Spanish predecessors, they hadn't solved the problems of the Muslim south.

After arrival in Manila, our little family had a short spell in a hotel and then moved into the house of the officer I was replacing, Cavan Hogue. In the gated village of Dasmariñas, Cavan's house was airy and spacious. There were play areas for the children, an outdoor entertainment patio and a bit of garden. It fitted our family requirements well.

Cavan was the embassy's political counsellor and deputy head of mission, with a laid-back manner and laconic delivery that disguised a sharp intelligence. He drove a purple Jeep, spoke Tagalog and Spanish, and played a guitar with which he entertained the locals at innumerable parties in Manila and at barrio fiestas in the countryside. His cosmopolitan wife, Mira, was a Filipina.

I was tempted to buy Cavan's Jeep, but resisted. I had other plans for transport, which included a cheap but airconditioned local car for ferrying the children to school and kindergarten and gymnastics around Manila, and something new and exotic from Europe for longer trips in Luzon. Obviously I had not absorbed the lesson I should have learned in Tehran: do not bring a sophisticated motor car into a developing country without the mechanical expertise to service it.

The local machine I selected was a canary-yellow 1974 Holden LJ Torana, sold to me at a discount by the local distributor who was establishing a Holden dealership in Manila. Originally derived from the 1966 British Vauxhall Viva, the Torana was a sporty six-cylinder compact of 2250 cc capacity with four-on-the-floor and an effective airconditioner. By 1974, it had morphed into an Australian design. We hired a local Filipino, Patricio, as our driver. Like Anthony in Rangoon but without Anthony's penile preoccupation, Patricio was a safe and reliable driver in the Jeepney and bus-choked maelstrom of Manila's traffic.

Like everything else in the Philippines, road systems were over-bureaucratised to the point of impotence. To reduce speeding on major roads, they didn't just tell the cops to stop cars exceeding the speed limit but formed a task force comprising the Land Transportation Office (LTO), Land Transportation Franchising and Regulatory Board (LTFRB), Philippine National Police Highway Patrol Group (PNPHPG), Metropolitan Manila Development Authority, Department of Public Works and Highways, and about a hundred non-governmental organisations. Patricio patiently negotiated dreadful traffic jams every day, especially at the intersection of Epifanio de los Santos and Ayala Avenue in Makati, to drive Anna to her Montessori school at Santa Ana and Adam to his Montessori kindergarten in Dasmariñas.

I had ordered our other car from Stuttgart. With fond memories of the Beamer 1800 we had driven in Tehran, I had selected a new BMW 520i. It would take several months to arrive, so I contained my elated anticipation and absorbed myself in my new job at the embassy.

The Australian Embassy was situated in the China Bank building in Paseo de Roxas in nearby Makati, a new business centre east of the old city which spread out along Roxas Boulevard on Manila Bay. Makati had been an airfield during the war and the original control tower was preserved in a park overlooked by the chancery. Apart from Tokyo, the embassy was the largest Australian mission I had worked in. I had three colleagues in the political section. Ranking between the political counsellor (me) and second secretary (Ali), was the dour first secretary, Kevin Boreham, who described himself as the meat in the Broinowski sandwich. Ken Berry was an enthusiastic new third secretary who made himself indispensable to the ambassador as a competent aide and fixer. The chancery also accommodated large trade, administrative and consular sections, a military attaché and an information officer.

The consul, Trevor Greenwood, had a sardonic sense of humour, with which he enlivened Monday staff meetings with tales about Australian tourists and others. Ageing Australian men would come in with their Filipina fiancées to get certificates of no impediment to marry. Conscious of the disasters that had befallen some Filipina brides at the hands of their Australian husbands, Trevor would take the women aside and ask them if they knew what they were getting into. 'Oh, sir,' said one young woman brightly, 'my family is very happy because they can join me in family reunions.' (Reflective pause.) 'Anyway, he is so old that I will remain technically virginal.'

Trevor and his staff also needed all their good humour and tenacity in coping with Vietnamese boat people. Following the fall of Saigon in 1975, these were flooding across the China Sea to Luzon and seeking asylum in countries like Australia. After some initial hesitation, Gough Whitlam had been far more generous in accepting Asian refugees than was John Howard in accepting Middle Eastern ones three decades later. With Canada and other receiving countries, Trevor set up a consular tent for processing Vietnamese at their point of disembarkation in Luzon.

My job was to supervise the political section, analyse regional and domestic politics and deputise for the ambassador when he was out of town on his provincial tours, or out of the country. For local tours Gerry Nutter sometimes requested a vintage World War II radial-engined Dakota. This was flown by its Royal Australian Air Force crew to Manila from their base at Butterworth in Malaysia. On these trips, Gerry often invited members of his staff along. Some provincial airstrips were unsealed and hair-raisingly short, but Gerry was determined to visit every province in the Philippines during his posting.

Ali had economic and aid responsibilities. She consulted with Ambassador Rosario Manalo, the senior official in charge of Association of South East Asian Nations (ASEAN) affairs at the Foreign Ministry, with the head of Family Planning, the felicitously named Rosario Concepçion, and with Jerry Sicat, head of the National Economic Development Agency. She liaised with Australian engineers and agricultural experts developing an integrated rural development project in the southern province of Zamboanga del Sur. Managed by Peter Goldston, an engineer from the Snowy Mountains Engineering Corporation (SMEC), the project included irrigation and the construction of a network of farm-to-market roads. The Australian base was in the town of Pagadian. Peter was an efficient manager, always in a hurry. He drove his small fleet of Toyota LandCruisers as if he hated them — flat out even over the worst road corrugations. Some of his vehicles literally fell apart from metal fatigue.

Monitoring political, military and sectarian affairs kept me fully engaged. I analysed the usefulness of the Clark air base and Subic Bay naval base to American (and Filipino) interests. I researched the so-called New People's Army and the Moro National Liberation Front, (a band of Muslim rebels in the southern island of Zamboanga). I developed a strong stomach for liquor, drinking brandy on early morning calls to Defence Secretary Juan Ponce Enrile and some of his colleagues. I had breakfast regularly with one of the two Catholic Cardinals in the Philippines; and the politically astute Chinese priest Jaime Sin would jovially greet me at the entrance to his palace, as he did all his visitors, with his well-worn joke: 'Welcome to the house of Sin!' In church–state affairs, he was conservative, but was responsible as much as anyone for Marcos's downfall in 1986. I got to know the intelligent, straight-shooting Chief Cabinet Secretary Alexandro Melchor and his staff, and through them developed an understanding of President Marcos' power base.

I tried to make an accurate assessment of President Marcos. Did he have much popular support? How corrupt was he? How serious and frequent were his violations of human rights? The ambassador had his own views, but he saw a lot of Ferdinand Marcos and his wife Imelda, who were both very good at charming ambassadors, especially when they took them on cruises on the presidential yacht. I hadn't had such experiences, and looked at Marcos through a more critical lens. I believed the president's public relations people unrealistically burnished his image and that his youthful achievements as a student and champion athlete at the University of the Philippines had been exaggerated, as was his record as a resistance fighter against the

Japanese in northern Luzon. More worrying, I decided that reports that came my way from Maryknoll and Columban parish priests about his corruption, manipulations, extra-judicial killings and electoral fraud were probably true. My colleague Charlie Salmon, a political counsellor at the American Embassy, and protégé of President Jimmy Carter's human rights advisor, Pat Derian, had similar views.

Meanwhile, the Marcoses kept diplomatic observers entertained with their sound and light shows. The president declared martial law, suspended congress and the writ of *habeas corpus* and introduced a 'New Society'. He gave long portentous speeches in which he frequently claimed the battle against Islamic and Communist rebels was being won, and would stage 'amnesty' ceremonies in which guerrillas from the MNLF and New People's Army would hand over their weapons. In a white *barong tagalog* brilliantly backlit by the strobe effect of press cameras, Marcos would declare that guerrilla warfare in this or that province was over. These events generated great headlines for next day's press in Manila. But, refreshed by the substantial *merienda* that followed the ceremony, the guerillas would return to their barrios, dig up other weapons, and, after a respectful interval, resume their resistance against the central government.

Imelda Marcos — Ferdy's Muse of Manila, his Rose of Tacloban — was even more entertaining and corrupt than her husband. Coming from the poor side of the wealthy Romualdez family of Leyte in the Central Visayas, she was ferociously acquisitive, and not just for shoes. She was uninhibited in her sentimentality, naming all the clapped-out buses in Metro Manila 'Love Buses', and singing cloying love songs on every social occasion. She was also remorseless towards her enemies, and quite lacking in irony or self-awareness. With no sense of time, she frequently kept the whole diplomatic corps waiting at outdoor events, often in blazing tropical heat, while she made her self-indulgent way from some previous engagement.

Imelda loved celebrities, frequently inviting them to stay at Malacañang. Rudolf Nureyev and the American pianist Van Cliburn were two of her favourites. She also courted Hollywood celebrities, but men rather than women, whom she generally disliked. Gina Lollobrigida came to town on a photo shoot but Imelda barely gave her the time of day. Francis Ford Coppola, Marlon Brando and Martin Sheen were another story. They came to film the concluding sequence of *Apocalypse Now*. Coppola's crew had constructed the jungle redoubt of the mad American Colonel Kurtz, portrayed by Marlon Brando, on the banks of the river at Pagsanjan. Anna and Adam were round-eyed in wonder when we took them to see the set. We had to look very closely at the Khmer temples, set among crashed helicopters, sandbags, hanging bodies and other detritus of war, to see that they were made of styrofoam and the bodies were dummies. But the multi-million-dollar tableau was scheduled for destruction in the final scene, and the Philippine Air Force had been paid to lend some Iriquois choppers for the sake of added verisimilitude. The story goes that on the day of the shoot, the choppers were diverted to Mindanao for a genuine emergency operation against the MNLF. Coppola was so incensed that he prevailed on Imelda to get her husband to order them back to Pagsanjan.

Imelda was keen to demonstrate that the Philippines was not just a conglomeration of émigré races but had an ancient indigenous culture. As Mayor of Metro Manila in 1976, she made a huge workforce labour round the clock on completing two monumental projects — a National Heart Foundation and a Cultural Centre. As the date of the IMF meeting approached, she was told of some stone menhirs that had been unearthed by road-building bulldozers at the Australian aid project in Zamboanga del Sur. Not prepared to wait for a check on their authenticity, Imelda sent a naval vessel to bring them to Manila, where she had them implanted along Roxas Boulevard in front of the cultural centre as examples of ancient Filipino civilisation. Gerry Nutter wisely left it to the navy to tell Imelda that an Australian geologist had determined that the menhirs were in fact naturally formed basalt plugs.

In 1974, Gough Whitlam had visited the Philippines as prime minister during a successful Asian tour. Now leader of the opposition, he came again in 1976 with his wife Margaret. The Marcoses were keen to entertain them, and proposed a visit to the Romualdez ancestral home in Leyte. Gerry had other business and sent me to mind the Whitlams. During the flight on the presidential jet, Marcos proposed to Gough scuba diving and a game of golf. Neither a diver nor a golfer, Gough politely declined but said I would deputise for him. Meanwhile, Imelda proposed to Margaret that she join her and her courtiers at an all-night disco party, a prospect completely alien to Margaret's tastes. She declined and flick-passed the invitation to me. Two days and nights later, weary from lack of sleep, I was golfed and partied out. Just as I had when eating live lobster in Japan in 1966, I wondered whether this was the right profession for me, or, if it were, whether my pay was sufficient.

Ali and I had quickly found our social feet. Two good friends of the embassy were Eki Cardenas and Bobby Reyes, senior officials who worked for President Marcos' chief cabinet secretary Alex Melchor at Malacañang. Eki invited us to many parties in Manila, and to barrio fiestas with his extended family in various Luzon provinces. Usually we went by road, to be greeted by a big banner saying 'Welcome Counsellor Broinowski and Party'. After judging a local beauty contest, we might attend an enormous banquet, the staple of which was roast *leçon* (pork). Then we might dance the *tinikling*, trying not to break an ankle between the clashing bamboo poles, and over many San Miguel beers would sing songs into a microphone with a local jazz band. The worse the singing, the more our hosts enjoyed themselves. Their own songs they performed with panache — Filipinos are natural troubadours. They also love nicknames. Eki, an eligible Manila bachelor, had girlfriends named Pinky and Boots and Cherry Pie. The foreign secretary, Carlos P. Romulo, had a social secretary named Bo Peep. The name of the president's son was Bong Bong.

After our first year we moved from Dasmariñas to occupy the old head of mission residence in Forbes Park. The ambassador had moved to a more splendid newly constructed residence in North Forbes. And my 5 Series BMW 520i had finally arrived at the port of Manila. Brilliant white with beige leather upholstery, it was more stylish and refined than the 1800 cc Neue Klasse we had enjoyed driving in Tehran. A reinforced safety cell surrounded the passenger compartment. The cockpit relocated the heater/cooler and radio controls nearer the driver, and the instruments were housed in a single binnacle behind the steering wheel. The speedo and tachometer were backlit at night by a subtle red glow which aided night vision. The smooth four-cylinder engine had Kugelfischer fuel injection and developed 130 brake horse power. A beautifully moulded drop-down tool kit was housed inside the boot lid.

Proudly I drove back to Forbes Park to show the car to an admiring family. And on the weekend we took it on its first day trip down to Las Piñas to view the early nineteenth-century church of San Jose with its famous bamboo organ. The trip there was fine, but on the way back the airconditioner iced up, leaving us sweaty and hot. As soon as I could, I took the car to the BMW service centre in Quezon City, but the proprietor and his head mechanic just scratched their heads. For the rest of the posting, we had to be content to drive any distance with the windows open.

In the following two years we drove the Beamer all over Luzon — to the top of the northern Cordilleras, east down the Cagayan Valley, south to Batangas, and south-east to Legaspi in the Bicol region, which was as far as one could go before running out of road. These were great trips, but another mechanical problem was beginning to worry me. When we climbed through a mountain pass, the engine would gradually lose power, as if the injectors were oiling up or were being starved of petrol. I first noticed the problem when we took a weekend trip to Baguio, a mountain resort where for centuries foreigners and rich Filipinos had escaped the Manila heat to play golf and walk in the alpine woods. Again, the service centre at Quezon City had no clue about what was wrong, and wouldn't touch the fuel injection unit, where I suspected the problem lay. The boss got quite defensive and angry when I pressed him. I cabled BMW in Germany, but they just referred me back to Quezon City.

So I had to face the frustrating fact that I had bought a lemon: a car I could drive around Manila and further afield in Luzon, provided I didn't mind the absence of airconditioning or avoiding high altitudes and steep hills. And the accredited service centre in the Philippines was not equipped to fix either problem.

The cause of the petrol starvation was finally diagnosed by the BMW Centre when I brought the car back to Sydney at the end of our posting in December 1978, but only after the second go (on the first occasion they completely misdiagnosed the problem and pointlessly tweaked the injectors). The mechanics eventually found that the fuel line from the tank to the injectors had been twisted because the tank had been installed incorrectly. Whenever atmospheric pressure fell, the line would gradually squeeze shut, thus starving the fuel flow to the injectors. It was all very frustrating, especially the absence of help or advice from the people at Stuttgart, who just didn't want to know. What use was a great instrument panel, a fitted tool kit, a beautifully balanced engine, or a crash cage, if the car wouldn't bloody go? The lesson about not bringing a sophisticated car into a developing country finally got through. I determined there and then never to buy another BMW, and I never have.

The problems of faulty German auto technology were put into perspective by an event at work. Some time during 1976 we had received intelligence from the Philippine Army that a Muslim rebel leader in Mindanao was interested in targeting our Pagadian project, maybe to kidnap or kill someone. I was in charge of the mission at the time and sent Ali down to talk with the rebels and then consult with the project manager, Peter Goldston, in Pagadian. Ali flew to Zamboanga City and made an overnight trip by rented jeep to Dumalinao to see the rebel, then to Pagadian to talk to Peter Goldston. She met the Muslim guerrilla and emphasised that the project was not a military plot, but a civil project to help local farmers. She was obviously persuasive: no one was kidnapped or hurt, and no Australians were evacuated. When Gerry Nutter returned to Manila, he was slightly appalled that I'd sent Ali on such a mission, but it was part of her job and I knew she had the physical courage for it.

A common characteristic in former Spanish colonies — Mexico as well as the Philippines — is a marked disparity between wealth and poverty. While the Roman Catholic Church reinforces the disparity, it's really the legacy of a system in which public office is given in order to enrich the recipient, who pays the donor back with favours and bribes. Even after revolutions, new regimes prove as corrupt as the old. With banners of social justice flying, all Philippine presidents have galloped into battle on behalf of the poor, promising social reforms that will erase poverty. They never succeed because to a greater or lesser degree all become corrupted by the system. I think Cory Aquino and Eddy Ramos were comparatively uncorrupted presidents. But was Ferdinand Marcos any worse that Joseph Estrada, or Gloria Macapagal Arroyo? Until he arranged the assassination of his only serious rival, the popular and charismatic Benigno Aquino at Manila Airport in 1983, I actually had a bit of a soft spot for Marcos. But when that happened, the people were right to rise up and kick him out of the country. It is amazing that, at the time of writing, his widow Imelda has regained her social status in Manila, and once again shamelessly flaunts her wealth. Filipinos are a forgiving lot. Or perhaps she was right when she said: 'Mass follows class.'

At the end of two years, I left Manila for a year of study at Harvard. I had long had the ambition to get a higher degree in a competitive scholastic environment. With Gerry Nutter's agreement, Ali remained in her job and the children remained at their Manila schools.

I had never been to the United States, but like many Australian kids, I had been conditioned to imagine it through comics and movies. I initially stayed with my sister Helen Caldicott and her family in West Newton not far from the university. Their house was in a tree-lined street of enormous houses with free-standing letter boxes with levers on them, sweeping lawns and no front fences. Like the other houses, theirs had a slate roof and attics with dormer windows. Squirrels hopped round the lawns, stocking up on acorns beneath autumnal oaks and elms. The whole scene was a cliché straight out of the *Saturday Evening Post*s my mother used to bring home from the Myer Library in Melbourne. I was delighted.

I took a studio flat in graduate housing at Peabody Terrace on Boston's Charles River, and embarked on a one-year Masters degree in Public Administration at the Littauer Centre. (The John F. Kennedy School was under construction at the time.) Two stimulating semesters followed, at the end of which I received my degree plus an offer to publish an essay in the prestigious magazine *Foreign Policy*. Written for Stanley Hoffman, Professor of European

History, the essay was about the profligacy and irresponsibility of American arms sales to the Shah. Malcolm Fraser was now the Australian prime minister, and he was quite a Cold War warrior, so I went to Washington to seek the advice of the Australian ambassador — Alan Renouf — about whether I should use my name or a pseudonym when the essay was published.

Put out to pasture following his time as Gough Whitlam's secretary of Foreign Affairs, Renouf had a somewhat jaundiced view of Fraser. He listened quietly while I explained my dilemma. After a few reflective puffs on his pipe, he said he thought I'd be 'fucking dead' if Canberra knew that I was the author of such an incendiary article. So by arrangement with the editors I became 'Leslie M. Pryor, a Western observer who has lived in Iran'. But an Australian journalist in Washington at the time, John Edwards, found out I'd written the article and published a story about it in the *Australian Financial Review*. When I got back to Canberra, no one in the department raised an eyebrow. I should have used my own name.

In June 1978, Ali and the children came over to Harvard for my graduation. The Russian writer and philosopher Alexander Solzhenitsyn was the guest speaker. He spoke of gloom and doom, and the victory of Soviet Communism over the world if Americans continued in their profligate and materialistic ways. As if to emphasise the gravity of his words, it rained on Harvard Yard, something God in Her wisdom had never permitted in three centuries of Harvard commencements.

It was wonderful to have a happy reunion with Ali and Anna and Adam, whom I had missed so much. I wanted to extend the reunion by driving us all across America to San Francisco before flying back to Manila to pack up and go home. My brother-in-law Bill Caldicott generously suggested that I borrow his VW Kombiwagen. He and Helen would fly across and drive it back east after our trip. Ali had to return to Manila, but the children joined me. Anna and Adam alternated in the co-pilot's seat to navigate and keep me awake.

Bill's 1976 babypoo-coloured Kombiwagen was a second-generation Transporter Type 2, or as it was called in popular German jargon, a 'bully' because of its bulldog stance. Its air-cooled 1.6 litre boxer engine was tucked under the back, driving the rear wheels with Kuebel-like drop gears. The driver sat over the front wheels, leaving plenty of room for passengers and cargo. The first Transporter had come off the VW Wolfsburg line in Lower Saxony in February 1950. As its proud creator Heinz Nordhoff remarked at the time, 'it was as full of faults as a dog has fleas'. The assembly line then switched to Hanover, and over the years the bully was improved, and adapted as a utility, van, tow truck, people mover, fire truck, bus and camper.

Bill's bully had a lift-up roof and a dinky little kitchen sink, gas stove and cupboards for provisions. We stocked the cupboards with plenty of shake and bake for chicken and lamb chops, said goodbye to Ali at Logan airport and headed down to New York on the first leg of our journey. After staying with Bob Immerman, an old friend from Tokyo days in his spacious apartment on West 81st Street, we motored on to Washington to stay with other state department friends, Bill and Peggy Breer, in North West. In the next few days, staying overnight at public camping grounds, we made our way north and west through Pittsburgh, Canton, Cleveland, Toledo, Gary, Indiana, and finally to Chicago.

Here we stopped and drew breath for a few days, taking stock of our journey and of how we were faring. Anna was keeping her 'rutter', or diary — a document that has sadly been lost over the years. Unlike our unfortunate BMW 520i in Manila, we were discovering that Bill's bully had a thoroughly reliable personality and a will of its own. It would not be hurried, but nor would it stop or starve itself of petrol up long gradients. Many times huge rigs, sitting well above the speed limit, would rocket past and blow us sideways in their slipstream.

And so on we went — through Iowa, Nebraska, down into Kansas and across Colorado. We stopped at the border junction of Colorado, Utah, New Mexico and Arizona, and bought Indian turquoise and silver jewellery for Ali. I was keen to spend a couple of nights among the high rollers at Las Vegas in Nevada, but Anna had other ideas. Disneyland in Anaheim, California, was on her agenda. When we got there, she and Adam were speechless with excitement. We went on Space Mountain and other rides which scared the hell out of me but delighted them.

And so up the coast to San Francisco, where Bill and Helen were waiting to collect the Kombiwagen. It had been great fun, but I was anxious to get back to Ali in Manila, and plan our trip home to Canberra.

It may have been interesting to speculate about whether Ali and I might have another joint post and where that might be. But at the time we just wanted to get home, put the children in school and re-establish our Canberra roots.

7

A Daimler and a Daihatsu in Canberra

Early in 1979 we moved back into our house in Doyle Terrace, Chapman, a suburb many miles to the south-west of Canberra in the sheep grazing country of Weston Creek. Designed by the Canberra master builder Gary Willemsen, the house had been in a treeless and bleak landscape when we bought it in 1974, but now the trees were beginning to grow, and the neighbourhood could almost be described as leafy. The garden had suffered from neglect at the hands of successive tenants, but we set about resurrecting it with enthusiasm while Anna and Adam re-established relations with neighbouring children. Anna was now a new scholar at Holder High School and Adam a year four student at Chapman Primary School.

In our weekend domesticity we were cocooned from the outside world, but not during the working week in the department. A great deal was happening on the world stage, especially in Vietnam, Iran, the United Kingdom and Afghanistan. Most of these events shaped international relations during the course of the next decade.

In January the Vietnamese consolidated their invasion of Cambodia begun on Christmas Day 1978, occupying Cambodia and removing Pol Pot and the Khmer Rouge. In the same month the Shah left Iran and fled to Egypt. In February, the Chinese retaliated for the Vietnamese occupation of Cambodia by invading the northern part of Vietnam 'to teach the Vietnamese a lesson'. And Ayatollah Khomeini returned from Paris to Tehran in triumph and popular adulation. In May, Margaret Thatcher became prime minister of Great Britain. In December, Deng Xiaoping announced the beginning of economic liberalisation in China, and the Soviet Union invaded Afghanistan.

Apart from Thatcher's elevation to the head of her government, all these events resonated with me because of my previous posting in Iran and my trip with parliamentarians to Vietnam and Cambodia in 1970. I would dearly have liked to be put in a branch assessing events in either Iran or Indochina, but personnel decided otherwise.

By the late 1970s Australia's export trade with Japan had become bigger than our combined exports to the United States and European Community countries. For the first time in Australia's history, its major bilateral trade partner had none of the traditional links of language and culture that had facilitated our trade with Britain or the United States.

We could see that in the Australian Commonwealth, governments and companies weren't doing very well at coordinating their trade activities, and tended to compete for Japanese contracts to Australia's disadvantage. The emphasis was on short-term micro rather than long-term macro planning. With a close interface between Japan's bureaucracy and private sector, the Japanese, on the other hand, were seen as masters of co-ordination, with the capacity to pick and choose among Australian suppliers, often driving down prices in the process.

In 1978, the Commonwealth government had asked Kenneth Baillieu Myer of Melbourne to convene an ad hoc committee to see what could be done. Like other members of the Melbourne-based Myer family, Kenneth was a wealthy and influential philanthropist with strong interests in Australian relations with Asia. He recommended a three-committee system with a secretariat to assist them. The Standing Committee on Japan (SCJ) would comprise the heads of seven Commonwealth departments. The Consultative Committee on Relations with Japan (CCRJ) would include those seven, plus representatives of the Australian business community, union peak councils, primary industry and the academic community. Among the members of the inaugural CCRJ in 1979 were Simon Crean, federal secretary of the Storemen and Packers' Union, David Asimus of the Wool Corporation, Bruce Watson, CEO of Mount Isa Mines, and Professor Wang Gung Wu of the Australian National University. The committee was chaired first by Sir Gordon Jackson of CSR, and on his retirement, by Sir Arvi Parbo of Western Mining. A third committee of SCJ members and senior public servants from state governments was convened to co-ordinate Commonwealth and state activities involving Japan.

I was selected to run a new secretariat to see to the needs of these committees. My main task was to set dates and agendas for committee meetings, and research and write papers on different aspects of the relationship, including speculative pieces on what might happen in the future. I was assisted by a small team, including Dr Alan Rix, an academic specialist on Japan, and Geoff George, a former intelligence officer.

The SCJ and CCRJ met monthly, the Commonwealth–State Committee infrequently. Some SCJ members, particularly the secretary of the treasury, John Stone, were irritated that they were not permitted to delegate their attendance. But experience of Commonwealth interdepartmental committees had shown that once a secretary delegated to a deputy secretary, the latter would in turn delegate at the next meeting to a first assistant secretary, and so on down the line until whoever represented a particular department would have no authority to decide anything. And this would lead to the kind of report devoid of clear recommendations that Prime Minister Gough Whitlam caustically rejected in 1973 when he was advised to take an 'on the one hand ... on the other hand', 'welcome though not seek', 'neither emphasise nor ignore' response to a problem.

In researching the secretariat's papers, we had fairly open access to the files of all Commonwealth departments, and did not have to clear our findings with any department before tabling them in committee. Nor were we subject to department line control or assessment reports. We had our own career structure, and the chairmen of the SCJ and CCRJ, Peter Henderson, Sir Arthur Jackson and then Sir Arvi Parbo, assessed our effectiveness.

The CCRJ wanted us to research every possible aspect of bilateral trade with Japan including domestic issues in Australia, Japan and elsewhere that could affect it. We examined environmental issues such as whaling, uranium mining, and woodchip exports; Australia's industrial relations problems and their effect on our reliability as a trader; the Australian and

Japanese financial and banking systems; Japanese interest groups and their effect on trade; the restrictive effects of agricultural and fishing lobbies on Australian imports. We looked at US and EC pressures on Japan to correct adverse trade balances, regional strategic and military developments, the formation of regional groupings such as ASEAN, and the reactions of Pacific island countries to Japan's proposal to dump radioactive wastes in their vicinity. We drew up a comprehensive list of bilateral and multilateral treaties and international agreements affecting trade.

One of our research papers concerned the application of new industrial materials in Japan and their effects on Australia's mineral exports. We predicted that Japan would continue to rely on iron ore and coking coal for its steel industry, but new industrial materials such as carbon fibres, ceramics and amorphous materials would encroach at the margins, especially in the motor car industry. We speculated that fine ceramics could replace steel and aluminium as energy saving, heat resistant materials in internal combustion engines, obviating the need for heavy cooling systems and saving fuel. Such materials would also be used in the nuclear, aerospace and mining industries.

Between 1979 and 1982, we had produced twenty-eight papers. Did any of them influence government thinking about Japan? Some research papers became standard texts in departments, and policy decisions on Japan allegedly became better informed. But did Kevin Rudd's briefing for his April 2008 visit to Beijing, or his June 2008 visit to Tokyo, include any of our material, much of it still relevant, or new research papers? It's highly unlikely that a harried and overworked public service would have had time to research events that may affect long-term trade with China or

Japan. Perhaps the need for an independent research outfit like ours now exists for relations with China.

For her part, Ali was absorbed in her new job in the ASEAN Section. Unlike my work, hers did have a connection with the experience she had accumulated during her previous posting in the Philippines, one of the five original ASEAN members. She worked with the section head, Robin Casson, a colleague, David Irvine, and an amiable and sharp new diplomatic cadet named Kevin Rudd. The most junior officer, Rudd did most of the section's filing and photocopying.

Concerning our domestic situation, personal transport continued to be essential in Canberra, where distances were long and public transport infrequent, especially from Chapman to the parliamentary triangle. Apart from the normal family ferrying duties, I wanted a fast and comfortable car for weekends to Sydney, winter cruising to the snow fields at Perisher and Thredbo, and summer trips to the beaches south of Batemans Bay at Broulee and Mossy Point. Such a car also needed to be fun to drive to Adelaide from time to time to see Ali's extended family.

Despite the problems I had endured with my XJ6 in Tehran, I was still bitten by the Jaguar bug. One Saturday morning in the *Canberra Times* I noticed an advertisement for a small Daimler. Intriguingly, this had a Mark 2 Jaguar body shell into which a small Daimler power plant had been dropped — an Edward Turner-designed, 76 x 70 mm, 2547 cc V8 aluminium engine originally designed for Daimler's own sports car, the bizarre-looking SP 250 of 1959. A successful hybrid developed at Brown's Lane when Jaguar bought the Daimler Company in May 1960, the little

Daimler was distinguishable from its Jaguar cousin only by a fluted radiator with a flying 'D' on top, and the subdued rumble of its V8 motor from twin exhausts. The takeover was prompted by record contracts for Jaguars from US distributors for 1961, when the company desperately needed the extra 56 acres of Daimler factory space to lift their production.

I bought my Daimler from a Commonwealth security guard at Government House in Yarralumla. It was a beautifully maintained white car with navy blue leather trim (my third white Jaguar). But as the guard handed over the keys, he advised me to keep a close watch on the oil level, as the V8 engine could be 'a bit thirsty'. On our first long trip out of Canberra, up to Cooma and then down Brown Mountain to the coast at Broulee, I noticed no discernible change during frequent oil checks. During a fitful sleep that night at our friend's house however, I suddenly sat bolt upright with an awful suspicion. Could I have been looking at the wrong dipstick — the one for the power steering? As a dewy dawn broke, I ventured out to the car and lifted the bonnet.

To my horror, my suspicion was confirmed. I had kept checking the power steering oil and overlooked the inconspicuous engine oil dipstick. The engine was almost dry, and had been so for the whole of the previous day, when I noticed it had been running a bit hot. I frantically raced into Batemans Bay, bought several quarts of engine oil and poured them into the engine. But it was too late. When I started it up, the engine emitted an ominous clunking. I had it towed to a Batemans Bay workshop, where it remained while several vital parts like pistons and rings and gudgeons were replaced. And with eight cylinders, the whole reconstruction was twice as expensive as it would have been if my engine had had four.

This time I couldn't blame the manufacturer. Suitably penitent, I picked up the Daimler several weeks later and drove it gingerly back to Canberra. I needn't have worried because for the next three years it ran beautifully, and was much admired among Canberra cognoscenti. Jeremy Webb asked if he could borrow it for his forthcoming wedding to his Belgian fiancée Arlene. Of course I agreed, and spent several days before the wedding detailing the car, including putting some navy blue leather food on the upholstery. Proudly, Jeremy's chauffeur took delivery of the car for the wedding rehearsal. He was to drive the bridesmaids in convoy behind the white Roller hired for the bride. All was fine until the party disembarked at the church to find that each bridesmaid had a vivid streak of navy blue leather food down the back of her ivory dress. Many censorious remarks and an urgent trip to the dry cleaner followed, and all was well on the day. Last time I checked, Jeremy and Arlene were still my good friends.

About this time, Ali and I bought a piece of land in East Jindabyne in the snow country. Two hours from Canberra, it faced west, overlooking Lake Jindabyne towards the mountains. From A. V. Jennings, the popular master builder of suburban houses, we bought a plan for a plain brick veneer house with a cement tile roof. We had it modified as a small ski lodge with a veranda extending the length of the house overlooking the lake, plus a big bunk room, and hired a local builder to construct it.

But the block was very steep, and even contemplating driving the Daimler up the scrabbly twisting drive gave me nightmares. So I looked round for a small four-wheel drive with which to commute from Canberra to the snow — one with heavy duty tyres and four-wheel traction, an all-terrain vehicle that would handle the steep drive and take us safely up to the skifields without going to the expense and inconvenience of hiring chains. In 1980 such a vehicle was quite a novelty, well before every aspirational couple in Australia seemed to be driving enormous, petrol-guzzling, over-equipped, leather-seated SUVs loaded with air bags to protect their children from accidents and ferry them to school, ballet and football practice.

Our four-by-four turned out to be a small Daihatsu which I discovered in a Canberra used car and truck yard. Founded in Japan in 1907, Daihatsu first specialised in three-wheel trucks. A famous model was the amazing Tri-Mobile of 1957, a common conveyance on the streets of Tokyo in the mid-1960s, carrying everything from bamboo scaffolding to chicken coops. The company was taken over by Toyota in 1967, but models kept being developed and produced under the Daihatsu brand name. Ours was a bright orange 1975 F-20 'Taft'. It had two doors, a solid chassis with a box section ladder frame, front and rear rigid axles with longitudinal leaf springs and telescopic dampers, four-speed gears with high and low ratios, and an enormous black kangaroo bar protecting the front end. The whole show was driven by a 2530 cc petrol engine, and we could switch from two- to four-wheel drive by twiddling a couple of dials on the front axles.

Not only was the Daihatsu fun to drive in the snow, it was a practical car on the beach. When my brother-in-law John Ballinger got bogged at Terrigal, it was an easy matter to tow him out. Another plus was that with its arresting colour and high roofline, the Daihatsu was easy to spot in the crowded departmental car park in Canberra after a long day's work.

In February 1981, Ali was invited to join the staff at Yarralumla. This took her out of the posting stream and fitted with our general wish to remain in Canberra for a few years. She became administrative secretary to the governor-general, Sir Zelman Cowan. She found it quite a challenge to fit in with the male-dominated staff — the Official Secretary David Smith, his male deputy, and three junior male commissioned officers from the army, navy and air force, supervised by a naval commander. In this male hierarchy, Ali was also replacing a man in a position never before occupied by a woman. In addition to arranging the governor-general's program, she undertook research for Sir Zelman's speeches. When Sir Ninian Stephen replaced Sir Zelman as governor-general in July 1982, he asked her to try her hand at drafting his speeches as well as researching them.

I was curious and intrigued by Ali's new role, which was quite different from normal departmental duties. As a spouse, I could attend functions whenever wives of household staff were invited. One on occasion, I sat next to Gough and Margaret Whitlam in the crowded Senate chamber of Parliament House when Sir Ninian opened a new session of Parliament with Ali standing behind him. Gough greeted me with his usual booming 'Comrade!' adding, 'You scrub up as a comely wife.'

On another occasion, the Queen and Prince Philip visited Australia and stayed at Yarralumla. One evening Sir Ninian hosted a small dinner for the royals with just household staff and spouses present. I don't know in which century the rule was laid down, but commoners are not supposed to initiate conversations with royalty, so it was left to the Queen to keep the conversation going. This seemed an unfair burden, especially after a day full of official functions and pretending to be interested in everything. But, after long years of practice, the Queen was doing well. One subject she raised briefly was a recent affair that was all over the press between Prince Andrew and the English stripper Koo Stark — whom she called 'that gel'. Another was a dilemma she had faced over the war in the Falklands. The Royal Navy had lost several ships to Exocet missiles fired at low level from Argentinian Mirage fighter bombers, including the frigates *Antelope* and *Ardent*, and the light cruiser *Sheffield*. A surviving captain of one of these had paid a call on Her Majesty on returning to Britain, and expressed inconsolable regret at having lost one of her ships.

Addressing the whole table, Her Majesty asked rhetorically what should she have done? After all, it *was* one of her ships. Silence greeted this invitation until Ali said, 'Well, Ma'am, you could always have said: "Off with his head".' What seemed to be a long and stony silence followed this quip, until it was broken by an appreciative laugh. 'Unfortunately,' said the Queen, with regret, 'such days are past.'

In the federal elections of March 1983, the conservative Liberal–Country Party Coalition was defeated by the Labor Party and Bob Hawke succeeded Malcolm Fraser as prime minister. Bill Hayden replaced Tony Street as Minister of Foreign Affairs. Shortly before that Peter Henderson, the secretary of the department had called Ali in to tell her they had decided to send me as ambassador to Vietnam. Would Ali go as my spouse? Ali reminded Henderson that she was an officer of the department, and would like to go to Hanoi as a diplomat. Henderson demurred, and said that wives were expected to go as wives, not officers. 'But we went as a couple of professionals to Manila,' said Ali. 'Yes, but Richard wasn't an ambassador there,' said Henderson. Ali replied that in that case she would apply for a posting of her own somewhere else.

So it was decided that Ali would have a separate posting as cultural attaché in Tokyo, with three months of language training at the American Foreign Service Institute in Yokohama to brush up the Japanese she had learned in the 1960s. Tokyo was not as far from Vietnam as a European country, and I could commute there during leave periods via Bangkok. Meanwhile, I stayed with Anna and Adam in Chapman while preparing for my first head of mission posting. They would join Ali in Tokyo at the end of her language training. I had no time to even begin mastering the difficult tonal language of Vietnamese, so I took a refresher crash course in French instead.

And thus we all prepared as well as we could for a new and difficult phase in our lives.

8

Toyotas and Tanks

In mid March 1983 Bob Hawke's new foreign minister, Bill Hayden, called me in to his office in Canberra to outline what he wanted me to achieve in Vietnam. Previously, in response to that country's occupation of Cambodia in 1978/9, Prime Minister Fraser had totally withdrawn Australian aid and otherwise reduced Australia's presence in Vietnam. Hayden regarded these measures as an overreaction. He was convinced Vietnam would become an important player in South East Asia, and wanted to build impetus back into the bilateral relationship.

He quite obviously had some priorities in mind, and gave me several tasks. He wanted me to re-start an Australian aid program, stimulate bilateral trade and tie up the loose ends of Australia's previous relationship with the now-defunct Republic of South Vietnam. To do that included signing over title of our quite extensive embassy holdings in Saigon to the government of the Socialist Republic of Vietnam (SRV), and addressing some of the concerns of families of the 50,000 Australian troops who had staged through Vietnam during the eight long years of Australia's military involvement. This meant trying to locate the remains of six Australian diggers 'missing in action' and looking at the effects of defoliants such as Agent Orange on the local population to determine whether complaints of returned servicemen about illnesses brought on by exposure to dioxin could be substantiated. As comprehensively and frankly as I could, I was also to discuss with the SRV government their plans for Cambodia, and when they were thinking of getting out.

During several weeks of pre-departure briefings, I called on all Commonwealth departments and agencies in Canberra with interests I needed to pursue in Hanoi. I also visited a number of state authorities and Australian companies that had had investments in the old regime that might be revived.

After farewelling their school and neighbourhood friends, Anna and Adam helped me pack our belongings, put things in storage and prepare for our departure. In late March we flew to Tokyo to join Alison, now cultural attaché in the Australian Embassy. After several days helping her adjust the children to their new home in Meguro, I took off from Narita airport for Bangkok. There I was to meet my predecessor in Vietnam, John McCarthy, to get some briefing on what to expect.

Over dinner in Patpong, John gave me a judicious and careful rundown on embassy staff, facilities, logistics and the quality of other heads of mission in Hanoi. The Australian photo-journalist Neil Davis joined us. He had spent several years during the war accompanying ARVN troops on their forays against the Vietcong, and in his amiable and reassuring way had a unique set of experiences to impart. He made some pungent comments about how the Americans had conducted the war, and how they could have been more effective if they had been tougher on nepotism and corruption in Saigon.

My mind churning with the novelty of it all, I spent a last sleepless night at the Montien Hotel on Suriwongse before heading very early the next morning for Don Muang airport and my flight to Hanoi.

I've noticed at international airports that the atmosphere of the destination often infuses itself into the departure lounge, and so it was with Don Muang. Unlike the orderly well-dressed people departing in large aircraft for Singapore or Kuala Lumpur or Tokyo, the passengers for Hanoi had a frontier look about them. They included Indiana Jones adventurers, earnest non-government organisation (NGO) types, mothers and babies, and a crowd of Communist officials with bad teeth and rows of biros lining their pockets. Accompanying the mob was a profusion of unwieldy boxes which had to be shoe-horned into the straining hold of the Boeing 737-200 aircraft assigned to take them. Thai International seemed to be making a political statement: we'll maintain an air link with Communist Vietnam, but the journey will be as uncomfortable as we can possibly make it.

All passengers eventually got on board. After what seemed to be an unusually long take-off we climbed to 30,000 feet and an hour and a half later began our descent into Hanoi's Noi Bai airport. After the bustle and energy of Bangkok, the first thing that struck me as I disembarked was the rural quiet around the airport. No snarl of traffic, no tall buildings, no elevated expressways, no massive power lines or commercial billboards. There were reminders of war — lines of bomb craters, now adapted as fishponds radiating asymmetrically out from the airport, a squadron of camouflaged MiG 21 jet fighters in earth revetments interspersed with surface-to-air missile batteries along the runway, and several kinds of Soviet military transport aircraft in blue and white Aeroflot livery — Antanovs, Ilyushins, Tupolevs and Yakovlevs.

These first impressions were interrupted by the need to concentrate on a bumpy ride in a crowded Soviet-made bus to the shabby airport terminal. Here, passengers were making frantic attempts to retrieve their luggage from an arthritic rubber conveyor belt on which a large can of white house paint had sprung a leak among the luggage, and unnoticed, was dribbling its contents onto boxes and bags and occasionally people.

Unsmeared, I was met by the Vietnamese head of protocol and some Australian members of my staff who ushered me into a small VIP room for a cup of bitter brown Vietnamese tea while my passport was processed. Then I went out to the car park where an embassy driver, Mr Dzu, greeted me proudly with the head of mission limo — a slightly battered, black, 1972 H 150 Nissan President equipped with a huge Y44 V8 engine. On the forty-five-kilometre run into Hanoi, I noticed that the President was inappropriately overpowered and outsized. The road was narrow and rutted, metalled in some sections, dusty and unsealed in others. It meandered along the tops of flood dykes and through villages. It was constantly crowded with trucks, motor scooters, buffalo-drawn wagons, bicycles — some with squealing pigs strapped on behind — and the occasional official-looking military vehicle. No one seemed to have any idea of road rules and simply chose their own speed and course. Our velocity varied from 1 to 30 kilometres per hour with Mr Dzu constantly blasting his horn.

Finally we came to the Long Bien Bridge spanning the impressively wide Red River on the outskirts of Hanoi. Everywhere in Vietnam traffic proceeded on the right, except on this bridge. Designed by Gustav Eiffel, inventor of the steel box-girder which he used in the Eiffel Tower in 1889, this humping leviathan — part suspension, part box girder — had been built with the latest French technology in 1903. It was hit but never destroyed by many American bombs during what the Vietnamese called the American War. To compensate for resulting structural weaknesses, motor traffic and pedestrians had been moved to the left, while heavy traffic such as railway trains had been diverted to the other, stronger, side. As we crossed, the whole structure trembled and swayed as a locomotive rumbled by the other way.

And so we drove into Hanoi, past the tranquil Petit Lac and its picturesque Ngoc Son Temple, the opera house, the post office, the old city of long houses, and on to the embassy on Pho Ly Thuong Kiet. This was in the tree-lined French Quarter, still remarkably intact despite some fairly heavy bombing by B-52s in April and December 1972 during President Nixon's efforts to get the Vietnamese to agree to his 'peace with honour' ceasefire solution.

The embassy occupied a pretty, white, two-storeyed French provincial villa. Upstairs was my residence, a comfortably furnished two-bedroom apartment with high ceilings and French doors. Downstairs was the chancery. At the back was an above-ground swimming pool surrounded by a wooden deck. Behind this was the Billabong Bar, housed on the ground floor of a three-storeyed prefab block of staff flats constructed some years earlier by SMEC. The flats leaked during the monsoon and were infernally hot in the dry months. Nor were they soundproofed. One could hear bathroom ablutions, not just in the next flat, but two along.

Bordering one side of the embassy compound was a once-beautiful French provincial house, now run down, overcrowded and housing what seemed to be about twenty families. Every evening at the same time a little girl practised her violin very loudly and very badly. And on many early mornings, the agonised screams of a pig being gradually slaughtered pierced the air. (Vietnamese slaughter their animals slowly because adrenalin released during the process tenderises the meat.)

Flanking the other side of the embassy was a square Corinthian building that housed the local branch of the Communist Party. I wanted to get Australia's hands on both buildings, and began negotiations that continued well beyond my time in Hanoi. My successor, Ian Lincoln, eventually acquired both to accommodate ever-expanding staff numbers. The residence/chancery was restored to its full colonial glory, first to house the senior trade commissioner, then as the residence of the ambassador. The chancery was later moved out to the new diplomatic housing area at Van Phuc, half an hour to the city's west.

I was fortunate to have competent and agreeable Australian-based staff. My political officers were initially Robert Scoble and Philip Stonehouse, later replaced by Lyndall McLean and Caroline Millar. Bob Deveraux was the senior administrative officer and Helen Kortlang the aid officer. Two officers from the Department of Immigration occupied a portable garage in the back driveway of the compound. We were also blessed with an

Adelaide law student with his 1936 Austin Ten. With glacial acceleration, thin tires and a slipping clutch, not a chick magnet.

Below: Riley 1.5 litre with Ali at rented flat in Mugga Way. It boiled all the way from Adelaide to Canberra, but its front suspension was state of the art.

Ali with the Hillman Imp in the Japanese pottery town of Mashiko. Bits kept falling off, but young Japanese petrol-heads were very impressed with its unconventional design.

Now *here* was a car with grunt. Skyline Prince GT with triple Weber carbs in Tokyo.

Honda rent-a-car in Kyushu. A motorcycle disguised as a sports car driven by a chain. But capable of 140 kph.

Another chain-driven conveyance at Yamanaka, Mount Fuji.

My first Jag. A beautiful 2.4 litre Mark 2. Guilt-stricken, I later traded it in after a year on a Vauxhall Victor plus some change. The used car salesman in West Terrace, Adelaide thought he'd won the lottery.

Holden Kingswood in Rangoon. Driven by the priapic Anthony, it went through several sets of tires but handled the most appalling Burmese roads with ease.

1973: A pit stop somewhere in Yugoslavia en route from London to Tehran in my new XJ6 – an exhausting trip we did in seven days because I promised Ambassador I'd be back for an Embassy event.

Yellow Terror in Forbes Park: Patricio's highly reliable Holden Torana – the children's taxi.

Right and below: My BMW 520i: A German lemon in Manila. It couldn't go up hill and its aircon never worked. Following unfixable problems with the XJ6 in Tehran, a triumph of hope over experience.

2.5 litre Daimler V8 at Jeremy Webb's wedding in Canberra. Navy blue leather polish applied for the occasion left the bridesmaids stained and unimpressed.

Daihatsu 4WD with triumphant extended family aboard after rescuing John Ballinger's Mini Moke Californian from incoming tide at Bendalong.

Head of Mission's Nissan President in Hanoi with local staff. A land barge with too much power for local conditions.

Happy NVA troops returning from Cambodia in their Soviet truck. They were as relieved at leaving as their Khmer brothers were at seeing them go.

Below: Motorcade en route to the Governor's palace to present credentials in Hanoi, 1983. All solid Soviet machinery.

Above: Three unsmiling commissars in their Soviet jeep marking the 30th anniversary of the Fall of Saigon, 2005

Left: With Head of Mission Mercedes on the Han River near Seoul. Quiet, reliable, powerful, it handled the chaos of Korean traffic with aplomb.

State of Korean auto art: my Daiwoo 2.2 litre Leganza before handing it on to daughter Anna. Amazingly, although now bent and rusty, it's still running.

My fourth and probably last Jaguar, a 1965 3.4 litre 'S' type. In 1990, it had an anthill protruding through the back seat and woodwork bleached white by a thousand summer suns. Now an entirely reliable car, it does 24 mpg and has been everywhere.

Second of our two Prius hybrids. Electric/petrol motors, 4.4 litres per 100 kilometres. A beautifully put-together electric pram, wonderfully economic transport between Sydney and Termeil on the New South Wales south coast.

Ali and Anna with one of US Ambassador Art Hummel's tiger cubs in Rangoon, 1971. The cubs were anonymously left at his gate after their mother had been shot by one of his hunting parties.

Two violinists in Manila, 1976. Anna has just recovered from breaking her arm at gymnastics.

Above: Former Australian Prime Minister Gough Whitlam with President Ferdinand Marcos at Orlot, Leyte. Gough would swim, but drew the line at waterskiing.

So Broinowski skis in Gough's place. Marcos is containing his impatience waiting for me to get suited up.

Deputy Prime Minister Doug Anthony signing a nuclear cooperation agreement with President Marcos at Malacañang Palace in 1977. Supplying uranium to the first Philippine nuclear reactor excited Australian uranium miners, but the reactor was never commissioned because it was built on an earthquake fault line. I'm behind Anthony looking the wrong way.

Presenting credentials to Korean President Chun Doo-hwan at the Blue House, Seoul in 1987. Chun and his successor Roo Tae-woo, the last two military presidents, ended up in gaol for corruption.

Welcoming President Roo on a state visit to Australia at Mascot Airport in 1988.

Kangaroo Quartet giving spirited performance at Embassy residence, Seoul. The Koreans love classical Western music. The Quartet was a demonstration that Australians do too.

On meeting Pope John Paul in Seoul, I ask him whether the Popemobile is sparing on gas. 'Not so good,' he replies, 'too many vertical surfaces.'

Presenting credentials to President Carlos Salinas de Gortari in Mexico City in November 1994. Supposedly one of Mexico's 'new breed' of incorruptible leaders, Salinas fell from grace early the following year on corruption charges, leaving the economy in a mess for his successor Ernesto Zedillo to clean up.

Being invested with the romantically named Aguila Asteca (Order of the Aztec Eagle) at the Foreign Ministry, Mexico City, April 1997.

Above and opposite: Wreath-laying at the tomb of the 19th-century national hero and symbol of Cuba's bid for independence from Spain, José Martí, Havana, Cuba, November 1994.

Discussions with Cuban Foreign Minister Roberto Robaina in preparation for Foreign Minister Gareth Evans' visit in 1995. A 'young turk', Robaina was a slick operator noted for his jewellery and dress sense, who fell out of favour with Castro around 1998.

Australian-based technical officer who kept the airconditioners running and the emergency generator serviced. This was keyed to start automatically as soon as the town power supply was interrupted — a frequent occurrence. Stripped to my underpants in sweltering heat during a tropical downpour, I once helped the tech change some heavy batteries used to automatically start the generator and housed in the suffocatingly hot roof space above the strong room. Unusual work for an ambassador, I reflected, even a relatively junior one on his first post.

One omission in my staff was a defence attaché. This seemed peculiar, as conservative Canberra analysts had been asserting ever since Vietnam's invasion of Cambodia in 1978 that the Hanoi regime was bent on continuing territorial expansion through Thailand. A professional Australian observer would have seemed essential to make an accurate assessment of Vietnam's military capabilities. Nonetheless, I was happy to make my own military observations and judgements and send them to Canberra, where they were apparently read with some interest by the intelligence community. And there was a cornucopia of Soviet and Chinese military hardware to be spotted — including small arms, rockets, tanks, APCs and towed and self-propelled artillery — all on generous display during military parades on Ho Chi Minh Square off Duong Hung Vuong. I also had access to the advice, willingly given, of a senior editor of the Vietnamese Army newspaper and some other former NVA generals.

Hanoi was the first posting where I had no need to purchase a car of my own — the government provided one as part of my package. I nevertheless took a close interest in the composition of our small fleet and how our tech went about servicing it. Shortly after arriving, I decided to sell the President and standardise our cars to Toyotas. We imported a new, 1983 Crown S 120 sedan with a 2800 cc DOHC engine. Beautifully made, solid and reliable, it was whisper-quiet and manoeuvrable, and served me and at least two of my successors with minimal problems as the head of mission vehicle. We also had a 1984 two-litre diesel-powered Toyota HiAce Commuter mini-bus, and a couple of four-cylinder Cressida sedans. Our transport fleet was augmented with a two-tonne truck — either a Toyota or an Isuzu, I forget which — for bringing sea freight, including beer supplies, up from Haiphong.

Giving representational dinner parties for Vietnamese officials and the diplomatic corps was a necessary burden, one made more onerous without a spouse to help. But I was blessed with several domestic servants supplied by the foreign minister. These we assumed did double duty as spies, but they were amiable and helpful. The team was run with an iron hand by the disarmingly diminutive Mrs Hai, who had an uncertain but deadly grasp of English. She addressed me as 'The Ambassador', and one day not long into my posting began, informed me that my generosity in lending embassy silver cutlery to A-based staff for their dinner parties had to stop because not all of it was returned. I demurred, saying they could use it sometimes. Mrs Hai shot back: 'Very sometimes, The Ambassador, very sometimes.' I also had a general maid, Madame Du, who was willing but a bit thick, and a cook, Monsieu Vuong, who wore a black beret and made superb omelettes, the ash from his cigarettes dribbling down his front. In addition there was my driver Mr Dzu, and several guards at the embassy gates. These, we suspected, were not appointed to protect us so much as prevent locals from forcing their way into the compound to claim asylum.

Hanoi was justifiably categorised by Canberra as a hardship post. Exhausted and shabby after the long war against the French and Americans, the city offered few amenities or diversions. Its stores were chronically short of basic foodstuffs and practically everything else. As for our health, we had access to the resident Swedish doctor who ran a clinic at the Swedish Embassy. But as in Burma, there was a complete dearth of medicines available at 'People's Stores' or pharmacies. Thus, like most Western missions, we had a regular weekly diplomatic bag run to Bangkok. There our designated courier (I put myself on the roster), would drop the safe-hand bag at the Australian Embassy, spend a few days shopping for things unobtainable in Hanoi that we all needed, such as meat, UHT milk, ice-cream, pharmaceuticals and clothing, plus a supply of videos for circulation among embassy staff. At the end of this all-too-brief sojourn, our courier would arrive early at Don Muang airport, hoping that the flight had not been overbooked and that our pile of foodstuffs packed in dry ice and sweltering in the hot tropical sun would find a place in the hold.

On weekends we created our own diversions. These usually began on Friday nights at the Billabong Bar, where we kept open house to other diplomatic missions in town as well as blow-ins from Australia and elsewhere. It was a convenient way of meeting and briefing visiting journalists. For a while, Soviet and Eastern European colleagues came too, but I stopped them because of the security risk and their unwillingness to grant us reciprocal hospitality in their own embassies. For late-night revellers, there was also a disco at the Swedish Embassy. On Saturdays, a group of us would sometimes prepare a picnic and take off out of town to surrounding villages in the Red River delta, or to the hills to the west and north. For these excursions we generally used the embassy's HiAce mini bus. It was a reliable vehicle with air and a good sound system. It never let us down, whatever the state of the country roads (usually appalling).

I determined that all staff, including me, should be qualified to drive and thus to obtain local licences before taking to the road. Notwithstanding the chaos on Vietnamese roads, the process was stern, intricate and involved three stages — a physical examination, a written exam and a road test. It applied equally to locals and foreigners. The physical was conducted by a panel of male Vietnamese doctors who wanted to listen to our hearts and check our general physical state. This went okay until one of my female staff complained that the doctors wanted her to take her top off. She refused, and I made representations to the Foreign Ministry. That part of the test was henceforth waived for foreign women. The written test was very complex, involving such questions as: how fast can a military vehicle travel along a dyke? How fast a civilian bus? How fast a dumpster or a self-propelled anti-aircraft battery? Or a fire truck, a) on its way to a fire, or b) on its way to lunch after extinguishing a fire? What are the duties of a civilian witness to a road accident? The duties of an off-duty policeman? As all questions were written in Vietnamese, an English-speaking official would provide a translation, and, at the price of three cartons of 555 cigarettes, the correct answers.

The road test involved three uniformed cadres sitting sphinx-like in the back seat of one's vehicle noting every move and directing the driver in sign language where to go. One of their tricks was to indicate to the examinee to proceed the wrong way up a one-way street. If he did he failed the test. Nevertheless, all my A-based staff got their licences, and many kept them as souvenirs ever after.

I used the HiAce for trips to Ha Long Bay near Haiphong and once up to the Vietnamese town of Lang Son and thence to Dong Dang near the Chinese border. There my daughter Anna, on her first visit to Vietnam, a secretary newly arrived in Hanoi and I accidentally strayed into a mine field. On noticing the dull brass detonators half hidden in the bush beside the path, we froze, and slowly retraced our steps back to the car, causing as little vibration as possible. From then on, I ventured into former battle areas with much greater circumspection.

I also took the HiAce on an epic road trip with other Embassy staff to Ho Chi Minh City. Apart from my colleague Henri Bastouille, the French ambassador, this was the first time a Western diplomat had been given permission to make the road journey all the way from north to south. Extending more than 1200 kilometres, Highway One was the scene of much bitter fighting during the French and American wars, and earned the sobriquet 'Street without Joy', from Bernard Fall's 1961 best-seller about the French Indochina war. On the trip we passed many wrecked towns and burnt landscape as far as Hue. At Danang we took on extra fuel and a relief crew which had flown in from Hanoi, and proceeded south through Hoi An and Nha Trang, along some spectacular beaches and lagoons, over headlands and through fishing villages, always with the dramatic Indochina mountain spine to our west. At Phan Rang we turned left and drove up through the southern highlands to Dalat, and then south-west along Highway 20 through Xuan Loc, Bien Hoa and into steamy Saigon.

The variety of motor vehicles on this southern journey was fascinating. Crowds of locals on bikes and motorbikes were a constant, but in the north were mainly government-owned and driven Soviet trucks — Urals and Pragas and Tatras and Zils — with the odd Gaz 69 command car and small and funky UAZ 469 jeeps. Most common seemed to be Zil 131s, which the Soviets boasted was the best and toughest truck ever made. Basically unmodified from 1966 to 1989, designed to withstand abuse from conscript soldiers, and able to run cheerfully on a wide range of cross-fuels, the Zil, according to a Ukranian general, would run on anything 'so long as it would burn'.

As we passed the seventeenth parallel and drove into former South Vietnam, however, the traffic changed. There were fewer Soviet vehicles, many more American, most of which seemed to be in private hands. Most common of these were former American Army 'deuce and a halfs' — the M 35 family of trucks of two and a half ton capacity, many in faded camouflage paint with signs neatly stencilled in black on their sides saying 'US Army — Not for Hire'. They were made among others by REO, Kaiser and GM. These were six-cylinder, turbo-charged monsters coupled to five-speed transmissions. They could run on diesel fuel, jet fuel, kerosene, heating oil or petrol with oil added to lubricate the injectors. In many of these the water pumps and/or radiator cores had long since given up the ghost. By welding a 44-gallon drum to the roof, with a pipe circulating water through the engine, their Vietnamese owners had ingeniously adapted the cooling into an 'open flow' system, The coolant, a rusty mixture of steam and boiling water, was pissed out sideways under pressure at windscreen height into oncoming traffic. The range of these vehicles was not measured by the diesel in the tank, but the water on the roof.

And so to Bill Hayden's to-do list. Restarting a bilateral aid program to Vietnam was part of the ALP's platform. But it was difficult to implement, not because the Vietnamese were ungrateful but because of the opprobrium from Australian friends and neighbours. Apart from Indonesia, which feared Chinese expansionism and regarded an independent Vietnam as a bulwark against it, the ASEAN countries were scandalised. How could Australia give aid to such an aggressor, one that had so recently invaded and occupied a neighbour? The Thais were alarmist, complaining that the Vietnamese were now only two hours' tank drive from Bangkok. The foreign minister of Singapore, Dhanabalan, was hugely self-righteous. The Americans flatly told Hawke we couldn't do it, and Hawke conveyed this to Hayden. But Hayden wasn't to be deterred. Backed by some clever footwork at section- and branch-head level in the department, he wisely chose to send our aid — educational aids, surgical equipment, other equipment and some emergency food aid — under United Nations Development Program auspices. It seemed to have a lower profile and was less offensive to Vietnamese watchers that way.

How to encourage trade? Several large Australian companies had made solid investments in the old Republic of Vietnam, including oil prospecting forays in the South China Sea. But most were now gun-shy and didn't want to chance further investments in the new centrally planned Vietnam. I arranged for a visit by BHP executives to discuss resuming their old oil leases in the South China Sea with Vietnamese officials. I like to think they went home with some favourable impressions, but nothing eventuated during my watch. What we did achieve, however, slowly and hesitantly, was a renewed Australian interest in Vietnamese tropical timbers, fruits and fish. An Australian company even came up to establish a cold store and fish processing plant on the Saigon River. It was the start of what has now become a substantial two-way flow in goods and financial and tourist services, contributed to in no small way by Australian Vietnamese. Indeed, I become quite emotional when I now visit Vietnam and see the huge range of Australian companies operating there with such confidence in so many areas.

How to tie up the loose ends of the war? Like military units of the Americans and other allies engaged in the Vietnam War, the Australian battalions, the RAAF helicopters and Caribou transports, and our military advisors, had begun to withdraw from Phuoc Tuy province and elsewhere in South Vietnam in November 1971. In some haste the Australian Embassy closed its doors, and the ambassador and his staff decamped just before victorious North Vietnamese and Vietcong units entered Saigon in April 1975. We had left behind a chancery on the seventh floor of the Caravelle Hotel on Tu Do Street, plus several residences and staff apartments in other locations in Saigon. These I had to inspect, and then sign them over to the SRV government in Hanoi.

I recall that my inspection and handover took place towards the end of 1983. Escorted by Foreign Ministry officials, I entered the now empty Caravelle Hotel, took the lift to the seventh floor, and walked past the reception area where, on my first visit in 1970, a section of Australian soldiers used to make tea and toast as they guarded the chancery, their armalites stacked in a corner. Everything was now quiet. It felt like a movie set or an archaeological dig. I walked along the corridor and entered the ambassador's office, once bustling with activity, now silent as a grave. In one corner, rats had eaten part of the carpet, and venetian blinds flapped fitfully in a breeze coming through a broken pane. The ambassadorial desk sat dusty and bare, his swivel chair cracked and listing to one side. Offices occupied by the political, economic, consular, aid and administrative staff, and the strongroom, were similarly silent and neglected.

In the offices of the military and defence attaches, however, I saw signs of hasty departure. Empty top secret red-bordered file covers with titles like 'Operations North of the DMZ' lay scattered among walkie-talkie radios, their batteries long-since dead. A desiccated half-smoked cigar lay in a cut-glass ashtray, a half-empty bottle of whisky on a shelf. A large map of South Vietnam covered one wall, with acetate arrows marking the advance of the enemy through the first four months of 1975, including the capture of Phuoc Long Province on 6 January, Ban Me Thuot on 11 March, Hue on 25 March, and Danang on 30 March. The final entry on the map marked the fall of Xuan

Loc, the ARVN's last stand before Saigon, on 21 April. On 30 April Communist forces entered Saigon and their Chinese-made T-62 tanks broke through the gates of the presidential palace. American and Australian Embassy staff had decamped several days before. The war was over.

We conducted an investigation of Agent Orange. Dr Fiona Stanley from Western Australia was one of a small team of medicos, epidemiologists and others who came to Vietnam for the exercise. Each morning in Hanoi, the team joined me in my jog around Thong Nhat Park before their program began. They visited hospitals in the north and the south. In the south they were shown babies, both alive and in formaldehyde, with malignancies and some shocking congenital deformities. Vietnamese hospital staff courteously explained that they strongly suspected that defoliants, including the widely used agents Orange and Blue, were responsible for the abnormalities, but the Vietnamese didn't have the equipment or epidemiological resources to prove it. One rather aggressive member of the Australian team was quite dismissive of the evidence. In the end, to Fiona Stanley's intense frustration, nothing was proven, and Australian soldiers claiming they had been adversely affected by dioxin received no compensation. The Royal Commission had been a political whitewash.

That situation changed in the 1990s, when a US Congressional Committee of Experts found there was indeed a connection between Agent Orange, and other defoliants, and the high incidence of cancers afflicting returned American soldiers. An Australian Administrative Appeals Tribunal subsequently determined that Australian soldiers who had served thirty days or more in Vietnamese war theatres in which defoliants had been sprayed, and had contracted any one of several listed cancers, was entitled to free medical treatment and a war pension that flowed on to his widow after his death. Tragically, none of the millions of Vietnamese afflicted by cancers due to dioxin have received similar medical assistance or compensation, except from a few NGOs — a drop in the bucket.

We made arrangements for an Australian Missing in Action team to visit the sites where six Australians were last seen alive, but never conclusively proven to have died. (In contrast, the United States had 2486 MIAs, a reflection on the disproportionate military commitment of the two countries to the war.) Our team included Colonel Barry Bradshaw, a Vietnamese-speaking veteran of the war, and was accompanied by a film crew. The six Australian MIAs included Flying Officers Robert Carver and Michael Herbert, last seen alive in their Canberra bomber as it took off from Danang in November 1970. The aircraft was presumed to have been hit by a missile near a village called Tun Duc, but the wreck had not been found. Two soldiers from 1 RAR, Lance Corporal Richard Parker and Private Peter Gilson went missing near their base at Bien Hoa north of Saigon in 1965. Private David Fisher, an SAS trooper, was seen to have fallen from the extraction rope of a helicopter in an area of heavy fighting near War Zone D, and Corporal John Gillespie went missing in the Long Hai Ranges in Phuoc Tuy Province in 1971.

We consulted known map co-ordinates, went to all possible sites, and with the help of our foreign ministry minders, questioned villagers. On one particularly hot day looking for Fisher around the tunnels at Cu Chi, we were accompanied by a former VC officer in full uniform. He was taciturn at first, but it emerged that he had lost his own wife, a VC combatant, during an ambush by an Australian unit, and he had never recovered her body. Yet here he was helping the enemy find our MIAs. None of our explorations were successful, but I note with some chagrin that another Australian MIA mission in 2008 had found the remains of three of the six — Parker, Gilson and Gillespie. They no doubt had our own groundwork and reports to help them. The story was all over the newspapers, which claimed it to have been the first attempt to recover Australian remains. I wrote a letter to the *Sydney Morning Herald* correcting the claim, but they chose not to publish it.

All these were important tasks, significant in their bearing on the course of bilateral relations. But my final task — finding out about Vietnamese intentions in Cambodia — had a wider, regional significance.

One of my crucial interlocutors in discussing Cambodia was the Vietnamese foreign minister, Nguyen Co Thach — a tough, intelligent and urbane man. He had served as one of Le Duc Tho's deputies during the Paris negotiations in 1972. He loved to discuss history, especially what he termed the two thousand year war for Vietnamese independence — against the Chinese over many centuries, the French since 1852, and the Americans and their allies since 1962. He told me with some asperity that his worst job had been shovelling shit from a French officers' latrine during a spell as a POW before their defeat at Dien Bien Phu. Quite accurately, Thach claimed that four of the five permanent members of the UN Security Council had at one time or another invaded and occupied Vietnam. (Britain had occupied South Vietnam at the end of the Pacific War.) He was aggrieved at stories put out by the pro-Vietnam War industry that Saigon had become a bloodbath of reprisals after its capture by NVA troops. Certainly, many former ARVN officers had been put in to re-education camps, but the Vietnamese had done nothing compared to the widespread reprisals carried out, for example, by the French in 1945 against Nazi collaborators. He asserted that Western countries like Australia had no need to fear the Soviet presence in Vietnam, which was ephemeral. The Russians had an alien culture and temperament that jarred with many Vietnamese and Vietnam would send them packing soon enough.

But the *Chinese* worried the Vietnamese — they were culturally close, patient, powerful, had occupied Vietnam for centuries, and were ready to invade Vietnam again at a moment's notice, just as they had in 1979. Thach said that after the war against America, all the government in Hanoi wanted was a peaceful environment in which to reconstruct the country. But Pol Pot, a 'crazy man', had not allowed this, and persisted in making murderous raids into southern Vietnam, slaughtering people and destroying villages. China had been rancorous towards Vietnam after it sent the Americans packing, and was again making aggressive sounds from the north. Beijing had not wanted NVA and VC forces to take Saigon so quickly. The Chinese had attempted to delay the Paris Peace Talks, and to keep North Vietnam fighting the Americans. They preferred an endlessly divided country and a continuous war with America to a united, powerful Vietnam.

In October 1978 the United States postponed plans to normalise relations with Hanoi, and in November Hanoi signed a friendship pact with Moscow. Hanoi faced two enemies — Beijing from the north and Pol Pot to the south-west. It had no hope of tackling China, but could surely remove the threat from the west. So, on Christmas Day 1978 Vietnamese forces entered Cambodia, quickly seized Phnom Penh and sent Khmer Rouge forces into full retreat along the Thai border. Thach indignantly said that if the Allies in World War II had been justified in pushing the Germans back to Berlin, surely the Vietnamese had the same right in Cambodia. It was a defensive move, with the additional benefit of stopping Pol Pot from continuing to prey on his people.

Thach added that the anticipated Chinese retaliation across Vietnam's northern border took place, but Vietnamese forces were ready for them, and drove them back after much bloodshed. In describing Vietnamese fighting spirit, he was fond of quoting Napoleon, who had said 150 years ago that 'The spirit is to the matériel as three is to one'. 'It's not the sophistication of the rifle or machine gun you hold that wins the battle, or the armour or fighter bombers you can call in if you are in difficulty, it's what's inside,' Thach would say as he theatrically thumped his chest.

I could relate to this sentiment. I had watched squads of Vietnamese infantry on the move, riding high on piles of firewood in battered Soviet trucks, with no air cover or supporting artillery, an iron cooking pot and a sack of rice their only form of sustenance. I would not willingly have met them as enemies, even with air or artillery cover.

I also made a habit of calling on the Soviet ambassador in Hanoi to get his perspective on events. A large man in a large office in a large embassy (a former French *lycée*), the ambassador would periodically invite me to breakfast. This was not a small meal, consisting of caviar and blinis and Russian bread and all manner of spreads as well as eggs, sausages and bacon. After about an hour of him talking and me listening, I would stagger back to my embassy, my head fuzzy from the several toasts in neat vodka I had consumed, to report the latest Soviet perspective to Canberra. The ambassador never gave me much enlightenment, but it was useful to report his proprietorial attitude towards Russia's little comrade, and the progress being made to install hydro power stations and other inappropriately enormous Soviet-designed infrastructural projects throughout the country. At the end of my posting, the Soviet Foreign Ministry invited me to visit Moscow to give them the perspective of a diplomat from a country which had participated in the Vietnam War on the 'wrong' side. It was an interesting visit in the middle of a Russian winter.

I reported Vietnam's declared intentions of quitting Cambodia to Canberra, with the comment that they made sense and were probably true. The 50,000 Vietnamese troops in Cambodia faced 30,000 Khmer Rouge in the western provinces, who were backed and financed by the United States, China, Thailand and Singapore. For Hanoi, the occupation was wearing and increasingly costly. My reports met with agreement in some quarters but with sour disapproval in others.

My views occasionally conflicted with those of the Australian Embassy in Bangkok, which at the time had joint reporting responsibilities for Cambodia. Reflecting the view of the Thais, Ambassador Gordon Jockel and his staff kept suggesting that Vietnamese forces might invade Thailand. The issue came to a head when Bill Hayden visited both Vietnam and Thailand in 1984. In a briefing in Hanoi, he was told by the Vietnamese that they had no intention of occupying any Thai territory, an assurance he then related at a press conference to accompanying Australian journalists. When Hayden got to Bangkok however, the embassy triumphantly informed him that even as he had been speaking in Hanoi, Vietnamese squads had entered Thai territory to get at military remnants of the Khmer Rouge. They had withdrawn after capturing or killing them.

This was probably true, but the incursions were tactical, and did not contradict the Vietnamese assurance that they had no intention of permanently occupying Thai territory. It was a ludicrous claim by Bangkok which did not add clarity to the situation.

During another visit to Hanoi, Hayden asked me to arrange a call on Vietnam's preferred leader for Cambodia, the former Khmer Rouge fighter, Hun Sen. I informed Nguyen Co Thach, and he quickly signalled Phnom Penh to see whether Hun Sen would fly to Ho Chi Minh City to meet the Australian foreign minister. He would, and Bill Hayden, John Holloway a senior Foreign Affairs officer, and I had a fascinating discussion with Hun Sen at a 'safe house' in Ho Chi Minh City — in fact, the residence of the former British ambassador to South Vietnam. Sipping tea out of fine bone china bearing the British crown, Hayden closely questioned Hun Sen about his plans for the future of Cambodia. After the meeting Hayden was convinced that Hun Sen was a Cambodian patriot with his own agenda, no satrap of the Vietnamese, and unlikely to do their bidding. He also remarked that Hun Sen's glass eye seemed to be the friendly one. After UN-sponsored elections in Cambodia in 1993, Hun Sen became co-premier and later prime minister, and Norodom Sihanouk was reinstated as a king, although stripped of his former power.

I have returned to Vietnam several times since my posting there, and each time I have been staggered at the economic progress in Hanoi and Ho Chi Minh City. Also, I must admit, at the growth of official corruption. But the country has re-identified itself. Once it was a pariah in its neighbourhood, feared by most of the ASEANs, despised and isolated equally by the Americans and the Chinese (although throughout its troubles with Hanoi, Beijing maintained a large embassy in Hanoi. The Americans had no diplomatic presence until the late 1980s).

Vietnam is now a powerful and respected member of ASEAN. I once predicted that during my lifetime it would eclipse Thailand as an engine of growth in the region. This hasn't happened yet, but it may in the near future. Meanwhile, the once-feared Communist Party of Vietnam remains in power, just as the Communist Party does in Beijing. Both countries are short on human rights, but their citizens gain in other important areas, such as economic predictability and increasing purchasing power.

On consultations from Hanoi in Australia in 1984, I met one day with a large group of Vietnamese refugees in western Sydney. Mainly men, they were disgruntled and angry at having been forced to flee their country and resentful that Australia now had official relations with the SRV. They were without jobs, partners and identity, and hated Communist Hanoi. Today they have jobs and families. Some run businesses such as bakeries and restaurants. Others are professionals. Their children are generally highly motivated and successful. They have blended seamlessly and productively into the Australian community of which they form a valuable part. Many visit relatives in Vietnam, particularly at Tet. One still occasionally sees the old red and yellow Republic of South Vietnam flag flying at rallies in Cabramatta or Dandenong. It was prominent at Randwick during the Catholic World Youth Day mass in July 2008. But by and large the anger has gone.

Today it would be risible to regard Vietnam as an expansionary power, an illusion fiercely held by many conservative watchers in Canberra and in the Australian press during the Cold War. If elections had been allowed in 1954 as agreed at Geneva, Ho Chi Minh would have been overwhelmingly voted in as the president of a united and peaceful country. Instead, millions of Vietnamese were killed for no gain at all over twenty long and agonising years.

9

The Kimchi Olympics

On my return from Hanoi to Canberra in 1986, Foreign Minister Bill Hayden asked me where I'd like to be posted next. I was taken aback by his question — officers rarely have the privilege of choosing their next post — but I thought quickly and suggested Seoul. I knew that trade between Australia and Korea was growing, that security dynamics on the peninsula were worth watching, and that the Seoul Olympics were scheduled for 1988. Bill agreed, and promptly informed the secretary of the department, Stuart Harris, of his decision. I was scheduled to go at the beginning of 1997.

While working in the Economic Division over the next twelve months I did a lot of preparation, including taking Korean language lessons. My grounding in Japanese helped. My teachers had contrasting styles. Choe-Wall Young-hi of the ANU was a dignified linguistic scholar who loved to explain the historical roots of grammar. My tutor Kwak Ki-song believed in machine-like drill to beat speech patterns into my skull, interspersed with percussive bouts of ping-pong.

Next, I had to expand my knowledge of Korea. I especially wanted to know more about the origins of the Korean War which had had such a strong influence in shaping both Koreas. The common view, perpetuated in the Australian press each year on the anniversary of the outbreak of the war on 24 June 1950, was that the North Korean Communists under their leader Kim Il-sung fell upon the fledgling and freedom-loving South Korea without warning and very nearly took it until General Douglas MacArthur made a brilliant landing at Incheon halfway up the western side of the peninsula and forced the Communists back across the thirty-eighth parallel. MacArthur then overplayed his hand by pursuing the North Koreans up to the Yellow River border with China and Chinese forces then joined the war and forced him back into South Korea. After two years of trench warfare along the thirty-eighth parallel, an armistice was negotiated in 1953.

I found this story superficial as it failed to take the war's origins into account. These were grounded in the opportunistic Soviet declaration of war against Japan in August 1945, when Japan was already on the verge of surrender. Soviet troops invaded Korea from the north on 8 August 1945. They looked like engulfing the whole peninsula before the United States, still regrouping after bitter fighting on Okinawa, could get its troops on the ground. But the Americans, beginning to see the strategic importance of Korea to their future interests in the western Pacific, decided to draw a line across the peninsula and tell the Soviets not to advance over it. On 15 August John J. McCloy of the American War Department instructed two young army colonels, Dean Rusk and Charles H. Bonesteel, to work out where the division should be. They decided on the thirty-eighth parallel because, as Rusk later said, it would 'place the capital city [Seoul] in the American zone'. Possibly deterred by the two atom bombs the US had dropped on Hiroshima and Nagasaki on 6 and 9 August respectively, the Kremlin accepted the division in silence. No Koreans were consulted or informed about the division of their country.

Neither the northern nor southern regime accepted the division peacefully. From 1945 to 1949, many battles were fought across the thirty-eighth parallel. South Korea initiated some, North Korea others. And, while North Korea was locked down in a Stalinist embrace under Kim Il-sung, South Korea was in ferment with its own civil war, fought between rich and poor, between peasants and the hated land-owning collaborators of the Japanese. Unlike General Douglas MacArthur in Tokyo, the commander of the American occupation in Korea, General John R. Hodge, was not tutored in local affairs, and was clueless about stopping the fighting. He failed to acknowledge the legitimate nature and strength of nationalistic feelings sweeping the country, and narrowly viewed the trouble as caused solely by dangerous pro-Communist rebels, whom he mistakenly believed were all in league with the North. He backed the American-selected and appointed Syngman Rhee as the autocratic president because he was anti-Communist, and he turned a blind eye to massacres of nationalists carried out by Rhee's Japanese-trained police.

Meanwhile, cross-border fighting increased. It was particularly intense in 1949. One battle initiated by the South occurred at Kaesong just north of Seoul on 4 May. Four hundred North Korean and twenty-two South Korean soldiers were killed, as well as about a hundred civilians. The South had committed six infantry companies, of which two, in the heat of battle, defected to the North. Another significant battle occurred on the last weekend of June 1949 on the Ongjin Peninsula northwest of Seoul. A week before the war began on 24 June 1950 Eisenhower's special envoy, John Foster Dulles, visited Rhee in Seoul and pleaded with him to stop military provocations. Rhee forcefully argued the other way, advocating a full-scale attack with American support against the North.

When the North Koreans counter-attacked the South on 24 June 1950, they meant business. Like the Vietnamese in their response to Pol Pot's attacks against Vietnamese territory from 1976–1979, Pyongyang saw an invasion with overwhelming force as the only way to stop cross-border raids. But Kim also wanted to unify the country under his rule. It had never before been divided, not least by a foreign power. The invasion was an act of civil war, not, as so many Cold War warriors in Washington (and Canberra) argued, part of a worldwide Communist conspiracy directed from Moscow. Stalin probably supported it, but it is doubtful that he controlled it, or even knew when it would begin.

After three years of bitter fighting, the last two spent in a bloody stalemate along the thirty-eighth parallel, an armistice was signed on 27 July 1953. North Korea and China signed it on one side, the USA on the other. South Korea did not sign, and still has not. North Korea lost over two million civilians and 500,000 soldiers. Chinese losses were around a million. About a million South Korean civilians and 50,000 soldiers died. The United States suffered around 33,600 'battle deaths'. Total casualties among other participants were around 3200, of whom 686 were

British and 339 Australian. The biggest winner was Japan, which received a flood of orders for trucks and other equipment from US forces that played a central role in rebuilding the country's war-ravaged industries. Another winner was Australia, which enjoyed a wool boom stimulated by the war. The biggest losers were North and South Korea, particularly the North, the infrastructure of which was totally destroyed by American bombing.

Since war's end the two Koreas have gone their separate ways. At first economic development was stronger in the North, which had coal and mineral wealth. By the 1980s, however, the South was streaking ahead. With a population of 42 million people, gross domestic product and income rose twentyfold from 1953 to 1986 as the country's manufacturing sector, backed by the government, successfully built ships, machinery, and later, motor cars and electronics. Even democracy was getting a foothold. The first three presidents, Rhee Syng-man, Park Chung-hee and Chun Doo-hwan, were all ruthless dictators, the latter two generals who staged coups against their predecessors. But in February 1988 Roo Tae-woo, another general, was elected president of the Republic. He in turn was succeeded by civilian presidents in free elections — Kim Young-sam, Kim Dae-jung, Roo Myo-hun and, at the time of writing, Lee Myung-bak. A former foreign minister, Ban Ki-moon, became secretary-general of the United Nations in 2006.

Bill Hayden had given me no specific goals to achieve in the Republic of Korea, but what needed doing was clear enough. The main job was to build on the tremendous bilateral trade flow. By the mid 1980s the ROK had become Australia's principal market, after Japan, for iron ore, coal, bauxite and non-ferrous metals, and a very significant market for beef and agricultural products. How could trade be expanded? How could Australia's rather obscure profile in Korea be raised, not just as a significant country in the Pacific, but as a sophisticated and culturally rich society, a worthy centre of advanced education for young Koreans? Australian diplomatic representation in Seoul had begun with A. B. (Jim) Jamieson in 1949, and had been managed by fourteen ambassadors before me. Each of my predecessors had done something to lift Australia's profile. My job was to build on the base they had set.

I arrived alone at Kimpo airport in Seoul from Tokyo on 2 September 1987. Ali had completed her posting to Tokyo in January 1986 and was in Canberra with Adam who was finishing high school at Telopea Park, and Anna was enrolled in Arts/Law at the University of Sydney. An early autumnal haze lay over Seoul, and the leaves of gingko trees lining the avenues were just beginning to turn golden. Superficially, the city looked to me like Tokyo — the same high blocky business towers solemnly blinking their red aircraft warning lights through the night, the same efficient subways, clean taxis and buses, garish neon-lit entertainment districts, advertising hoardings and department stores. Much the same architecture, too, in ancient Buddhist temples and palaces set in orderly parks. This impression of Japanese-ness was reinforced by the arrogant grey bulk of the Chong-Ang Cheong building, the Japanese imperial administrative centre constructed during the colonial period at Gwanghwamun at the end of the main avenue of Sejongno. It had been deliberately sited to cut off the view of the Gyeongbukgung Palace behind it.

During the 1990s, the Koreans dismantled and removed the building, turning the site into a vast forecourt for the palace, and a parade ground for guards in ancient Korean battledress.

But my early forays around Seoul revealed a city different from metropolitan Tokyo — not just in the crowded and noisy markets, fragrant eating houses and surprisingly numerous Christian churches, each with its blue fluorescent cross illuminating the night sky, but in the topography of the metropolis. Rugged granite mountains intruded into the heart of the city and its surroundings, and tunnels were cut through them into which the traffic, driving on the right, disappeared and re-emerged at great speed.

As for Koreans, superficially they looked *en masse* the same as the Japanese, especially the businessmen in their dark suits, white shirts and sober ties. But they had a pleasing lack of decorum, and were not imbued, like the Japanese, with much of a sense of personal space. After a business lunch, Korean men also exuded a strong aroma of *kimchi* (garlic-impregnated pickled cabbage) which a visiting Australian wit dryly observed was enough to kill a brown dog on a chain. Koreans also loved physical exercise and fitness, and were forever charging up mountainsides in full alpine gear including deerstalker hats and corduroy trousers, and carrying ropes, crampons, tents, ghetto blasters, spirit stoves, picnic hampers and flasks of lethal-strength *soju* (clear grain spirit) or *dongdongju* (fermented rice wine). It was great fun to set off on a Saturday morning in the middle of winter, climb for hours up rugged boulder-strewn paths to the summit of a local mountain, and there join boisterous clumps of fellow hikers and share roasting meat and drink at their impromptu snow-covered barbecues.

Another difference from Japanese cities were the manifestations of tension and emergency underlining the fact that the country had been bitterly fought over and all but destroyed less than forty years before. There were tank traps, barbed wire, gun emplacements and watch towers against a northern invasion along the Han River and up the road to the border. Most Korean hotel rooms had emergency lighting and clear plastic containers on the walls of guest rooms containing bottled water, axes and rope ladders in case of sudden fire. Also, in Seoul, emergency drills occurred at regular intervals, more frequently as the 1988 Olympic Games approached. As amplified air raid sirens wailed the traffic would stop, people would disappear into underground shopping malls and the city would lapse into eerie silence.

My house was on a high mountain to the north of the city at Seongbuk-dong. Behind a traditional Korean stone wall were some good spaces for entertaining, including a large reception room, a tennis court and gardens with grand views over the city. The drive up to the house was very steep, but the views were worth it. It was staffed by Mr Kim the butler, Mr Kim the cook, Mrs Kim senior maid, and Mr Kim the gardener. To distinguish the Kims, and to their vast amusement, I called the butler Big Mr Kim (Kun Kim Shi Ajoshi), and the cook, very slightly shorter and wider, Little Mr Kim (Chagun Kim Shi Ajoshi). The most common Korean family names are Lee, Min, Kim, and Park. I learned the trick of saying 'Ah, Mr Lee!' on meeting someone I'd been introduced to before but forgotten his name. I had a good chance of being right once in maybe six times. If I guessed right, the Mr Lee in question was unfailingly amazed at my good memory.

THE KIMCHI OLYMPICS

I presented my credentials to President Chun Doo-hwan at the Blue House in October 1987. This enabled me to get down to the serious business of representing Australia, and to host, right at the start of my appointment, a long-planned visit by the Melbourne Symphony Orchestra. Under the direction of its conductor Vanco Cavdarski, the orchestra played works by Kodaly, Tchaikovsky, Mozart, Glinka and Dvorak at two sold-out concerts in Seoul and a standing room only concert in Pusan. Three Korean soloists were invited to play with the orchestra — Kwon Hae-ryeung and Kim Hyung-kyu both played Greig's Piano Concerto in A Minor, and violinist Kim Min played Mozart's Concerto No. 5 in A Major. The concerts were good-quality 'soft' diplomacy in a country that reveres Western classical music more than we do.

The Australian Chancery was in the Salvation Army building on Saemunangil in downtown Seoul, but I moved it to the more spacious and modern Kyobo Building nearby on Sejongno. My hard-working and generally amiable Australian colleagues included a senior trade commissioner, several political officers, a military attaché and his assistant, immigration and information staff. All were backed up by competent locally engaged staff. There were also outrider groups including representatives of the Australian Meat and Livestock Corporation, and a lively Australian business community.

The embassy had a fleet of several cars, mainly Japanese. My head of mission car, however, was a black 1985 Mercedes Benz 280 E. One of the W 123 series of Mercedes made between 1976 and 1985, it had a six-cylinder engine of 2746 cc with twin overhead camshafts, Bosch K-Jetronic electronic injection and a smooth automatic transmission. It was a solid example of Teutonic engineering, with plenty of grunt when required, which in Seoul traffic seemed to be most of the time. My driver, Mr Lee, was a dignified self-effacing man with a broad face and prematurely greying hair. He knew Seoul and its environs intimately, and always calculated the best route to an appointment, and when I had to leave to arrive on time. If some Korean drivers were aggressive and pushy or the urban traffic grounded in gridlock and smog, Mr Lee was unperturbed, and always found an alternative route.

Mr Lee was also a competent tennis player, and a great practice partner on the residence court after a gruelling day at work. He had some older male friends with whom he played regularly, including a former cabinet member, 'Minister Min'. On one of Adam's visits to Seoul from Pembroke, the Adelaide boarding school he was now enrolled in, Mr Lee invited us to play doubles against Minister Min and his equally ancient partner, Dr Koo. Adam, a relaxed and stylish player, had sparred at the Institute of Sports in Canberra with Jason Stoltenberg, and was a bit impatient at facing such old opponents. But they took the pace off the ball with wonderful drop shots and lobs with pinpoint accuracy, and Adam and I overhit our shots. After two energetic sets in which we did all the running and our opponents won, we discovered that Minister Min and Dr Koo had been Korea's best two tennis players in their youth.

The Merc was a wonderful touring car. Officially I used it to travel to such places as the Hyundai Heavy Industries shipyard at Ulsan to help launch the *Portland*, a bulk ore carrier for Alcoa Australia; to inspect a complex of four nuclear power reactors at

Kori; celebrate Anzac Day at Kapyong (several times); call at the Pohang Iron and Steel works where much of Australia's coking coal and iron ore went; and visit many other industrial sites around the peninsula.

I also used it at weekends and holidays for touring: east over the mountain spine to the forests of Soraksan National Park where wonderful skiing was available in winter; south down the western coast through the Taean Haean Maritime National Park to Gunsan and Mokpo; through the centre to Gwanju, Jeonju, and Cheongju; and several times to the south-eastern corner of the peninsula at Pusan. With Ali, who stayed with me for a year during 1988, and whatever friends were with me at the time I would wander back to Seoul up the eastern coast through Ulsan to the temples, pagodas and royal tombs and shrines of the ancient Shila kingdom at Gyeongju. One of the best touring areas was among the bays and inlets of the southern part of the peninsula. The highways in the Republic were fast and smooth, and some of the straighter sections had been marked out as runways for the Korean Air Force's jet fighters. Most country roads were also quite serviceable.

I recall that the other cars in the small embassy fleet were Japanese rather than Korean. Japanese cars were regarded as of better quality, and we could bring them in duty free, which ensured high resale prices. But in motor car production, as much as in every other industrial activity, the Koreans were fiercely motivated to compete with and to equal or surpass the Japanese. They began to do this in shipbuilding during the 1970s, and with their auto industries during my watch in the 1980s. They would repeat the process with whitegoods and electronics in the 1990s, and then copy the Japanese by moving their industries offshore to the United States, South East Asia, and later, China.

South Korea began making motor cars a long time after Japan, but they followed a similar pattern. Their first car, the Sibal, was assembled in August 1955 by Choi Mu-seong, a mechanic who mounted an engine on a modified American Army Jeep. In 1960 Sinjin Motors, with technical assistance from Toyota, launched its Publica. Three motor car companies started up in 1962: Kyeongseong Precision Industries which became Kia Motors; Ha Dong-hwan which became Ssang Yong Motors; and Saenara Automobile, with technical assistance from Nissan.

Mergers, co-production and technical agreements followed, many with Japanese companies, and all strongly protected by the Korean government. The Asia Motor Company began in 1965 and Hyundai in 1968. The main companies at the end of the 1980s were the Hyundai Motor Company, Kia Motors, GM Daewoo, and the Ssang Yong Motor Company.

With its small, four-cylinder Excel, offered with a variety of trims and body styles, Hyundai entered the American market in 1986. That year it sold 126,000 vehicles, a record for entry-level cars into the United States. But Excel's faults and poor quality control soon became apparent, and Hyundai became the butt of many jokes, including on the popular *David Letterman Show*. One joke laboriously had it that Hyundai stood for 'Hope you understand nothing's driveable and inexpensive'. The Koreans were mortified, and in response invested heavily in quality, design and manufacture. By 2004, Hyundai tied with Honda for vehicle quality in the American market, and by 2006 was ranked third overall in world motor car quality, after only Porsche and

Lexus. By 2008, Korea had the fifth largest automobile industry in the world in terms of production volume and the sixth largest in terms of export volume. In the same year, Hyundai's Santa Fe and Elantra became the US magazine *Consumer Report*'s 'top pick' for safety and reliability, beating such high-quality stalwarts as the Honda Civic, Toyota Corolla and Toyota Prius. The company says it will market its first hybrid electric vehicle, the Avante, in 2009.

Hyundai enhanced its credentials as an environmentally conscious company in 2008 by starting a five-year plan to transform 50 square kilometres of desert 660 kilometres north of Beijing into grassland. If it succeeds, it will end dust storms that annually shroud Beijing (and Seoul) and block desertification.

I had personal experience of Korean car quality only after retiring in Australia. In 2002 I bought an Italian-styled Leganza from Daewoo. A pleasingly squat, four-door sedan with 2002 ccs under its bonnet, a manual five-speed box on the floor, beautifully laid-out instrumentation and fine leather upholstery, the Leganza went like a rocket between Canberra and Sydney and elsewhere around New South Wales. At least it did until its timing belt broke one Saturday on the Princes Highway south of Kiama. Towed into Gerringong and then back to the Sydney, it spent several weeks having the engine painstakingly reconstructed at the Daewoo dealer. With 20,000 kays on the clock, and still under warranty, I handed it on to Anna and her partner Duncan. They were creative types, blithely unconcerned about leaving the Leganza unwashed and unserviced. They also bumped into things and collected an interesting mosaic of body dings. They still thrash the Leganza around Sydney with their small daughter, Ava — our grandchild

— singing away from her crashproof seat strapped to the rear bulkhead. After over 150,000 kilometres of such heavy treatment the car still runs, although bits keep falling off. I have my fingers crossed that it will continue to go, and regularly nag Anna and Duncan to wash it, or at least the rich layer of black brake carbon off the front wheels, and have the beast serviced.

Each year during my posting, the Americans staged a large military exercise somewhere on the South Korean peninsula. Known as 'Exercise Team Spirit', this involved elements of the US Army, Navy, Marines and Air Force, as well as the Korean Armed Forces, in amphibious landings, air warfare, and bombing raids, some with simulated nuclear weapons, all directed at North Korea. And every year the North Koreans reacted to what they saw as a reckless display of military strength by railing against the 'imperialistic provocations' of the Americans and their lackeys, putting their own massive forces across the peninsula on red alert, their dug-in artillery pieces vectored on Seoul. As I write, these exercises still go on. On 26 August 2008 the North Koreans stopped disabling its nuclear facilities at Yongpyon, partly because the United States has still not taken North Korea off its terrorist blacklist, partly because Chinese Premier Hu Jintao was visiting Seoul at the time, and partly because the US had just held another joint military exercise with South Korean forces, described with some justification by North Korean radio as 'war manoeuvres to practise invading the north'.

One of the uncomfortable realities of Korea is that if war should once more break out Australia, under the terms of the armistice, would be obliged to become involved. I thought it relevant therefore to ask the US ambassador, Jim Lilley, why such exercises were held. Would it not be better to ease off, especially as the 1988 Seoul Olympics approached, and work towards eventual peaceful integration without such provocations? Jim candidly said that this indeed was the goal of the State Department, but the US military did not necessarily share such ambitions, and were more concerned to remain in control of what they regarded as one of the best arenas for war games in the western Pacific. They had their own network of bases, their post exchange stores and movie theatres — an extensive microcosm of American culture — right here in Korea, and were not about to give it up. They were unconcerned that their military presence and activities were a source of anxiety to the State Department, or of continual provocation to Pyongyang.

I reminded Jim of Australia's role in the Korean Armistice and ANZUS obligations and suggested that it would be a good idea if the ambassadors of America's allies could be fully briefed about US military assets in the country, see where they were deployed, and know something about the game plan if the North decided to invade again. After all, the Americans still technically commanded Korean forces in wartime.

Jim was receptive, but my suggestion took six months to percolate through the American military hierarchy and a tour was arranged. Eventually, after a false start because of bad weather, a small group of ambassadors, including from Turkey, Canada, Australia, New Zealand and the United Kingdom, assembled in May 1988 at Yongsan, a US military base of 630 prime acres in the centre of Seoul. From there we were whisked by US military choppers around selected American bases. At one we were taken underground to an impressive surveillance centre where every military activity in the North was graphically displayed on huge screens. I doubt that President Kim Il-sung could have gone to the toilet without his every movement being monitored by the Americans, but then not all intelligence is useful.

A popular destination for every visitor to the Republic was Panmunjom, the village on the DMZ north of Seoul where the 1953 armistice was negotiated across a green baize table in a tin hut. A line was drawn down the length of the table, one side being South Korean territory, the other North. Outside, North and South Korean soldiers, selected because of their height and physical strength, have ever since the armistice glowered silently at each other. Gawking tourists were warned not to take photos or make sudden movements as they looked north and west into North Korea.

I escorted many official Australian visitors to Panmunjom, usually followed by a call at Camp Casey, a bleak collection of brick buildings and Quonset huts that in the 1980s housed the US Army's Second Infantry Division. There, guests were subject to a dogmatic military explanation of the Korean War delivered with machine-gun rapidity by polished and pressed American non-coms. No room was left for ambiguity or speculation and questions were not encouraged. I said to one young sergeant that he must have researched his well-rehearsed delivery very thoroughly. 'No sir,' he dead-panned, 'I make it up as I go along.' I laughed at his cynical wit. Most Australian visitors took it all as gospel and went home convinced that the forces of evil were alive and well in North Korea, only held back by a handful of brave young American warriors.

For two years before the 1988 Seoul Olympics, illuminated numbers on the Seoul Town Hall counted down the days until the Games began. Vast construction efforts were taking place just south of the Han River. The Jamsil Sports complex housed the main stadium which was connected by fast rail to Olympic Park, with its quirky art gallery, gymnasium, cycling velodrome, weightlifting hall and other gymnasiums. In a palpable atmosphere of mounting excitement, Koreans in Seoul were briefed about the peculiarities of foreigners and the need to treat them with courtesy and give them directions. My colleagues and I were kept busy looking after a growing number of visitors, including State premiers, Federal ministers and sports bureaucrats including Phil Coles, John Coates and Kevan Gosper. I was helped in these endeavours by Leith Doody, a businessman appointed as Australian Olympic Attaché. Ali was now with me to share the burden and the fun. Adam joined us too, and wangled a practice session with one of our Olympic tennis players, John Fitzgerald.

The Minister of Sports, Graham Richardson, arrived in Seoul with his friend, the stockbroker René Rivkin. I took them to the Chosun Hotel, where I'd reserved a suite for the minister. The hotel had been booked solidly for months, and I'd got the best accommodation I could, which included a small anteroom for meetings and a bedroom/bathroom annex. Looking around, the minister pronounced, 'This isn't good enough, Ambassador.' At this, Rivkin said, 'Don't worry boss, I'll fix it.' Fingering his gold worry beads, he disappeared into the elevator, returning triumphantly some minutes later. 'Come with me,' he said, and we all trooped up to the top floor, where he had snared a gigantic suite complete with fake marble fireplaces. So the minister was comfortably accommodated for the Games.

On 17 September 1988 a magnificent opening ceremony was held at the main stadium with numerous tableaux reflecting Korea's long and proud history. One hundred and sixty nations were represented by 8391 athletes. North Korea boycotted the event, as did Cuba, Ethiopia and Nicaragua. However, the much larger boycotts of the previous three Olympics were avoided, making Seoul the Olympics in which the largest number of countries had participated so far in the history of the Games.

A day or two before the Games opened I held a barbecue at the residence for the entire Australian team, their coaches, officials, Australian media and assorted hangers-on. For days, anxious coaches had been appearing at the gates to survey the grounds. They were worried about the steepness of the drive, and whether their charges could negotiate it without straining a well-tuned muscle. On the day, the Australian band Sirocco set up on the tennis court, Graham Richardson and assorted others gave rousing speeches, old Olympians like Dawn Fraser sang songs and the barbecues were mobbed. I had four massive grills set around the gardens, on which sides of beef and lamb, and chickens were roasted. There were Australian oysters and prawns and plenty of fruits and vegetables. Mr Kim, the cook, had been storing these provisions for days in improvised cold containers. As the weather got hotter and hotter, Ali and I had nightmares in which we gave the team food poisoning, and they were too sick to even march at the opening, let alone compete.

We need not have worried. The athletes devoured great helpings of food and came back for seconds and thirds. It was no surprise to read twenty years later about the American swimmer Michael Phelps' voracious appetite at the 2008 Beijing Olympics — three fried egg sandwiches, a five-egg omelette, corn-based porridge, French toast and chocolate-chip pancakes for breakfast; 450 grams of enriched pasta and several ham, cheese and mayonnaise sandwiches washed down by 1000 calories of energy drink for lunch; and 450 grams of pasta and a family-sized pizza for supper. Our athletes in Seoul had similar appetites, with bodies like blast furnaces to turn it all into energy.

Australia's results in 1988 were nothing to write home about. We won three gold medals, six silvers and five bronze, placing us fifteenth after Japan and ahead of Yugoslavia. Nonetheless, we have improved our performance since. As an Australian colleague observed in an email to me in August 2008, calculating the total number of Olympic medals won per head of population for the ten countries with the highest number of medals in the history of the Olympics, we have, after the Beijing Olympics, the following table:

Australia	2190	Russia	507
Great Britain	770	Germany	500
South Korea	646	Italy	467
France	625	USA	362
Ukraine	586	China	75

Not that such figures existed or were available in Seoul in 1988, and we were surprised and proud of every medal we won. Ali and I were invited by President Roo Tae-woo to join him and his wife in their box at the hockey stadium for the women's final between the Koreans and the Hockeyroos. Hockey was not then a sport with grassroots support in Korea, and their players had to do nothing but practise for ten years, with rich incentives to get gold, including an apartment and car each. On our way to the stadium with Mr Lee, I suggested to Ali that we should contain our triumph if we scored a goal. By her uncharacteristic failure to comment, she seemed to agree. When Australia scored the first goal I leapt to my feet and gave a resounding, 'Yes!' Ali, President Roo, and his wife remained seated in po-faced silence. We went on to win the game and the gold.

The Australian Men's Hockey Team did less well. They were knocked out of their tournament early, and at a reception at the residence were given a public dressing down by the businessman John Elliott. He lined them up in the living room, and, between fags, told them in a grating voice: 'The Olympics was about winning. You blokes are a disgrace to Australia and should just go home.' I recall their sad faces. One or two were crying, with regret, remorse or anger at Elliott. It was an unedifying scene.

Life would have become anticlimactic after the Games, except for three events. The first was a State visit to Australia by President Roh Tae-woo towards the end of 1988, his first overseas visit as president. Following the usual practice, Ali and I went ahead to greet him on arrival in Sydney and accompany him around Sydney and Canberra. His discussions with Prime Minister Hawke and his cabinet in Canberra covered the usual regional and bilateral issues, including progress in science co-operation, aviation, culture and trade. He was greeted everywhere he went by members of the 12,000-strong Australian Korean community. A state dinner was held for him at the new Parliament House in Canberra.

The second was a visit by Prime Minister Bob Hawke to Seoul in January 1989. He and his mainly commercial entourage talked to ministers about expanding two-way trade — then valued at almost $3 billion — and differences the two counties continued to have about Australia's anti-dumping actions and Korea's ban on Australian beef. He praised Roh for his 'northern policy' of seeking rapprochement with the Democratic People's Republic of Korea (DPRK), and said Australia was trying to re-establish contact with that country, first made and then broken during Whitlam's Labor government in 1973. Hawke then announced his visionary Asian Pacific Economic Co-operation (APEC) organisation which would bring countries around the Pacific together to discuss economic co-operation. The Koreans were, I think, flattered that Hawke had chosen to announce APEC in Seoul, and they gave him and his party a magnificent lunch of traditional Korean dishes at a pavilion at the Blue House.

The third event was a visit by David Hill, Managing Director of the Australian Broadcasting Corporation, who was interested in my taking over the management of Radio Australia, the ABC's overseas broadcasting service. David stayed with me at the residence, and through a long and tiring weekend, including a fairly heavy drinking session in the entertainment district of Itaewon, outlined the attractions of the job. He did most of the talking and I did most of the listening, and by the time I saw him off at Kimpo airport, he'd convinced himself that I was the man to replace the current General Manager Peter Barnett. But I had two conditions. I wasn't going to take the leap from foreign affairs into the ABC until I'd completed my three-year posting to Seoul at the end of 1989. And I wouldn't do it unless I could persuade Ali, now living in New York and working at the Australian Permanent Mission to the United Nations, to cut short her posting and join me in Melbourne. David agreed to both demands, and generously offered to pay for my trip to New York. There, Ali agreed to come home, and her boss, Ambassador Peter Wilenski, agreed to release her.

When I finally left Seoul I did not expect to return very often. But since 2002 I have visited annually to arrange internships for Australian students in journalism at English-language Korean newspapers. My visits invariably take place at the same time of year as my first visit — in autumn as the gingkos turn to gold. I take delight in re-visiting old friends and old haunts, and seeing how the city is changing. My greatest pleasure is to walk down the tank stream, or Cheong Kye Cheon, that wends its way from the centre of Seoul near the Kyobo Building to the Han River. It is a marvel of rehabilitation — a small river that for centuries was choked up and eventually all but buried by rubbish and over-building, now excavated and set free. Running several metres below the cityscape, the clear stream burbles over pebbles with footpaths on either side, the walls of which depict, in glazed terracotta, the glories of ancient Korean dynasties — kings and princes and royal parades by warriors. It is a narrow valley of peace, a marvellous place of tranquillity.

10

Radio Static in Melbourne

Radio Australia began as a government propaganda service at the beginning of the World War II in 1939. By the 1970s it was a star in spreading good news about Australia around the world. It used short wave, a signal which bounced like a ping-pong ball between the earth's surface and the dense ionosphere until it reached its target. Its programs in English, Indonesian, Mandarin, Cantonese, Japanese, Thai, Vietnamese, French and Tok Pisin (for Melanesians), had a total weekly listenership of around ten million, ranking it in the top half of international broadcasters.

Radio Australia managed to free itself from government control in the 1960s and, unlike the Voice of America run by the US Department of Information, was widely seen by its listeners as an impartial reporter of news and current affairs. Its programs generated bags of fan mail and its broadcasters, especially the Indonesians, were mobbed like film stars whenever they visited home. A world opinion poll conducted in 1971 put Radio Australia at the top of the International Shortwave Club for fast and accurate news and friendly presentation. With 200,000 letters a year, half from Indonesia, it was more popular and trusted in the South East Asian region than the BBC World Service. Cabinet meetings in Fiji were known to be interrupted to allow ministers to get up-to-date news on regional affairs.

I arrived in Melbourne from Seoul in early January 1990, full of anticipation at the challenge of managing this legendary service. For the first couple of weeks I narrowed my horizons to focus on getting to know my staff and my job. I took a serviced apartment in Prahran, and in the evenings wandered along Toorak Road in South Yarra looking for reasonable restaurants for dinner, which I usually ate alone. Every morning around 7am, I drove out to Radio Australia's headquarters and studios at East Burwood, putting in ten- and twelve-hour days in meetings with journalists, broadcasters, managers and the heads and staff of the various language sections.

After diplomatic life in Seoul, especially the heavy entertainment load to which I willingly committed myself during the 1988 Olympics, this new Melbourne routine was a welcome contrast. It was a busy but orderly time without heavy evening engagements, broken only by weekly trips to attend ABC Executive meetings in Sydney and the occasional media interview. One of these was a laconic conversation with the comedian Steve Vizard on his show *Tonight Live* on Melbourne's Channel Seven. I recall deadpanning some responses to Steve's characterisation of me as a stripe-panted diplomat trying to manage journalists at Radio Australia. I don't think the image of me as a sober radio executive or RA journalists as hard-working professionals was dented too badly.

An unexpected plus in my new job was my daily commute to and from Radio Australia headquarters in East Burwood. An ABC-supplied car was part of my salary package, and from Prahran I drove east along High Street against the heavy incoming flow of commuter traffic to Melbourne in the mornings, and west against the flow back towards the CBD at night. My first ABC car I inherited from my predecessor Peter Barnett. It was a maroon VL Holden Calais, a hybrid based on the German Opel of the early 1980s, but with a longer nose cone, polycarbonate front bumpers and slightly kicked-up boot lid. It had a 3.0 litre six-cylinder engine from Nissan, which was fed by electronic fuel injection and mated to a Nissan four-speed automatic. As Jeff Brown observed in *Modern Motor* in March 1986, VL Holdens really marked the end of an era of Australian designed and made motor cars. General Motors-Holden's had a minor hand in developing the Nissan six. As GM-H's retiring chief engineer, Joe Whitesell, had explained at its launch, 'We simply could not afford to put in a $300 million engine plant, and we needed a competitive engine. We searched the world — not just Japan. We went to the US; we looked at engines in Europe; we looked at engines in England, including the Jaguar six; and we finally sorted it out and came down to this engine from Nissan.'

After a few months Peter's car reached the 40,000 kilometre replacement point, and the ABC bean counters said I could have anything in the range of Holdens, Fords, Mitsubishis or Toyotas, providing it was Australian-made. In a fit of reckless originality, I chose a white Holden Calais with grey leather seats. Jeremy Clarkson of *Top Gear* would have said that this car had about as much character as a glass of cold water. He would have been right, but it came with rego, insurance, petrol and servicing, and I was not complaining.

While I waited for the Calais to be built and delivered I drove a battered ABC general purpose sedan — a Toyota Lexcen. Prompted by Prime Minister Hawke's Minister for Industry, John Button, who wanted to reduce the number of motor car models made locally, the Lexcen was a re-badged Holden VN Commodore named after the late America's Cup yacht designer Ben Lexcen. To return the compliment, Toyota had allowed GM-H to re-badge its Toyota Corolla and Camry as a Holden Nova and Holden Apollo respectively. The myth of Holden being Australia's own car had slipped further. The Lexcen reeked of cigarette smoke and its radio was stuck on a Melbourne hard rock station, but it did its job.

When my new Calais arrived at East Burwood, it triggered all the usual responses in my car-loving nervous system. It had that peculiar and wonderful new car smell of lacquer, rubber and leather, and its tight 3800 EFI V6 Buick engine ticked as it cooled after its first run home to Prahran. With its widened and restyled Opel Omega design, the Calais was one of Australia's first 'aero-styled' cars, wind-tunnelled to eliminate extraneous noise. Later cars with this shape have become fatter and wider until they look like frogs, but my Calais was comparatively thin and sensible. Its hi-fi system sounded great in the nearly windless silence. It represented a return to full family-sized Holden cars, and had won all three major Australian motor car magazine awards at the end of the 1980s for the nation's best sedan. It once again took GM-H to the top of the passenger car market in 1989, replacing the Ford Falcon.

In April, my solitary settling-in period ended when Ali joined me from New York and we celebrated her homecoming with dinner at my favourite Thai restaurant in High Street. We took a short-term lease on a spacious federation-style house on High Street in Glen Iris, then moved into a comfortable house owned by a cousin in Surrey Hills, not far from my parents' small weatherboard house in the same suburb where I had spent the first fourteen years of my life. To our delight our son Adam, now an Arts/Law student at Monash University, decided to join us. Anna couldn't because she was studying acting at the National Institute of Dramatic Art (NIDA) in Sydney, but it was the closest thing I'd had to family life since just before I'd been posted to Vietnam in 1983. To replace a beautiful black cat called Wingnut whose company we enjoyed in Glen Iris until he was stolen sometime in February 1990, Ali and Adam had rescued a tabby kitten from death row at the Burwood RSPCA and presented it to me on my fiftieth birthday in May 1990. I called the cat Furflex after the door lining used to restore an old Jaguar I had just purchased.

The Calais was office transport, but the Jaguar was a hobby, a calming and healing diversion after a full-on fifty-hour week at the ABC. It was a 1965 'S' type with a 3.4 litre engine. Derived from the Mark 2, it had hooded eyes, four-on-the-floor with electric overdrive and an extended boot. It was the first medium-size Jaguar production saloon to have independent rear suspension and dual fuel tanks. It was sleek and elegant, although when I first saw it at an auto wrecker's yard in Oakley these qualities were hard to discern.

Painted a dull mid-green, my S-type had red dust annealed around the bodywork and a heavy duty towbar on the back. The interior woodwork on the dash and doorsills was bone-white, devoid of polish and blistered by a thousand country suns. The leather was cracked and dry, and when I lifted the daggy sheepskin covering the rear seat, an anthill constructed of the same red dust that coated the bodywork reared up like a baby alien emerging from an astronaut's chest cavity.

'She's been a hard worker,' said the small oil-stained salesman who passed as the day manager at the yard. 'Belonged to a shearer mate out the Mallee. Never been bent.'

He pressed the starter button and we watched a thin cloud of oily blue smoke rise into the early Saturday morning air. 'Of course,' he added after a reflective pause, 'the engine's gunna take a bit of work.'

So I imagined would the cooling system, the gearbox, the clutch, steering, suspension and electrics. Not to say the upholstery, head-lining, rubber seals, carpets, instruments and woodwork.

But my mind shifted into overdrive as I imagined my sleek S type, with new woodwork, leather and mechanics, wire wheels and a two-pack respray in British racing green, purring its way around Melbourne's streets and further afield. I wrote out a cheque for $3000, handed it to the small salesman, and the car was mine. On the way back to Surrey Hills, the gearstick came loose in my hand and the rear-view mirror fell off.

Throughout my three years with the ABC, several garages around Melbourne practically lived off the money they earned from repairing and restoring my Jaguar. They included Mike Roddy Motors in Moorabbin, the Jaguar Performance centre in East Hawthorn, and later in Canberra, Peter and Paul Dunster, who were fond of racing vintage motorcycles and ran a Steptoe and Sons look-alike operation out at Mitchell. My garage in Surrey Hills was also usually cluttered with seats awaiting new leather, rubber door-linings, or bits of woodwork drying after being varnished. Restoration of the Jag was very much a work in progress. After eighteen years it still is. But more than almost any modern car I have driven, it continues to delight me as I drive it up and down the Princes Highway between Sydney and our property on the New South Wales south coast.

At first, my professional life at Radio Australia went well. David Hill was all consideration, charm and hospitality. In Sydney he introduced me to other ABC executives, including the three other output directors: Paddy Conroy, head of television, Malcolm Long, head of radio, and Helen Mills, head of concert music (in charge of the ABC symphony orchestras). I met large numbers of production heads, journalists and managers. It was an altogether new and exciting prospect after the staidness and predictability of foreign affairs.

At one function, however, the Deputy Managing Director Stuart Revill drew me aside to tell me I wasn't uniquely the object of David's charm. Since becoming managing director in 1986 Hill had initially treated all his new managers the same way, but had soon brought them down with a thud. Too busy with networking and getting to know my Melbourne staff, I only half-registered what Stuart was saying. Pretty soon however, his words came back to haunt me.

My fall from grace came suddenly and unexpectedly in early 1990. David asked me to write a report on the efficiency of the three transmitters Radio Australia used at the Cox Peninsula outside Darwin. He wanted to brief the ABC Board, which was scheduled to have its next meeting in Darwin. I prepared a concise few paragraphs detailing the design of the transmitters, the rehabilitation of their log periodic aerials following near-destruction by Cyclone Tracy on Christmas Day 1974, their technical capacities, their target areas of broadcast (North Asia, Papua New Guinea and the Pacific), and which language services we sent over them.

I wrote the report in one morning, sent it up to Sydney, and went off with a clear conscience to a luncheon at Rippon Lea, the magnificent federation-style reception centre in Elsternwick owned by the National Trust of Victoria. The luncheon was to mark the inauguration of the ABC's mini-series *Embassy*, about the adventures of the Australian ambassador and his staff in Ragaan, a mythical country somewhere in South East Asia, but filmed in Fiji. Halfway through the launch, with wine flowing and speeches about to begin, I got a frantic call from my secretary. David Hill was on the warpath. No, he wouldn't speak to me over the phone, I was to get back to East Burwood pronto. I excused myself and took off for the office. I called David who in great agitation and with considerable vehemence told me my report was fucking garbage, not what he wanted at all. What he *did* seem to want, but never spelt out, was a report suggesting the transmitters were incapable of handling the amount of programming we assigned to them from East Burwood — a not-too-subtle way of telling the board that Radio Australia was too big and that it needed to be reduced.

I won't say that war was declared between Hill and me at that point, but it was clear that we had different perspectives. I saw my job as to manage RA in a changing environment but not to reduce its staff or output, or move precipitately to terminate the short-wave service and replace it with other forms of delivery. Never the most patient of men, Hill seemed to want radical changes: a smaller, tighter, less expensive service using fewer journalists and broadcasters and different means of dissemination. Either that, or closure of the service altogether. I believe he saw me initially as a radical change agent of a kind I was neither managerially equipped for nor motivated to become.

I also quickly found that in the struggle for its share of what seemed to be an ever-diminishing ABC budget (in 1990, we received $15 million of an ABC budget of $500 million), Radio Australia suffered from several strategic and operational disadvantages. First, it was concerned with the needs of foreign audiences (who had no votes), whereas the ABC's main focus was the parochial one of catering to its domestic Australian audiences (who did). Into this mix Hill added ratings, as if the ABC should constantly compete with commercial radio and television. He would repeatedly assert at executive meetings that Radio National should close down because of its small elitist audience. Radio Australia was in an even worse position because calculating accurate listenership statistics was difficult. If ABC programs were to be cut, argued most managers, they should be from Radio Australia before other parts of the organisation.

Second, Radio Australia was the only output division not in Sydney. Its broadcasters and journalists had developed a siege mentality, full of Melburnian suspicion about the Sydneycentric mindset of ABC management. Sydney managers reinforced this image by referring constantly to the 'BAPH states', that is, Brisbane, Adelaide, Perth and Hobart, as if they were outsiders whose offices were too big and audiences too small for the budget allocation given to them. Melbourne was not included here, but the view in East Burwood was that Radio Australia, as well as Melbourne metropolitan radio, were considered by Sydney management to be poor and not particularly relevant cousins.

Third, Radio Australia's very existence continued to be questioned, by politicians in Canberra as well as within the ABC itself. Should it broadcast unflattering views about Australia or the neighbourhood to outside audiences? Indeed, did its managers even know what was being broadcast in its Asian language programs? Were its regional audiences as large and wide-ranging as its managers claimed? What in fact *were* its target audiences? Were its transmitters powerful enough or numerous enough to broadcast clearly to them? Should it use another form of delivery altogether? And because it was unfamiliar to the vast majority of Australians who had not heard its broadcasts, it lacked a political constituency.

These issues had been dealt with over many years and by many different inquiries, including the successive Green, Dix and Waller reports of the 1970s. These by and large upheld the autonomy of Radio Australia, as did another report conducted in 1988, two years prior to my taking over management of the service. This was by Dr Rodney Tiffin, a senior lecturer in the Department of Government at the University of Sydney. He concluded that Radio Australia should continue to broadcast via short-wave for the foreseeable future, particularly into the Asia Pacific region, where it should strive to maintain its status as the most authoritative broadcaster. It should continue to be an autonomous division of the ABC, accountable directly to the managing director. All its foreign language services should continue in short-wave except Japanese: because of the sophistication of broadcasting in Japan, the Japanese service should be delivered by a more up-to-date medium.

Tiffin also recommended that Radio Australia's transmitters be substantially upgraded, a complex bureaucratic exercise for Radio Australia since they were located in four widely separated sites around Australia — Canarvon in Western Australia, Shepparton in Victoria, Cox Peninsula in the Northern Territory, and Brandon in Queensland. Further, they were not owned by the ABC, but the Commonwealth Department of Transport and Communication, and were operated and maintained by Telecom.

Throughout my watch I was the meat in the ABC sandwich, between David Hill and the board he controlled by the force of his personality on one hand, and the Public Sector Union and Australian Journalists' Association who challenged every voluntary redundancy I managed to negotiate on the other. I oversaw with absolutely no satisfaction the constant diminutions in the service I had to preside over. These included cessation of Japanese language broadcasts which I initially resisted on the grounds that many Japanese continued to listen to shortwave; halving the French service to one hour a day in 1991, and halving it again to thirty minutes a day in 1992; a reduction of the Indonesian service from eight to seven hours a day in 1992 and reductions in the number of hours broadcast in Mandarin and Cantonese.

These reductions accorded with a general Australian trend in the early 1990s towards small government and the start of a revolution in information technology. One of my managers seriously argued that the ABC's Victorian library, meticulously managed by its devoted librarian at Radio Australia, should be abolished because books were information storage systems of the past, took too much space, money and time, and that electronic literature should replace them. I successfully opposed closing down the library.

Against the trend and Hill's negativism, I did score a few minor successes. I began broadcasting to Australian civilian hostages taken by Saddam Hussein in the months leading up to his invasion of Kuwait in August 1990. We brought sporting stars like the legendary Australian Rules Football legend Ron Barassi into the Burwood studios to record morale-boosting messages to the hostages. Learning of the service, the Royal Australian Navy asked if we would also broadcast to the crews on Australian frigates assigned to the Persian Gulf. I agreed to do this while Hussein continued to hold the hostages. When they were released I terminated the service, informing the navy that the special broadcasts beamed at the Middle East were costing an arm and a leg in transmission charges, and that unlike civilians held in solitary confinement in the Iraqi desert, the crews on Her Majesty's Australian ships had their crewmates' support as well as single-sideband communications with Australia. If Gunner Smith's wife was having a baby, he would hear of its birth through the navy network. But the Opposition portrayed my actions as unpatriotic or anti-American (the two were conflated in the minds of some of them), and the Shadow Minister for Defence Services, Jocelyn Newman, brought a successful censure motion against me and Radio Australia in the Senate. I recall receiving no backing from Hill, moral or otherwise.

Sometime during 1991 Hun Sen, the prime minister of Cambodia, made an official visit to Australia. Having met him with Bill Hayden in Saigon in 1984, I prevailed on Foreign Affairs to include a visit to East Burwood in his program, and arranged for him to inaugurate a Radio Australia Khmer language service during the visit. We recruited Khmer-speaking staff from the Cambodian community in Melbourne.

Overriding these slim pickings was a constant guerrilla war with David Hill in Sydney. I had to fly there at least once a week, sometimes twice or even three times, to attend senior executive meetings at Ultimo. Seldom did the agendas include anything of substance about RA, and I felt my presence was redundant. Hill rarely expressed any interest in RA, and I generally felt invisible, However, after one session he invited me into his office. He sat at one end, I sat at the other, and he placed the ABC's senior personnel manager, Harold Wall, in the middle to take notes. As Hill and I conversed, Wall began to look like the audience behind the net post at a tennis match. Hill said I was working pretty hard, but asked me if I really thought the management of Radio Australia was my 'cup of tea'. I said it was a unique management experience for me, but that I felt I was adjusting to it pretty well. He then asked sarcastically whether I realised that at least one of my executives was actively undermining me, and trying on his own field marshal's uniform in anticipation of my demise. In fact I had suspected this, and also that one of my managers was systematically and critically reporting my doings back to Hill in Sydney. But I blandly told Hill that by and large I thought I had the support of my management team.

I could see the writing on the wall, but I had no intention of quitting before my three-year contract ended. As a survival technique and as a means of conserving my strength, I began forward planning my life without David Hill or the ABC. I took a couple of weeks' leave and decided to look for a piece of land in the country where Ali and I might retire in ten years or so. Neither of us was committed to such a scheme, but the search for the land at least lifted me out of my gloom. We thought the south coast of New South Wales looked promising, so one early autumn morning in 1992 I loaded up the now re-sprayed and semi-rehabilitated Jaguar and headed off. Ali had writing deadlines to meet and remained in Surrey Hills.

I stayed at South Durras north of the fishing port of Batemans Bay with Cecile Jamieson, a gifted pianist with whom I often played violin and piano sonatas and the widow of Jim Jamieson, my former colleague in Tokyo. On arrival, after two days of trouble-free motoring through Gippsland and southern New South Wales in the Jag, I was briskly led into the front room where Cecile had pinned a large map of the Shoalhaven Shire on a wall, marked with coloured pins indicating properties on the market. Over afternoon tea Cecile and her friend Elizabeth, the widow of another Tokyo colleague Philip Searcy, briefed me about each place and the timetable they had devised for visiting them over the coming few days. It was like a military operation.

We combed through the area. Many of the properties represented the broken dreams of divorcing couples, some were follies of eccentric design. One or two came within sight of meeting Ali's and my specifications. But none was right until on the late afternoon of day two we inspected a parcel of land

400 metres up the Old Princes Highway at the hamlet of Termeil (in truth a combined servo and post office). With 2.5 hectares of open meadow sloping down to a creek, a patch of rainforest, and more meadow rising up the back, it was beautiful. At the back post marking the edge of the property we turned and looked north towards the highway. The sun flickered through a tall stand of *Eucalyptus maculata* gently swaying in a light breeze. I decided there and then to negotiate a price with the owner. This was the beanie-topped Matt O'Brien, ex-NSW cop, ex-rugby player, maker of drink coasters and bird feeders in his workshed beside the horse stud from which our property had been subdivided.

I settled on a price with Matt, and Cecile, Elizabeth and I returned triumphantly to South Durras for evening gins and tonic. When I returned to Melbourne Ali was as delighted as I was with the land. But apart from bulldozing a dam and putting up a shed, we left it to gather interest, like money in the bank, while plans for its future development gradually formed in our minds.

My relationship with Hill did not improve, and after two years of my three-year contract had expired, he suddenly replaced me with another ABC executive, Derek White, and transferred me to work with the head of radio, Malcolm Long, on an international television service to augment Radio Australia. Designed to bounce off one or more geo-stationary satellites positioned over the equator, the signal would cover most of South and East Asia as far north as southern China. We had high hopes for the service, and devised programs we hoped would reflect Australia's multicultural diversity and foster international understanding. We would have the best of ABC television, including news and current affairs, plus specially produced programs highlighting Australian culture and education. Sports programs would include AFL and rugby for expatriates, but also sports popular in Asia, such as golf, tennis, and badminton. There would also be programs reflecting Australia's Asian connections: Chinese New Year in Little Bourke Street, shopping at Cabramatta, and dragon boat races on the Yarra or in Darling Harbour.

Funded by government subsidies and commercial sponsorship, the service was launched by Prime Minister Paul Keating in 1993 and broadcast live to fifteen countries in South East Asia from the ABC's studios in Gore Hill. But funding cuts made the service non-viable and it was taken over by Channel Seven in 1998. Its program quality suffered and it was reduced to mainly Australian news and wall-to-wall rugby and AFL football for expats. Seven lost money, and the service was again taken over by the ABC. It was called ABC Asia Pacific, and then, in 2006, Australia Network. Following a restructure of the ABC in early 2007, Australia Network became part of the ABC's International Corporate Strategy and Governance Division.

There is little forensic evidence of the nature and extent of the Australia Network's audience in South East Asia, but it is restricted largely, I suspect, to Australian expatriates. My suspicions were confirmed in November 2008, when I watched Australia Network from my hotel room in Bangkok. It ran a documentary entitled 'Jews of America', then an ad for 'Japan's About Face', a documentary on Japan's self-defence force. This was followed by 'East West 101', an Australian police drama, and then half an hour of domestic ABC news. Not bad fare altogether, but not the kind of uniquely Australian material we had originally envisaged for the service. It would certainly not have been compelling viewing for a Thai audience who would be watching their own dramas in their own language, or, if they had curiosity about world events, the BBC or CNN news.

Meanwhile, Radio Australia suffered a major contraction. At the end of my time, the ABC sold off the dedicated East Burwood site to a born-again Christian church. I was invited to the dedication service the church put on to 'bless' the site. The pastor told me that the hand of God had indicated that this was the place for his new church. Candles were placed every three metres or so around the perimeter, and a service was conducted in a big tent. This attracted what seemed like half the population of the eastern Melbourne suburbs, including lots of young aspirational families and single mothers looking for companionship and spiritual support.

Against the fierce resistance of many of its staff who had made their homes in the Burwood neighbourhood, Radio Australia was then transferred to Southbank, the new ABC headquarters on the Yarra in Melbourne's CBD. Here journalists and broadcasters had to compete with those of domestic ABC radio for a limited amount of studio (and car parking) space. At a time when the Keating government was urging more Australians to be Asia-literate, and when knowledge about Australia in the region was clearly deficient, a major instrument for projecting the country and its views into the area was being downgraded.

Radio Australia suffered further blows at the hands of Bob Mansfield, a company director commissioned in 1996 by the Howard government to review the ABC. Mansfield recommended stopping funding both Australian Television International and Radio Australia, the money saved ($26 million per annum) to be ploughed into domestic ABC programs. Both overseas services survived, but RA was cut in half. In an incredibly short-sighted move sanctioned by the Foreign Minister Alexander Downer, the transmitters at Cox Peninsula were then leased for ten years to a British evangelical Christian group which, having no doubts about the continuing effectiveness of short-wave, went busily about its business of broadcasting born-again messages to Muslims in Indonesia, the largest Islamic country in the world. RA is now in the ridiculous situation of buying back limited air time at Cox by arrangement.

As of 2008, the picture has become even more complicated. We still have RA, but Television Australia is now Australia Network. To listen to RA anywhere outside Australia is a confusing business, especially for those without a sophisticated understanding of computers. It involving trying to make a selection between an extremely attenuated short-wave service broadcast out of Shepparton in Victoria and Brandon in Queensland (and sometimes from Cox), finding some local radio station that takes RA programs and broadcasts them on local AM or FM frequencies, using a computer or mobile device via Really Simple Syndication (RSS) podcast feeds, or through a digital signal to selected radio stations via one of three satellites — Intelsat 2, Intelsat 8 or Intelsat 10. Meanwhile, RA has only the vaguest idea of the size of its audiences and where its listeners are. In my view putting something on the web is a poor substitute for a vigorous direct broadcast that tests the material openly in a public forum and demands long-term listener commitment.

As for Australia Network, about the only way to watch it in Asia is to stay at one of the few hotels that screen it, or check with local commercial TV stations to see if they broadcast it.

In the uncluttered airwaves of the 1950s, a short-wave signal from Victoria could be heard clear across the world in London. The decolonisation process in Asia saw the emergence of twenty new countries, each wanting to be heard via its own short wave service. In this increasingly competitive environment countries accustomed to projecting favourable images of themselves, such as the British, French, Dutch, Japanese and Koreans, simply devised stronger and better ways of broadcasting their voices. The new systems cost money, but those who controlled the finances knew that long-term national benefits of maintaining strong international profiles outweighed any short-term political costs.

The Australian experience has been the reverse of this. When there is no political constituency for expenditure, no discernible votes to be had, the long-term investment has not been made. Australia's voice has been diminished by opportunistic cost-cutting decisions that make a mockery of Radio Australia's once powerful voice. From being the clear choice of most listeners to international radio in the Asia Pacific from the 1960s through to the 1980s, it has sunk in the number and strength of its short-wave hours broadcast into the region to fifteenth place, trailing not only such services as VOA, the BBC, China Radio International, the Voice of Russia, Deutsche Welle, All India Radio, NHK, Radio France Internationale, Radio Netherlands, but also Israel Radio International, the Voice of Turkey, and the Voice of Pyongyang.

Is the cliché that we 'punch above our weight' in diplomacy true? Maybe it was immediately after World War II when Australia played an important role in setting up the United Nations. Maybe also when we helped some newly emerging countries in the Asia–Pacific region become established after the departure of the colonial powers. And, fleetingly, in helping the post-Pol Pot election process in Cambodia in the mid 1990s. But nowadays, I think not. We are seen as too close to the policies of the United States to have an independent voice about world events. Furthermore, we lack the means of insisting that we do. With a team of professional journalists devoted to projecting Australia abroad up until the early 1990s, the News and Information Bureau was abolished in the interest of cutting costs. Radio Australia has been gutted for the same reasons. As a substitute, 'public diplomacy' sections have been set up in some embassies and high commissions, but collectively they represent an uncertain and unpersuasive voice.

11

Yank Tanks in Central America

My contract with the ABC expired in December 1992. I had no income and no job. What should I do? It was a time of recession and fairly high unemployment. I had approached a couple of law firms but neither they nor I was particularly interested. Very fortunately, however, I had signed a secondment agreement with the department before coming to Melbourne in 1990: it allowed me to return to DFAT at my old level. Ali was enjoying herself as regional head of the department in Melbourne and wasn't inclined to up stakes again, but I really had no options except for Canberra.

And so, on the first Sunday in the New Year of 1993 I loaded the Jaguar with books and clothes, sat my cat Furflex in the back seat on top of the pile and bade farewell to Ali. The Jag, sleek in its coat of British racing green and with a new set of Dayton wire wheels, hubs and spinners, purred up through Northcote, Brunswick and Coburg to the Hume Highway. Throughout the long night drive to Yass and Canberra, Furflex sat perched on the squab behind the rear seat, his yellow eyes reflecting the glow from the instrument panel and the lights of oncoming traffic. His composure was only disturbed twice — once for a toilet stop, and once when I had to brake suddenly to avoid a semitrailer cutting in from a side road. The furrows of Furflex's claws on the back of the driver's seat are still visible today.

The cat and I quickly found a place for rent in a leafy complex of townhouses at Wybalena Grove in the northern Canberra suburb of Cook. Every evening, I would return to the house after work, where Furf waited faithfully for me beneath the same cotoneaster bush. He was now a big handsome three-year-old tabby, and being territorial and an RSPCA death row survivor, spent much of his time seeing off other cats who intruded on his space.

After my experience in the ABC it was logical of the department to assign me to manage the corps of journalists from the old Australia News and Information Bureau (ANIB), now a part of the department. I was looking forward to this, but I had a shaky start. Without being aware of it, I was suffering from short-term memory loss, repeating things I had told staff earlier the same day. I also found my normal exercise regime of morning jogging and weekly tennis excruciatingly tiring. I was physically unco-ordinated, and my serve, normally a strong point, had become highly erratic. The fact was that I had taken a battering at the ABC, and was physically and emotionally exhausted. I was a bit shocked when Bob Cotton, divisional head of personnel, called me in to express his concern. He tactfully told me to take a couple of weeks off and get some rest. After the break, I returned to work physically stronger and in a better mental state.

Once a spirited and independent information service dedicated to spreading good news about Australia to the world, by the late

1980s ANIB had lost its autonomy and been reduced to a resentful adjunct of DFAT. My task was to manage a cynical bunch of journalists churning out news releases for overseas missions as part of Australia's much-reduced program of what later became known as 'public diplomacy'. Like the half-hearted cultural activities on which DFAT spent small amounts of money, the journalists' output was not valued by the department's senior officers, many of whom had been led by experience to distrust the press. But it was my job to tell the journalists, against the evidence, that they were performing a valuable function. The negative dynamics I faced had an eerie resemblance to those between Radio Australia and senior ABC management in Sydney. Nobody seemed to think about Australia's interests, everybody was concerned about their own. The most absorbing part of the new work was the conferences I attended early each morning with a couple of other officers to brief Secretary Peter Wilenski and his deputy secretaries about foreign affairs' coverage in daily press.

I persevered with the journalists for the better part of 1993, but I needed something more creative to do. Another overseas posting looked increasingly attractive. Although Ali enjoyed Melbourne, she was also looking for a more demanding job. So we made a joint application for the best of several pairs of head of mission positions that were becoming available — Mexico and Jamaica. Situated respectively on the isthmus between North and South America, and in the middle of the Caribbean, the two countries were more or less contiguous. Commuting between them on reunions would be much easier than between Seoul and New York or Hanoi and Tokyo. As luck would have it however, Ali was offered a senior position in the Australia

Council in Sydney the day before she could have accepted Jamaica, and with my agreement, she turned down the job of high commissioner in Kingston.

I went ahead and accepted the appointment as ambassador to Mexico, thus beginning another episode of what Ali and I ironically called our 'apartnership'. In my case, this involved mentally putting our marriage onto an impersonal plane so that I could practise my not particularly robust capacity for self-sufficiency, and get on with whatever job I had to do.

At such times I wondered whether the job was worth it, in this case running an Australian diplomatic mission without the moral and intellectual back-up of a partner and wife. What could I expect to do in Mexico, or indeed in Guatemala, El Salvador, Nicaragua, Honduras, Costa Rica, Panama and Cuba, the seven other countries in Central America to which I would be jointly accredited from Mexico City? Apart from a two-year stint in Iran, all my professional experience had been in Asia. I knew nothing about Latin America.

As with all my previous postings, I began preparing for Central America with an extensive reading course. I got in touch with the Australian academic Inga Clendinnen, who sent me some of her writings about the Aztecs. I looked at the Indian world of pre-Colombian America, and then at the invasion of Mexico by Hernán Cortéz and his four hundred-odd conquistadores in 1519, his improbable conquest of the Aztec capital Tenochtitlan and subjugation of the Aztec King Moctezuma in 1521. From the Spanish conquest until modern times, Mexican history seemed to reinforce all the Western clichés about Latin American instability: generals galloping madly into battle fired up by revolutionary ideals, only to settle into a life of repressive exploitation of the wretched underclasses — invariably the indigenes — until another general, with new idealism, carried out a coup and repeated the cycle. I was struck by the similarities with the Philippines. There, as in Mexico, the Roman Catholic Church of Spain gave moral sanction to the exploitation.

From the beginning of the twentieth century, a modern Mexican state gradually emerged from this chaos. Church repression gave way to a constitutional secular government. The rule of law was established and a degree of economic growth and prosperity followed, at least for the rich and the middle classes. By the time of my posting, the Mexicans were enjoying a 97 per cent literacy rate, even distance learning to the provinces via satellite. They were making progress towards universal health care. The suave Harvard-trained politician Carlos Salinas de Gortari had been elected president in 1988, and spent much of his time carrying out neo-liberal reforms. He had fixed the exchange rate, controlled inflation, and the economy was buoyant. By 1993, foreign investment in Mexico's stock market had increased 98 per cent and the country's reserves were at a record level of $24.5 billion. *Forbes* magazine included thirteen Mexican billionaires among its list of the world's richest people, and asserted, I thought debatably, that, 'You can't any longer think of Mexico as the Third World'.

In the Americas Division of Foreign Affairs in Canberra, Salinas was seen to represent a new age of Latin American leaders — shrewd, principled, Ivy League-trained technocrats who were the antitheses of the corrupt politicians of the past. The cliché about Mexicans being a lazy bunch of characters sleeping off a bellyful of tequila under their oversize sombreros in the shade of a cactus seemed far from the collective DFAT mind. They sensed a new element of stability and principled governance. My job was to get close to Salinas, his cabinet colleagues and the Mexican bureaucracy and look afresh at trade opportunities for Australian firms, not only in Mexico itself but in the United States. With its new status as Latin America's only member of the Organisation for Economic Co-operation and Development (OECD), and as one of three founding members of the North American Free Trade Association (NAFTA), Mexico seemed an ideal country through which to mount a trade push into North American markets.

To crack this Latin American nut however, it was essential to have a working knowledge of Spanish, so I embarked on an intensive three months of full-time language tuition in Canberra. I then went to Melbourne for a somewhat emotional farewell dinner with Ali and returned to Canberra to settle Furf in with his new owner, Dr Anthea Hyslop, a most amiable cat-loving friend and neighbour in Wybalena Grove. I was determined not to sell the Jaguar as I had my other cars before my other postings, and arranged to have it garaged at my sister Susie's Border-Leicester sheep stud in Kangaroo Valley. I asked her and her husband John Ballinger to take it for a weekend run when they had the time.

I then returned to Canberra, made some farewell calls and charted my course on Qantas to Los Angeles, and south on Aeromexico to Mexico City. After calling on the incumbent Australian ambassador, the amiable Keith Baker, I went on to Cuernavaca, a beautiful town 85 kilometres south of Mexico City, a place of slow pace and benign climate. Originally called

Cuauhnahuac by its Indian inhabitants, Cuernavaca had been destroyed and rebuilt by Cortes in 1525. It later became a refuge, a divine place of perpetual springtime for the rich and powerful of Mexico City.

In Cuenavaca I spent a month consolidating my Spanish while living with a Mexican family, Federico and Concepçion Gomez and their young children Felipé and Dolores. None of the Gomez family spoke English, so communicating in Spanish was essential for survival. I quickly settled into a routine: an early morning jog around the narrow cobbled streets near the Plaza de Armas, a leisurely breakfast with the Gomez family where we talked about our plans for the day, formal morning lectures at language school, lunch with fellow students, and three hours of conversation practice in the afternoon. In the evenings Concepçion taught me to cook *quesadillas, enchiladas* and *burritos*. To celebrate the completion of my course and my last night in their house she made *mole poblano*, a complex Mexican dish in which roast chicken is smothered in a chocolate sauce infused with chilli, peppers, peanuts, almonds, cinnamon, aniseed, tomato, onion and garlic, with tequila as an artfully intoxicating accompaniment. It's not a dish for the faint of heart, either in its preparation or consumption.

And so to Mexico City. When first observed in 1519 by the conquistadores from the lofty saddle between the twin peaks of the active volcanoes of Popacatépetl and Iztaccihuatl, Tenochtitlán had been a breathtakingly splendid city of gleaming adobe houses, stone villas, palaces and pyramids set on straight causeways constructed across an immense glistening blue lake. Four hundred and fifty years later, now Mexico City, it had become a vast megalopolis choking on its own air- and water-borne effluents. Except for tiny reed-choked remnants around Xochimilco, the lake was filled in and built over. Surviving Indian architecture was limited to the downtown area around the Zócalo, the historic and spacious heart of the city surrounded by the National Palace, Metropolitan Cathedral and Federal District headquarters. There were more ruins outside the city, notably the great brooding Mayan causeway of the Sun and Moon pyramids of Teotihuacán. With every avenue and overpass in the city ending in bottlenecks, traffic was chaotic, locked in a perpetual rush hour.

In due course my mind adjusted to the hustle of the Distrito Federal (Federal District) and my body to the rarefied smog-filled air of the high basin surrounding the city. The official residence was at Sierra Negra 215 in Lomas de Chapultepec, a leafy suburb on foothills slightly above the worst of the smog. A large house with five bedrooms, several bathrooms, capacious reception areas and spacious grounds, its rear wall adjoined a public park full of gum trees. It came with domestic staff, including Tina, a Peruvian cook of infinite resourcefulness. She could cheerfully expand a meal like Norman Lindsay's magic pudding, a feat she performed often as Mexican guests unexpectedly brought their friends to sit-down dinners.

The head of mission car I inherited from Keith Baker was a rather clapped-out black Mercedes 300 of mid-1980s vintage in need of some major mechanical work. My driver, Cirilo, was a courteous and soft-spoken man whose daily cunning at choosing alternative routes to work to avoid city traffic equalled that of the tennis-playing Mr Lee in Seoul.

On the Monday after moving in to the residence from

Cuenavaca, Cirilo drove me to the embassy. It occupied the tenth floor of a new building in Polanco, an inner suburb close to the town centre. There I met my staff, ten Australian-based officers from Foreign Affairs and Trade and Immigration, and sixteen locally engaged people including an accountant, a property clerk, an information officer, a translator/research officer, receptionist, four immigration clerks, and several drivers and driver/messengers. I also met the commercial manager and assistant marketing officer of Austrade.

I settled in by reading the files and calling on diplomatic colleagues. I began with the ambassadors from Canada, New Zealand, the United States, Japan, China, the Republic of Korea and the countries of South East Asia. After several weeks my assistant Alicia Rosado arranged for me to present credentials to President Salinas, which would formally recognise my position as Australia's ambassador and enable me to call on Mexican secretaries and officials.

The ceremony occurred with several other new ambassadors in a vast gilded room at the National Palace off the Zocalo. Groups of schoolchildren waved the flag of whichever ambassador they had been assigned to cheer for, and a military band interpreted the relevant national anthem at the appropriate time and in their own way. President Salinas turned out to be short, slim and bald, with prominent ears and a quiet manner. He listened politely to my enthusiasm about his presidency (delivered in Spanish), and my hope that during my time in Mexico we might see further advances in bilateral relations. He said he hoped so too.

I came away with the disconcerting impression that Salinas had only half his mind on the ceremony. Perhaps he had a presentiment about cataclysmic things about to happen. And they surely did. Shortly after my presentation, Mayan rebels — the Zapatistas — arose in rebellion in the south-eastern state of Chiapas under their leader, the masked and pipe-smoking Sub-Commander Marcos. Luis Donaldo Colosio, Salinas's chosen successor as president, was gunned down in Tijuana. The secretary-general of the ruling Nacionalista Party, Jose Francisco 'Pepe' Ruiz Massieu, was shot dead in downtown Mexico City. Alfredo Harp Helú, one of Mexico's richest men and close friend of Salinas, was kidnapped. And numerous terrorist attacks broke out across the country, including one that rocked the government palace of Acapulco.

The effect of these and other scandals shook Salinas, and threw international perceptions — no doubt including Canberra's — right back to the view that Mexico had reverted to its old unstable ways. A catastrophic withdrawal of speculative fund investment in Mexico followed, including billions of US superannuation dollars invested in Mexico as unsecured short-term loans. President Clinton negotiated a $50 billion bailout package to keep the economy afloat, but the danger was that Salinas' successor, Ernesto Zedillo, would once again postpone badly needed political and economic reforms to prevent a repeat of the kind of economic crisis that had successively destroyed economic gains in 1954, 1976, 1982 and 1987. In fact, Mexico more or less recovered its sanity and resilience under Zedillo, and continued its uneven progress as before. By the end of 1997, economic growth was peaking at 7 per cent as if nothing catastrophic had occurred.

Not that catastrophic events won't continue. The drug trade through Mexico into the US is pernicious and expanding. It was bad during my watch, but by 2009 whole armies were involved and thousands were being killed. It will continue until the US government can reduce or stamp out the demand.

By the end of 1995 I was getting on top of the work and beginning to enjoy urban life in Mexico City — concerts at the Palacio de Bellas Artes, exhibitions at the Museo Nacional de Antropologia, visiting the houses of Frida Kahlo, Diego Rivera and Leon Trotsky, listening to the mariachi bands in the Plaza Garibaldi, and playing music in a piano trio. This included two talented young Mexican women, a pianist and a cellist. We gave several concerts, and were invited by the British ambassador, Adrian Beamish, who had vaguely heard that Broinowski played something, to contribute an item at the annual Commonwealth concert he gave at his residence. After a fashion show by the Malaysians and several other non-musical items from other embassies, we launched into the first two movements of Beethoven's Archduke Trio. This stilled the chatter among the crowd, and received standing applause. Adrian, who played with a small recorder group, and from his Oxbridge perspective considered Australians to be a fairly uncultured lot, admitted to me later that he was impressed.

One afternoon I was rudely reminded that despite its civilised veneer, Mexico City could still be fairly lawless. I was parked in Polanco waiting for a friend without Cirilo when two men approached and shoved a 0.38 calibre automatic pistol into my chest through the open window, demanding my cherished 20-year-old Rolex GMT Master watch. I gave it to them, but as they dashed off, I leapt out and chased them. One of them swivelled and fired a shot which whistled past my head, before they jumped into a waiting taxi and took off. Trembling with anger, I was restrained by a large rabbi who emerged with his flock from a nearby synagogue. In a kindly way, he made the obvious point that even my beloved Rolex wasn't worth a bullet in the head.

A keen pleasure was to explore Mexico outside the Distrito Federal (DF). I could do this during official calls on state governors, managers of businesses trading with Australia, or by visiting pastoralists interested in Australian cattle. I could also make trips at weekends or during leave. By early 1995, however, the Mercedes 300 had several hundred thousand kilometres on the clock and was too tired to provide reliable country cruising. The department wouldn't consent to another Mercedes, but they would agree to me buying a reasonably comfortable American car. After consulting all the literature, I chose a Chrysler LHS. Widely advertised at the time as a new breed of wonder machine from Detroit, the LHS had a V6 motor, front-wheel drive, a spacious and quiet interior and a fantastic sound system. I took the opportunity of Ali's first reunion visit to Mexico to fly with her and Cirilo up to San Antonio in Texas, where we took delivery of an LHS from an accredited dealer. It was an elegant, opalescent grey sedan with leather upholstery, woodwork panels in the dash and doors, and coffee cup holders on every horizontal surface. We drove it back to Mexico City via Nuevo Laredo, skirting through wild desert country to the east of the Sierra Madre Oriental, through Monterey, and then up to Saltillo, San Luis Potosi, and on to DF.

For six months, the Chrysler was a joy to drive. Cirilo and I used it on numerous exploratory trips. We travelled east through the Puebla corridor to the coastal city of Veracruz where Baz Luhrmann created the film *Romeo+Juliet*. We drove south and west on Highway 95D through the silver mining town of Taxco down to the fabulous Pacific resort of Acapulco, from where during Spanish times a galleon loaded with silver would sail annually west across the Pacific to the Philippines to trade for oriental spices and silks. We went south over the rugged and remote landscape to Oaxaca, the lively artistic centre of Zapotec Indian culture 250 kilometres from DF.

About the only place I didn't take the Chrysler was to the Yucatán Peninsula, which was too far from Mexico City to justify the road journey. Instead, accompanied by Dr Denise Brown, a Canadian academic friend who had written her PhD thesis on Mayan Indians, I flew to Merida and we hired a locally made Volkswagen to drive to Chichen Itza, Uxmal, Ticul and other Mayan sites where the jaguars grunted at night in the hot flat limestone jungle.

On these and other trips, I got used to Mexican road manners and signs. Drivers on newly constructed highways were better behaved and more considerate than in the rough and tumble of city driving. In cities and towns another hazard were the local police, who would stop cars and try to solicit bribes, known locally as *la mordida* (the bite), for real or imagined traffic offences. Usually, but not always, they were deterred by diplomatic plates. Road signs were conspicuous, especially those warning of *curvas peligrosas* (dangerous curves), *derrumbes* (earthquakes), *topes* (speed bumps — often high enough to take out your suspension if hit at speed), or *puentes angostos* (narrow bridges). On steep hills we were enjoined to *frenar con motor* (use your motor to brake).

Into its seventh month, to my great disappointment, the Chrysler suddenly began showing disturbing mechanical inconsistencies. Its front suspension seemed to lose resilience, its brakes their steel grip, and the automatic transmission its silky smoothness. Cirilo took it into the local Chrysler agent in DF, but they were disinclined to honour the warranty, and wanted to charge for whatever temporary repairs they pretended to make. Appeals to the San Antonio dealer were ignored. I quickly got tired of the prevarications and send an email to our Austrade representative in Detroit asking him to intercede on our behalf with the Chrysler head office. He did so, and some weeks later came a formal apology and authorisation for a full reconstruction of both the brakes and suspension at a major Chrysler outlet in Mexico City. In my mind however, this did not redeem them. No car, especially a sophisticated beast, should have been released onto the market with such design flaws. It was as bad as the BMW 520i I had had in Manila, but without the excuse of breaking down in a developing country.

While the Chrysler was in dock, I used the embassy's General Motors Suburban. This was a vast mother of an SUV, on huge tyres driven by a massive V8 engine. It seated nine adults while shouldering smaller vehicles off the road, floating over bumps and *topes*, and swaying ponderously around corners. With the airconditioner on full bore, and cruising at 100 kmh, it would guzzle about eighteen litres for every hundred kilometres of country driving. This, and other American behemoths like the Hummer, go some of the way to explain why the United States, with 5 per cent of the world's population, consumes about 40 per cent of its petroleum. But the Suburban was great for collecting delegations of visiting Australians or unwieldy packages from the airport, which was the main reason we had it in the embassy stable.

In my office safe were eight sets of credentials, all signed by the Australian governor-general, former Foreign Minister Bill Hayden, on behalf of Her Majesty the Queen of Australia. They introduced me to each of the heads of state to whom I was to be accredited. I had now done Mexico, and seven remained. During the next six months, Alicia Rosado worked hard with the protocol departments in San Salvador, Guatemala City, Tegucigalpa, Managua, Panama City, San Jose and Havana to fix dates for presentations. In due course, these were set and off I went. In each city, as in DF, bands played, schoolchildren were bussed in from the countryside to wave Australian flags, I presented my letters to the various presidents, and we had short discussions in their studies about bilateral relations and the state of the world. During these ceremonies I was reminded of an interesting fact that Ali had observed during her time at Yarralumla: national anthems are always in inverse length to the size of the country. The smaller the country, the longer the anthem. One Central American country's anthem had three movements.

Strung out over six months these ceremonies went without a hitch, except in Costa Rica. For that occasion, I was joined on the plane from Mexico City by the ambassador of Denmark who was scheduled to present on the same day. During a relaxed conversation over a drink, we decided to compare our credentials. They looked similarly elaborate, but were addressed to different men — his to President Jose Maria Figueres Olsen, and mine to President Rafael Angel Calderon Fournier. I called a flight attendant and, trying to keep the panic out of my voice, asked her who was the president of her country. As if answering an idiot child, she replied, 'Figueres Olsen, of course.'

As we taxied into San Jose airport, a black limousine drove to the plane. An expensively suited and tanned gentleman reeking of aftershave alighted and introduced himself as the chief of protocol. Drawing him aside, I said I had a problem. 'Ah, Mr Ambassador,' he said lugubriously, 'we all have our little problems. What is yours?' I told him and his face paled. 'Indeed, we do have a problem.' Sending my Danish colleague ahead in another car, he explained on our way into San Jose that my gaffe couldn't be worse. Figueres had narrowly defeated Calderon in an election in May 1994 and they were bitter enemies. But, he said, it was too late to cancel the ceremony. The president was briefed and prepared. The schoolchildren were arriving, and the palace band had been rehearsing the Australian national anthem for a week. Taking me straight to his office in Costa Rica's diminutive Foreign Ministry, he took out a heavy plain white envelope and in his best copperplate, inscribed it to 'His Excellency, President Jose Maria Figueras Olsen'. 'Just present this as if it contains your letters,' he said, 'and cable your ministry urgently to send a correct set as soon as you can.'

The double ceremony went without a hitch, although I felt I was participating in a charade as I solemnly handed my empty envelope to President Figueres. During our chat after the event, he said with a glint in his eye that he had an Uncle Olsen somewhere in Queensland. In view of the favour he had that day extended to me in overlooking a 'small irregularity', would I look him up? Indeed I would, and subsequently tried to, but without success.

As Ruth Pearce, head of DFAT's Americas Division, observed during a post-liaison visit she made to Mexico City in 1996, I was accredited to too many countries to do them all justice. I agreed, but nothing changed. My trips out of Mexico City to other countries were always tightly scheduled, and calls on ministers, officials and resident ambassadors were usually rushed. The personalities and mindsets of ministers and officials were subtly different from country to country. But one thing Central American capitals seemed to have in common was a US ambassador ensconced in a fortress-like embassy and imbued with a unique sense of exceptionalism. Ever since the Monroe Doctrine and the Platt Amendment, the United States had granted itself the right to interfere in Central American affairs, direct the training of local militias and constabularies, overthrow leftist governments or check the activities of nationalistic indigenes wanting land reform. Such policies were pursued by US ambassadors and their military and intelligence staffs with tragic results in El Salvador, Guatemala, Honduras, Panama and Nicaragua, not to mention further afield in Chile and the Dominican Republic. Although the ambassadors I called on were always cordial and welcoming, I found little to distinguish in their thinking about the United States' entitlement and capacity to exercise force where required.

The exception was of course Cuba. A large and seemingly disembodied United States presence existed in a tall building near the Hotel Nacional in Havana, but it was unofficial, without normal diplomatic recognition by or contact with the Cubans. I never made contact with these people, few of whom were from the State Department. But I had plenty to do with the Cubans. For instance, I had to try to get them to repay a long-standing Australian loan for sugar milling equipment, help the Western Mining Corporation negotiate an agreement to extract nickel in an eastern province and to arrange a visit to Havana by the Australian foreign minister, Gareth Evans.

The signature of the Western Mining agreement was celebrated at a dinner hosted by Fidel Castro. He and his cabinet sat on one side of a long table, and the CEO of Western Mining, Hugh Morgan and I, our wives and a bunch of his Canadian lawyers sat on the other. Castro professed a strong curiosity about Australia and the Antipodes, and his aggressive questioning turned the dinner into a quiz show. After Hugh and I had exhausted our knowledge, Ali, visiting me at the time from Australia, took over. Sitting beside Fidel, she matched him in knowledge and wit, and, unable to restrain her own curiosity, turned the session into one about Cuba and Latin America. She asked Fidel whether he expected relations with Washington to normalise during his incumbency. He doubted it. I think the discussion, and the dinner, resulted in a draw.

The Evans visit was nerve-wracking. I had carefully prearranged a meeting between Evans and Castro through the Cuban Ambassador in Mexico City. But as we waited in the Hotel Nacional on the Malecon, I remained uncertain when, or even if, the meeting would take place. After three days in Havana with no word, Evans became increasingly impatient, and paced restlessly around his hotel suite. Then, at yet another cocktail reception, a security officer in a black suit and sunglasses nudged me surreptitiously and asked me and the minister to get in a car behind him. I grabbed Rebecca Weisser, a junior member of my staff who had helped me with the visit, and we headed off at breakneck speed through Havana. At an undisclosed safe house outside the city, Castro was waiting. He not only engaged Evans in a lengthy discussion, but posed with him for photographs and accompanied him to the airport afterwards. Evans was jubilant and I kept my job.

The Havana into which Castro and his revolutionaries had marched in 1959 was a fabled city. It was the home of Ernest Hemingway, the playground of Frank Sinatra and Sammy Davis Jr and their Rat Pack, and a profitable working environment for American mobsters who ran most of the casinos and brothels. When Castro took over, American trade, aid and intercourse (as it were) were frozen. But an enduring legacy, increasingly cherished by the locals, remained: ageing American cars, the so-called Yank Tanks of the 1950s. As noted by Simon Bell and George Fischer in *Classic American Cars of Cuba*, Cuba had been the world's leading importer of American automobiles in the 1950s. Perhaps 10,000 of these machines, in hot primary colours or two-tone fantasies, remained in various stages of decay in and around Havana and in more distant barrios. They included Buicks, Cadillacs, Chevrolets, Fords, the Chrysler stable of Dodges, De Sotos and Plymouths with their freakish tailfins, Hudsons, Packards, Pontiacs, Ramblers and Studebakers.

Short on engineering innovation but heavy on chrome and style, most of these machines would be unregistrable today without modifications such as seatbelts and toughened glass windscreens. Equipped with basic inline six cylinder engines, synchromesh or powerglide transmissions and solid rear axles, only some had power steering and brakes. They were kept running by ingenious owners who cannibalised parts from similar models, hand-forged components or fossicked around repair shops and country barns for parts from Lada saloons and Russian trucks and tractors. Modifications on some were so extensive that it was difficult to discern the original make and model from the Frankenstein's monster adaptation. As unofficial taxis called peso taxis or *boteros*, many of them were employed to augment the overcrowded 'camels' — twin-humped Russian buses sometimes nicknamed by the locals as *Peliculas de Sabado* (or 'Saturday night movies'), as they tended to be filled with sex, violence and bad language. Unfortunately, *boteros* were off-limits to tourists and I never got to travel in one.

A small number of classic Yank Tanks in Cuba were imaginatively restored by their owners, who proudly paraded them at weekends around the seaside breakwater of the Malecon, or along the tree-lined Prado leading down to the El Morro castle at the entrance to Havana Bay. I saw some lovely examples, including a bright red 1960 Chevy Impala, a silver 1954 Oldsmobile Super 88 with a rocket ship as its bonnet mascot, a two-tone blue and white 1957 Buick Roadster with faux vents along its sides, a green 1951 Dodge Kingsway, a copper-coloured Chevy 210 with twin rocket-shaped wind splits, and a customised 1955 Chevy refitted with a Hyundai engine. Cars like these were available for rent at around $US90 per day from large operators such as Caribe and Panautos Rent a Car. Many were parked strategically outside Havana hotels such as the Nacional, Melia Cohiba, Inglaterra and the Hotel Havana Libre to entice *gringos* who could afford a day of nostalgia. I could afford the money but not the time.

YANK TANKS IN CENTRAL AMERICA

*   *   *

Back in Mexico City in early 1996, I was aware that the Keating Labor government was making a bid for a non-permanent seat on the UN Security Council in September. The bid was taken over and continued by the conservative government of John Howard, who had defeated Keating in the March election. I was instructed to get endorsements from all eight governments to which I was accredited. I promptly received assurances from the Mexican government. Six of the other governments also indicated they would support Australia (whose rivals for the seat were Portugal and Sweden). In a move I did not support because I thought it unnecessary, the Australian ambassador to the UN, Richard Butler, was sent down to help me reinforce our bid in a swing through Central America. We received the same assurances, but at least some of these were withdrawn before the vote took place. In the end, Australia did not win the seat.

I can identify two main reasons for our failure. One was an arrogant assumption in Canberra that Australia was held in such high international regard that merely putting our name forward would win us a seat. The trouble with this was that we did not acknowledge, or bother to contest, the efforts by Sweden and Portugal to secure the seat for themselves, with the support of the Western European group. In Central America, both countries had honorary consuls and aid programs. We had neither, and our diplomatic presence from Mexico City was stretched, to say the least.

Second, I had been appalled on being instructed by the department at the end of 1995 that it no longer required regular reporting from the post on the Central American countries. During mid-term consultations in Canberra, I asked the division head where they would now get their information. From CNN, was the laconic reply, as if a bland, US-centric news service needed no challenge from professional Australian observations in the field. This carelessness was matched by another DFAT phenomenon — a sudden emphasis on administrative correctness at posts, even at the expense of effective diplomatic representation. I prided myself on running a reasonably tight administrative ship, but I bridled at the undue emphasis now placed on accounts and staff management. The administrative tail was wagging the diplomatic dog. I must admit also that I was not particularly keen to serve Alexander Downer as my minister. I had known him briefly during his time as a diplomatic officer, and was not impressed with his foreign affairs priorities or his personality.

I mulled over these developments, and decided with only a few regrets to take early retirement at the conclusion of my posting to Mexico in May 1997. Ali had retired in 1996 and was doing a PhD at the Australian National University. On my return to Canberra in July the secretary of the department, Philip Flood, hosted a small farewell reception for me. On of the guests was Don Aitkin, vice-chancellor of the University of Canberra. Out of the blue, he asked me if I'd like an adjunct professorship at the university. 'It gives you a title and a room in the Faculty of Arts, but no money,' he said. I had been wondering with some trepidation what to do in my retirement, and accepted his offer with alacrity. At least it would keep me off the streets, and I would get to drive my Jaguar again.

12

Every Man Needs a Shed

It was January 1998, hot as a baker's oven. Ali and I were in the Jaguar, 50 kilometres east of Mildura on the Sturt Highway heading for Adelaide. The open windows and vents admitted blasts of super-heated air, but it was even hotter with the windows closed. The water temperature gauge was off the red end of the dial. The engine was almost incandescent, an inviting target for a heat-seeking missile. Just before we melted into our sandals, a waft of cool air forecast a change, and we limped into Mildura to find an airconditioned motel.

As it turned out, it wasn't the engine that suffered permanent damage in that hot spell, but the tyres. As we crossed the South Australian border heading for Renmark and Adelaide, a rhythmic vibration started in the back and shifted to the front. I was amazed to see that all four tyres had grown blisters like gunports on a Catalina. This was the result of the car sitting undriven for long periods over the previous three years when I was in Mexico, first at Susie and John Ballinger's sheep stud at Kangaroo Valley, later at cousin Gillis' cattle property at Cobbity outside Sydney. But apart from the tyres and a dramatic oil leak, the car was in remarkably good shape. Gillis had even fitted a new battery before I drove it back to Canberra.

So began my retirement. Was the experience an omen?

Ali and I had sold our family house in Chapman and bought a conveniently located apartment in a complex designed and built by Garry Willemsen near the parliamentary triangle in Brisbane Avenue, Kingston. While Ali completed her PhD in Australian–Asian relations at the ANU, I commuted to my office at the University of Canberra. To keep busy, I gave occasional lectures and one or two graduation speeches.

I also scratched an itch that had been bothering me ever since I joined the old Department of External Affairs in Canberra in 1963. I had been stung by the occasional ignorance or inaccuracy in reporting about Asia in the Australian media. Not that all Australian journalists in the region were mediocre. Indeed, we have a long tradition of brilliant and insightful correspondents including G. E. 'Chinese' Morrison and William Henry Donald reporting from China at the turn of the nineteenth century, and Cyril Pearl and Frank Clune early in the twentieth. Nor were all the offending stories written or presented by Australians. But there were enough to prompt me to start a scheme to send the best of our aspiring journalists as interns to South East Asian English-language newspapers. I thought that by priming the pump of journalistic recruiting with young graduates who had worked in busy and crowded newsrooms of newspapers in the region, we might improve the quality of reporting on Asia overall. When they eventually became foreign correspondents, they'd have a 'feel' for Asia seared into their impressionable brain pans.

In 1999, I obtained $6000 from the Myer Foundation in Melbourne, and, with a couple of colleagues in the Department of Communications, selected two students, Fleur Leyden and Lyndall McFarland, to work for four weeks in Asia during the 1999/2000 Australian summer break. We sent Fleur to the *Bangkok Post* and Lyndall to the *Philippine Daily Inquirer*. As my funding base expanded to include contributions from the Australia Korea Foundation and other universities, I increased both the number of students and newspapers to which I sent them. By 2009, with the help of colleagues from the Royal Melbourne Institute of Technology and the universities of Canberra, Sydney and Western Sydney, I have sent sixty-six interns to nine newspapers in Seoul, Bangkok, Jakarta, Manila, Kuala Lumpur and Phnom Penh. Keeping track of them after their return to Australia has been as hard as herding cats. But we do know that many are working as journalists both in Australia and abroad. Viva Goldner, whom I sent from the University of Canberra to the *Jakarta Post* in 2002, even won a Walkley Award and now works for a newspaper in Beijing. The program will continue if I keep getting funding.

Another thing that kept me off the streets was writing two books. The first was *A Witness to History*, a biography of my grandfather Robert Broinowski. Divorced from my grandmother Dais in 1926, who banished him and was thus virtually unknown to me. But I felt that his life as secretary to three defence ministers in the first decade after Federation, and as Usher of the Black Rod and later clerk in the Federal Senate, reflected much post-Federation history and events that were worth recording. The book was published by Melbourne University Press during the Centenary of Federation in 2001. My second book, *Fact or Fission* (Scribe, Melbourne, 2003), was about Australia's early Cold War ambitions to acquire nuclear weapons, its later renunciation of such plans and the moral complexity we now face in trying to reconcile uranium exports with our opposition to nuclear weapons proliferation.

Both books have had unexpected spin-offs. *Witness* resulted in a section of the rehabilitated rose gardens around Old Parliament House in Canberra being named after my grandfather, who established the gardens during the Great Depression of the 1930s. And *Fact or Fission* has opened up opportunities to write about nuclear issues, or debate them at forums in Australia and elsewhere.

A further post-retirement project has been building an architect-designed, three-pavilion house on the land I found with the help of Cecile Jamieson at Termeil on the New South Wales south coast. There, plenty of gardening, painting, and the oiling of timbers weathered by salt air have kept mine and Ali's ageing bodies in reasonable trim. But we have given away another exercise — riding our bikes the 6 kilometres to Bawley Point every morning for a swim (although we still drive there most mornings).

The reason for not riding was an accident I had while racing Adam back from the beach to the house during our New Year holidays in 2007. He didn't see me coming up behind him and swerved into my path. I somersaulted over him and landed like the victim of a spear-tackle head-first on the hard road. Even wearing my helmet I was badly concussed and taken by ambulance to Ulladulla General Hospital with Ali repeatedly assuring me that she had my wallet and watch and that Adam was taking care of the bikes. A local doctor in stubbies and thongs dressed my wounds, but failed to do an X-ray on my skull, which was fractured.

Three months later I had forgotten all about the accident. But one morning I drove my ride-on mower into the front gate, and started jogging sideways. I also found I could not type or play my violin without bow stutters. John Lawton, a doctor from Adelaide staying with us at Termeil at the time, asked whether I'd recently hit my head. When I told him about the bike accident, he suggested an immediate return to Sydney to get a CAT scan on my skull, and then taking it to my doctor. I presented the CAT scan to John Baffsky, my local GP in Edgecliff. His face went pale and he marched Ali and me to a taxi rank on New South Head Road, telling us to go straight to St Vincent's Hospital in Darlinghurst, where he'd line up a brain surgeon to operate on me immediately. The surgeon on duty was Richard Parkinson from Adelaide. That night, he drilled a hole in my skull and drained a massive subdural haematoma that had been pushing my brain to one side.

During my groggy recovery in the intensive care unit the next morning, my three-year-old granddaughter Ava visited me with her mother, Anna. Wearing her nurse's uniform with a red cross on the front, Ava solemnly handed me a box of chocolates and asked whether she could have one. She then observed that I had a pipe sticking out of my head, and proceeded to test my reflexes by hitting my knees with her rubber hammer. She then wandered off to ask other patients in the ward whether they were sick, and to offer them the same treatment.

* * *

During my travels for the government I had managed to keep few things for any length of time. But after twenty-five years my S type Jaguar was an exception, a constant in our motoring lives. With careful tuning I even reduced its former extravagant fuel consumption to about 12 litres per 100 kilometres. But as petrol prices kept rising, I became less and less inclined to use it as regular transport, and kept it permanently in the shed at Termeil for occasional weekend forays.

For daily driving, we managed with increasingly fuel-efficient machines. My first car on retirement in late 1997 was a new six-cylinder, front-wheel-drive Mitsubishi Magna, which I purchased from Canberra's main Mitsubishi dealer, National Capital Motors in Mort Street, Braddon. Made at the former Chrysler plant at Tonsley Park south of Adelaide, the Magna was breathtakingly ordinary. White with a stark grey fabric interior, it was undistinguished in performance, economy and reliability, no better or worse that any of the other Australian-made sixes — Commodores, Falcons and Camrys. It was mere transport, and Ali and I drove it around New South Wales, Victoria and South Australia for two uneventful years during which we clocked up over 48,000 kilometres.

One fateful day however, I checked the Magna in at National Capital Motors for its 50,000 kilometre service. 'It'll be ready in the afternoon,' they assured me. I returned at four o'clock, to be met by the foreman who gave me a shifty look and said in the kind of flat voice Australians sometimes use to hide a catastrophe, 'It's not exactly ready. Why don't you sit down and have a cup of tea?' I did so, and after what seemed like a long time, I strolled out to the workshop to see what was going on. There was my car, bent like a banana. Some idiot had broadsided straight into the driver's side during a test run. It was a write-off. The company grudgingly gave me a substitute car free of charge for a couple of weeks while I sorted out the insurance and arranged to buy another. But I did not ask to see the police accident report. Probably there wasn't one. Nor did I insist on speaking to the driver who had taken it on its last test run. God knows how he had managed to have such a comprehensive prang without being seriously injured. Maybe he *was* injured, or even dead, although there was no blood sprayed around the cabin. I should have been more suspicious and inquiring.

As an antidote to the Magna, I looked for something exotic, nippy and small. I trawled through showrooms along Parramatta Road looking at four-cylinder Japanese and Korean cars, and nicely put-together European compacts beginning to make an impact on the Australian market, including diesel- and petrol-powered Citroens, Renaults, Peugeots and Fiats. I was particularly taken with a Fiat 500, a growly little shoe of a thing that would have given me much excitement. But what I selected was a 2.2 litre Daewoo Leganza, the Korean-made car I had handed on to Anna and her partner Duncan in 2003. If ever a car needed to prove its ruggedness and reliability under pressure, Anna was the ideal taskmaster. She's as ruthless with the Leganza as is the Stig pushing an Aston Martin around a disused British runway for *Top Gear*. Long may she and Duncan drive it.

I next bought another car on my most-favoured list — a Subaru Impreza RV station sedan. This was not exactly a WRX, which out-performed police cars and was every ram-raider's wet dream, but its compact 2 litre flat four boxer engine still had plenty of grunt, especially if one kept up the revs. With permanent four-wheel drive and a tight five-speed gear box, it was very well-behaved and sure-footed, even driven hard in wet conditions. Its engine had a dissonant grumble a bit like the power plant of an air-cooled Volkswagen.

From 2002 Ali and I really began to pile on the kilometres in the Impreza — at least 2000 per month, or 24,000 per year. This was due to a move we made from Canberra to the terrace house Ali had bought in Paddington during my posting in Seoul. The distance from Sydney to Termeil is a third as much again as from Canberra, and we were driving there most weekends. I was now becoming aware of our rising fuel bill. In 2003, petrol had climbed to over a dollar a litre and was still rising.

During a family reunion at Susie Ballinger's sheep farm at Kangaroo Valley in 2004, I noticed that she and my other sister Helen had hybrid Toyota Priuses. Driving from sheep auction to sheep auction around New South Wales, John Ballinger had become concerned about his rising fuel bills, and had initiated a switch from his Camry. Helen and her partner Mary Cunnane, both passionate anti-nuclear greens, had also bought themselves a Prius.

After a long and earnest talk with John about the advantages of his Prius, Ali and I decided to join the green family movement. During a trip to from Sydney to Termeil in January 2005 we called on Bob Schubert, a senior salesman at South Nowra Toyota to see what sort of trade-in he would give us on our Impreza. No doubt mindful of all the business the Ballingers had generated with South Nowra Toyota — not just selling them Camrys and Priuses, but diesel utes and various makes of used Toyotas to assorted offspring — Bob gave us a very good price on our Impreza. We were now proud owners of a new, silver 2005 Prius.

The car was a revelation, not least in learning to drive it. Slip the black ignition lozenge into a slot on the dash, depress the brake pedal, press the large ignition button. No sound of a starter motor because there isn't one, but the black panel, improbably distant from the driver under the windscreen, lights up like a spaceship. Hidden electrical devices begin to whir. The machine is alive! Keep the brake pedal depressed, slip the stubby gear shift on the dash into 'D' on the gate, release the foot/hand brake, and ease gently forward on the accelerator. Still no sound as the car moves off on its electric motor. Depress the accelerator a bit more, and the 1.5 litre petrol engine kicks in. If you choose to push it, acceleration is brisk, but in the middle of the dash is a touch screen like a television with vertical bars telling you how much fuel you're using — a strong disincentive to heavy throttle use. The screen also gives a visual display of which motor is driving the car at any particular time, and of the electricity being generated by braking or cornering as it flows back into the battery.

Apart from these innovations the Prius was very comfortable, and voted so in a recent poll conducted by an American auto magazine. It might have had little individuality or spirit, but it handled well, and was a tremendous fuel miser. During the three and a half hours from Sydney to Termeil, we'd consume 4.4 litres per hundred kilometres, or with a tail wind, 4.2 litres.

In a *Top Gear* program broadcast in Australia on 24 November 2008, Jeremy Clarkson bucketed the Prius. He claimed the nickel for its batteries came from a mine in Canada, the batteries themselves from Europe, and in the course of manufacture the car caused more environmental damage than a Land Rover Discovery. He then pitted a Prius against a BMW 3 litre in a race around his disused British airfield. The Prius went flat out while the Beamer idled along beside it, only overtaking at the end. Clarkson triumphantly claimed the Prius consumed seventeen miles per gallon compared to the Beamer's nineteen. 'Thus,' said Clarkson portentously, 'it's not what you drive, but *how* you drive that counts.' Of course it is, you prat, I thought, but in any fair test the Prius wouldn't be driven flat out (when its fuel consumption rises alarmingly), but at moderate speeds at which it would beat the Beamer hands down.

In retirement I've also satisfied a yearning to see outback Australia, something I was never able to do during my peripatetic life overseas. The idea for a safari was kick-started by a mate, Andy Buttfield, an electrical engineer from Adelaide whom Ali has known since childhood. (In fact, he used to take her out.) One hundred and eighty five centimetres tall, Andy has a loud voice, a determined personality and a deep scepticism about government — local, state or federal. He's also a bit of a global warming sceptic and a member of the Centre for Independent Studies, a Sydney-based conservative think-tank. I hold none of these attributes against him, because Andy has a twenty-four carat heart, and has organised some exhilarating private safaris around Australia. I've joined a dozen or so Old Codgers (as we call ourselves) on three of them.

The first wasn't a road trip, but an easy week-long winter cruise on the Murray River from Renmark in South Australia to an old customs house on the Victorian border and back again. We hired a large multi-cabined houseboat, on which each of about twelve Old Codgers had their own cabins. After a non-taxing seven hours or so on the river we'd pull in each night at a likely bank, haul driftwood together for a massive fire and have a barbecue accompanied by plenty of red wine and ribaldry. Being an engineer, Andy has a keen desire to fix mechanical things. With equal enthusiasm, he'd repair a pump, a fuse board or a blocked toilet, the last by diving overboard in his underpants and sticking his arm up the offending pipe till he'd dislodged the shit. He also has contempt for natural bush hazards. On long walks along the banks of the Murray in a pair of grubby khaki shorts and bare feet, he'd walk straight through a lagoon that barred his way to the boat, no matter how deep or how likely he was to be bitten by snakes.

Our second safari was a more serious affair. Some of the original dozen Codgers, plus a few new ones, assembled at Cairns. There we hired three new, four-litre diesel Toyota LandCruisers, the undisputed king (and certainly the largest) of four-wheel drives then on Australian roads, and drove them up to the top end of Cape York. Like the crew in *A Perfect Storm* who provisioned their boat before their fateful voyage to the crab fishing grounds on the Newfoundland Bank, we stripped a large Cairns supermarket of all its steaks, fruit, vegetables, bread and beer, and packed the lot into Eskys with dry ice. The return trip, mainly up the east Queensland coast, took nearly three weeks. The LandCruisers took a frightful hammering on severely corrugated gravel roads, sand dunes masquerading as roads, and across rocky outcrops which never pretended to be roads. We were delayed from time to time when Andy did his good Samaritan act by trying to help hopelessly underequipped fellow travellers extract themselves from gullies and ravines.

Our equipment included geo-satellite global navigators, winches to haul each other out of sand dunes, a large tarpaulin under which the whole party could sleep, and fishing tackle for catching barramundi on the numerous tidal beaches along the eastern Queensland coast. (We never caught any.)

We also had a very comfortable portable toilet, a collapsible aluminium camp chair with a plastic toilet seat set in the frame. Each night we would position this over a hole we dug on the most prominent point of the campsites, rewarding the user with spectacular views of the surrounding countryside. The toilet seat was a comfort and joy except in a high wind. Then, the user could not simply drop his used toilet paper down the hole, but would have to reach down blindly and place it there so that it wouldn't blow away and catch in some nearby bush. Another comfort, rigged up by a LandCruiser enthusiast from Townsville, was a hot shower that fed off his cooling system.

On the last night of our return journey to Cairns, we used up the last of our meat — almost three-week-old steaks in vacuum-packed plastic. In the twilight they glowed through their wrapping like spent-fuel rods in a reactor pool, exuding a poisonous stench when we carefully opened them downwind of the camp. Geoff Pritchard, a pharmacist, and I were duty cooks, and we used all our combined alchemy to disguise the flavour of the meat, adding onions and garlic and beer and oatmeal and

Worcestershire Sauce. No one was fooled as they socked down their dinner with the last of our beer, but no one died of dysentery either.

During the trip, our LandCruisers had taken a severe battering in some of the most rugged and inhospitable country in Australia. But after we gave them a thorough washing they looked innocent and unmarked as we drove them through the gates of the hire company. God knows how much petrol we consumed on the trip, but I think each vehicle probably averaged about 16 to 18 litres per 100 kilometres.

Our third safari was in Arnhem Land in June/July 2008. A group of about thirty men and women, mostly Rotarians from Sydney, flew via Cairns to Gove on the north-eastern tip of Arnhem Land. After spending a night at the Nhulunbuy Motel, we flew south to Baniyala, the homeland of one of the Laynhupoy nations in the Northern Territory. They numbered close to 200 people, led by an enlightened headman, Djambawla Marawili. By common agreement, they allowed no alcohol, kava, drugs or pornography in the settlement.

There, on Tuesday, 1 July 2008, the former president of the Australian Labor Party, Warren Mundine, opened a new airconditioned house designed to accommodate school teachers from Darwin. The three-bedroom, two-bathroom house was built by young Aboriginal men under the guidance of Andy and another Sydney Cove Rotary Club member, Robert Bradshaw. It was completed after eleven weeks in November 2007. Funds came from the Commonwealth government with substantial top-up cash and services from the Rotary Club. Teachers had been coming from Darwin for some time to teach at the local school, but usually for only one or two days because they had nowhere to stay, except to camp out on the verandah of the schoolhouse. Andy reasoned that a lack of education was the only thing holding the youths back from employment. With the school house as an inducement, teachers might stay in Baniyala from Monday to Friday, and the kids might get a proper education. As it was, the highest ambition of Baniyala's young men was to become an Aussie rules football star, preferably playing for Essendon.

The day of the opening was a gala occasion. That night, the Baniyala people held a dance for us accompanied by their own rock band. The famous group Yothu Yindi came from the neighbourhood. We joined in the dancing and later put on a barbecue. Catering for 200 locals and about 50 visitors, the barbecue matched in scale the one I threw for the Australian Olympic team in Seoul in 1988. The difference was that this time I was foraging for wood, lighting fires and helping with the cooking and serving.

The next day, refreshingly without hangovers or other signs of excess, twelve of us left Baniyala by road, our eventual destination Darwin. Our vehicles were three Nissan Patrol four-wheel drives. With 'common-rail' 3 litre turbo-charged diesel engines, the Patrols were willing and agile machines, but lacked the sheer grunt and ruggedness of the LandCruisers we had hired on the Cape York trip.

Our route took us west across the Central Arnhem Road through several Aboriginal settlements to Bulman and Weemol then further west and south on the Mainoru Road, hitting the Stuart Highway at Maranboy. From there we drove north to Katherine, stayed in a local motel and early next morning took a boat trip on Yellow Waters. The pre-dawn glow revealed the wonderfully extravagant variety of the local flora and fauna — white sea-eagles, long-necked turtles, magpie geese, brumbies, king fishers, narcissus birds who spend all their time gazing at their reflections in the water, jabirus and, like innocent floating logs, crocodiles drifting among the ubiquitous *Pandanus spiralis*.

None of this travel would have been possible in the Wet, when most of the territory is underwater. Markers improbably high in the trees and buildings showed us where the waters had come to in the last Wet. At Katherine we also visited Ray Whear, a ranger I met by chance on the flight up from Sydney to Gove. Ray works for Aboriginal nations by shooting feral pigs, horses and buffalo from his helicopter, cataloguing sacred sites and starting burn-offs during the Northern Territory Dry.

From Katherine we drove north to Pine Creek, and then turned east onto the Kakadu Highway and up to Jabiru near where the Ranger uranium mine and its radioactive leachings are situated. Our route then took us west along the Arnhem Highway past various tourist lodges and Aboriginal craft centres to Darwin.

After a meal, a hot shower and a few hours' sleep in a Darwin motel, some colleagues and I took a taxi to Darwin airport. It was midnight on a Sunday, the fag-end of a long weekend. The airport was like a pub scene from Baz Lurhmann's *Australia* — full of beer-soaked revheads who had migrated north for the annual V8 super car race weekend. Like us, many were catching a scheduled Qantas flight to Sydney, leaving Darwin at the deeply depressing time of 0140 hours on Monday morning. But the aircraft, a Boeing 767, was delayed, at first for only half an hour, then for an hour, then all night, because in the interests of cost-cutting, Qantas did not have in their Darwin workshops an essential widget to repair a device which kept the aircraft in the air. 'Better to be safe than sorry,' said the unctuous announcer without the hint of an apology.

I was lucky enough to find a cab to take me back to the Darwin motel I had vacated several hours before. During the journey, I felt I could cheerfully have strangled Geoff Dixon, the Qantas CEO who keeps making inordinate profits for Qantas shareholders by reducing the services available to 'customers' and sending the bulk of heavy Qantas maintenance offshore. It's time Qantas and other companies providing essential services to the Australian public started giving their customers and employees the same consideration as their shareholders, I fulminated.

Indeed, before and since that delayed Darwin to Sydney flight, Qantas aircraft have been involved in an increasing number of incidents delaying their schedules. These have included running off the end of runways (Bangkok), gas bottles blowing holes through fuselages (Manila), automatic pilots becoming decoupled from the flight surfaces they are supposed to control (Western Australia), and an increasing number of late take-offs, arrivals and cancellations of flights due to cost-cutting and bad maintenance. In November 2008, I flew business class around Asia to place ten journalist students as interns on Asian newspapers. From Sydney to Seoul I flew on Asiana, to Bangkok and Phnom Penh on Thai, and to Kuala Lumpur and Manila on Malaysian Airlines. Only on the Manila to Sydney leg did I fly Qantas. Unlike all the other flights which had been on time, the Qantas plane, another Boeing 767, was ninety minutes late in leaving Manila because the crew had to replace and 'calibrate' a new cockpit computer that measured fuel. Also unlike the other flights, Qantas provided none of the little touches that can make flying pleasurable, like disposable toothbrushes and toothpaste or aftershave in the toilets. I was travelling business class but I was not even offered a drink before dinner, which was itself a spartan affair. Cost-cutting? Competing in the cut-throat business of international air transport? Saving money for CEO bonuses? Whatever the reason, I won't fly Qantas if an alternative airline is available until they have substantially improved both their reliability and their service.

I now return to the motor car industry and its uncertain future, especially in the United States. In November 2008 Rick Wagoner, Alan Mulally and Robert Nardelli, the chief executives of General Motors, Ford and Chrysler flew from Detroit to a Senate hearing in Washington. It was a begging expedition. They claimed they weren't seeking a bailout, but billions of dollars to enable their companies to retool for 'innovation'. They brought no supporting documents or calculations. At the hearing they were roundly criticised by congressmen and women for making the trip in their corporate jets instead of taking seats on scheduled airlines, and for not having documents supporting their shameless bid.

The Washington press was indignant too. In the *International Herald Tribune* on 13 November 2008, Thomas Friedman asked why the American public should subsidise innovation programs for Detroit. How could the companies be so bad for so long? A very un-innovative business culture and arrogant, visionless management explained a lot. General Motor's vice-chairman Bob Lutz was quoted as saying that hybrids like Priuses 'make no economic sense' and that 'global warming is a crock of shit'. But Friedman also blamed the entire Michigan delegation in the House and Senate, who year after year had shielded General Motors, Ford and Chrysler from environmental concerns, high fuel consumption, and the full impact of global competition that should have forced the Big Three to design and build greener machines decades ago.

Are the two surviving Australian offshoots of the Big Three — General Motors-Holden's and Ford — more enlightened? Certainly not if we judge their philosophy from commercial television ads for utes and SUVs that pull jumbo jets along runways, destroy fences in sheep paddocks, roar suicidally up precipices in the outback, or of gimlet-eyed macho vandals skidding V8s sideways around city streets. Of course, similar themes appear in ads for European and Japanese cars.

At the beginning of the 2000s, millions of dollars of taxpayers money were spent propping up Mitsubishi's sprawling Tonsley Park factory in Adelaide's south as it churned out dowdy six-cylinder 380s. But the new Magna did not sell and the company closed the operation, just as Chrysler had done at the same plant a decade before. In 2008, Kevin Rudd introduced his $6.2 billion Car Industry Rescue Plan. This was meant to be a lifeline to the remaining auto industry and its skilled Australian workforce. But it won't rescue General Motors-Holden's, Ford or Toyota unless they get serious about introducing much more imaginative innovations in motor car technology. Toyota's undertaking to make hybrid Camrys in Melbourne is a small step in the right direction, but why should Prime Minister Kevin Rudd have to bribe them to make this car when a Toyota spokesman, Mike Breen, said Toyota would make the hybrids in Australia even without the subsidy?

Nor will adapting heavy petrol cars to hybrids be enough to save the major car companies. The Prius, which is not made here, is streets ahead of the hybrid-modified Camry in fuel consumption, as well as American hybrid SUVs beginning to be promoted for 'discerning' customers in the *New Yorker* and other top-end American magazines. But other makers are starting to catch up in fuel-efficient technology. BMW has begun to employ micro-hybrid drive that dramatically reduces fuel consumption in traffic. Diesel electric engines are being test-bedded by Mercedes. Citroen will have a C4 diesel/electric hybrid by 2010. Hyundai will launch its first LPG/electric hybrid, the Elantra LPI HEV in 2009. And encouragingly for American makers, General Motors will introduce its Astra-sized Chevrolet Volt, a plug-in hybrid, in 2010 in the US and 2012 in Australia. Another plug-in is Nissan's Mixim, which was unveiled at the 2008 Frankfurt Motor Show, and is due for display in Japanese and US showrooms by 2010, and global release in 2012.

Such innovative developments in fuel-saving technology have not yet impacted on the Chinese, who love their cars and crowd into gigantic motor shows displaying the latest cars being made in ever increasing numbers in Chinese factories. Most of these cars borrow, steal or otherwise adapt American, European or North Asian designs. They include the Chery (an identical copy of a GM-Daewoo Matiz), the Lifan 320 (a Mini), the Shuanghuan Noble (the Smart car), a Hummer made by the Dongfeng

Corporation and the Roewe (Rover 75 manufactured in China after Nanjing Automobile Corporation bought the intellectual rights from Britain). Like South Korea in the 1970s, China's export markets are currently restricted to non-mainstream countries such as Libya, Belarus, Algeria and Uzbekistan. But within a decade, Chinese motor car sales in established markets will likely eclipse those from Europe, the United States and Japan itself. Meanwhile, the Indian motor industry is also gearing itself to compete for sales in global markets.

Throughout my career, I have been disappointed at Australia's inability to commercialise its inventions and market them abroad. There have been some remarkable successes like the Cochlear Ear and the T-VASIS landing system for aeroplanes, but these are few. The nuclear physicist Ted Ringwood invented Synrock, an artificial method of locking spent nuclear fuel into granite. After his death the technology moved offshore to America, never to be heard of again. Dr. Zhengrong Shi, the Chinese–Australian inventor of advanced photo-voltaic solar panels moved his business to Wuxi in China because he could find no backers to sustain his company Suntech in Australia. Many other Australian inventions and technologies have followed the same pattern, especially computer games and other software innovations. The degradation of Australian technology can be seen with particular clarity in the defence industry. After World War II Australia was producing fighter planes as good as any in the world (piston-driven P 51 Mustangs and then Avon Sabre F 86 jets). By the 1980s, Australian companies were lucky to secure offset contracts to make the tail-planes or landing gear for FA-18 Hornets. We can make ship hulls, but have to fill them with foreign (ie American) electronics which Australian companies cannot make. The Swedes, Dutch and Swiss can do these things. We should be able to also.

The same pattern emerges with Australian automotive technology. At the end of the nineteenth century, Australia led the world in steam cars, including the Thomson and Pioneer cars designed in Melbourne in 1897, and the steam car David Shearer made at Mannum and exhibited at the Adelaide Chamber of Manufacturers' Exhibition in 1900. Today we are among world leaders in making solar-powered cars that each year prove their reliability in the road race from Darwin to Adelaide. And a bright young cohort of engineering students at Deakin University in Victoria recently won an international competition sponsored by Ford to design a 21st-century equivalent to the company's famous Model T. Their lightweight car is known as the T2, or T-squared, a highly manoeuvrable three-wheeler built of light materials, with no gearbox, driveline or steering rack. It runs on compressed air, a full tank of which costs 80 cents, enough to travel 80 kilometres, less if one owns a scuba-diving compressor. But the inventors of T2 are not particularly hopeful of finding a backer to finance manufacture of their car in Australia.

Like many Australian youths, I began my love of cars in blissful innocence of the environmental roadblocks that lay ahead. At the age of sixteen I had no way of predicting the crises that began to afflict the industry in the 1980s — the fall or merger of great motor car makers, globalisation of the means of production, competition, overproduction, the stubborn insistence of many manufacturers on persevering with petroleum as the world reached peak oil consumption. Nor would I have been able to predict two other emerging phenomena: the desperation of the governments of established auto producing countries including Australia to subsidise their inefficient car makers as a way of avoiding massive unemployment; and the determination of emerging powers such as China and India to eclipse established Western and North Asian countries in motor car production and gaining global market share.

There is a connection here with diplomacy. Just as decisions about motor car production in Australia are made in the boardrooms of Detroit and Tokyo, so our policies on foreign affairs are more often than not formulated by others, particularly in Washington. They include the definition of national security, who our enemies are, which wars we will fight in and what military equipment and tactics we will employ in doing so. In both respects — motor car production and foreign affairs — Australia sometimes fails to behave like an independent country with its own ideas, skills and capacity to produce and market independent policies products and strategies.

Sentimentalists of my age and stage will always find joy and solace in maintaining and running their motor cars, especially classic ones like my Jaguar, and displaying them at rallies. But unless they are incurable optimists they probably realise that as in so many other aspects of our lives, the golden age of personal motor transport has come to an end. I probably won't any longer polish up the Jaguar and take it for a long drive simply for pleasure as I used to do with my black Riley in the early 1960s. But maybe Adam will. He always gets a glint in his eye when he comes up from Melbourne and opens the shed door at Termeil. I'm sure he and the Jaguar see him as its next owner.

Acknowledgements

Throughout my career I never kept diaries. Consequently I have had to rely on the collective memories of myself, Ali and our children, Anna and Adam. Several diplomatic colleagues jogged my memory, including Chris Conybeare, Allan Gyngell, Ian Lincoln and Gerry Nutter. David Manson and his brains trust of automobile enthusiasts picked me up on inaccuracies about cars. I am also indebted on certain technical points to Tony Arditto, a Jaguar specialist from Westmead, Georgine Clarsen, a motor historian at the University of Wollongong, my neighbour at Termeil Bruce Dalton, the proprietors of the Milton Tyre Service Barry and Darren Solomon, and my car-collecting South African friend from Bawley Point, Michael Truter. Adelaide friends Barney Hewitt and Ivan Shearer filled in some historical detail. The staff at the Mitchell Library, the Japan Foundation, and the Sydney bookshop Auto World, all provided much needed and sometimes quite obscure information that has enabled the project to continue.

Finally, I thank my agent Lyn Tranter for helping me find a publisher, and Brigitta Doyle, Jacqueline Kent and Michael Visontay for their editorial guidance, perseverance and support.

References

Baker, Kevin, *Economic Tsunami: China's Car Industry will Sweep Away Western Car Makers,* Rosenberg Publishing, New South Wales, 2007

Bell, Simon and Fischer, George, *Chariots of Chrome: Classic American Cars of Cuba.* Boston Mills Press, Boston, 2004

Broinowski, Richard, *A Witness to History: The Life and Times of Robert Broinowski,* Melbourne University Press, Victoria, 2001

Broinowski, Richard, *Fact or Fission: The Truth About Australia's Nuclear Ambitions,* Scribe, Melbourne, 2003

Carson, Iain and Vaitheeswaran, Vijay. *Zoom: The Global Race to Fuel the Car of the Future.* Penguin Australia, 2008

Casey, Richard, *Friends and Neighbours,* East Lansing, Michigan, 1955

Chapman, Giles and Porter, Richard, *My Dad Had One of Those,* BBC Books, London, 2007

Clarkson, Jeremy, *I Know You Got Soul,* Penguin, London, 2005

Davis, Tony and Wright, John, *Spotlight on Holden Commodore 1978–1988,* Marque Publishing Company, Blakehurst, New South Wales, 1994

Davison, Graeme, *Car Wars: How the Car Won our Hearts and Conquered our Cities,* Allen & Unwin, New South Wales, 2004

Dymock, Eric, *The Vauxhall File Model by Model,* Dove Publishing Limited, Great Britain, 1990

Falconer, Delia (ed.), *The Penguin Book of the Road,* Penguin Australia, 2008

Halliday, Jon and Cumings, Bruce, *Korea the Unknown War,* Viking, 1988

Hodge, Errol, *Radio Wars: Truth, Propaganda and the Struggle for Radio Australia,* Cambridge University Press, Victoria, 1995

Kamaki, Satoshi, *Japan in the Passing Lane: An Insider's Account of Life in a Japanese Auto Factory,* Pantheon Books, New York, 1982

REFERENCES

Kinzer, Stephen, *Overthrow: America's Century of Regime Change from Hawaii to Iraq,* Times Books, New York, 2006

Lewin, Tony, *The Complete Book of BMW: Every Model Since 1950,* Motorbooks, St Paul, United States, 2004

Loffler, Don, *She's a Beauty: The History of the First Holdens,* Wakefield Press, 1998

McCarthy, Tom, *Auto Mania: Cars Consumers and the Environment,* Yale University Press, New Haven and London, 2007

Mueller, Mike, *Cars of the '50s.* MBI Publishing Company, St Paul, Minnesota, 2002

Pahlavi, Mohammad Reza Shah, *Mission for My Country,* Hutchison and Co, London, 1961

Popham, Peter, *Tokyo: The City at the End of the World,* Kodansha, 1985

Reader's Digest Book of the Road, Reader's Digest Australia Limited, 1999

Renouf, Alan, *The Frightened Country,* Macmillan, Melbourne, 1979

Robson, Graham, *Cars of the Rootes Group,* Motor Racing Publications, Croydon, England, 1990

Skilleter, Paul, *Jaguar Saloon Cars,* Haynes Publishing Group, Somerset, 1980

Spry-Leverton, Peter and Kornicki, Peter, *Japan,* Michael O'Mara Books Limited, London, 1987

Styles, David G, *Riley: As Old as the Industry, 1898 to 1969,* Dalton Watson Fine Books, Deerfield Illinois, 2002

Sullivan, William H, *Mission to Iran: The Last US Ambassador,* Norton and Company, 1981

Thant Myint U, *The River of Lost Footsteps: Histories of Burma,* Farrar, Straus and Giroux, New York, 2005

Index

Ackroyd, Joyce, 19
Adelaide, 47–50
Ahmadinejad, President, 86
Aitkin, Don, 218
Akasaka Mitsukei, 45
Alaungpaya, King, 59
Alcoa Australia, 164
Andrew, Prince, 129
Antelope, HMS, 129
Aoyama-dori, 26, 34
Apocalypse Now, 109
Aquino, Benigno, 114
Aquino, Cory, 114
Ardent, HMS, 129
Arditto, Tony, 243
Arroyo, Gloria Macapagal, 114
Asakusa, 46
Asimus, David, 121
Aung San, 61
Aung San Su Chi, 79
Australia
 – decline of manufacturing technology, 238–239
Australian Embassies
 Hanoi, 135–136
 Manila, 104–105
 Mexico City, 205
 Rangoon, 68–69
 Saigon, 76, 144–146
 Seoul, 163
 Tehran, 83
 Tokyo, 26–28
Azabu, 25

Azabu Prince Hotel, 24, 26
Baffsky, John, 223
Baker Bates, Merrick and Crystal, 38
Baker, Keith, 202
Ball Macmahon, 54
Ballinger, John, 127, 202, 219
Ballinger, Susan, 13, 202, 219
Ba Maw, 61
Bandung Conference, 62
Baniyala, 231–232
Ban Ki-moon, 159
Barnett, Peter, 176, 179
Barassi, Ron, 188
Bastouille, Henri, 141
BBC World Service, 74
Beamish, Adrian, 207
Bell, Simon, 215
Belloc, Hilaire, 60–61
Bentley, Geoffrey, 18
Berry, Ken, 105
Billabong Bar, Hanoi, 139
Bishop, Tony, 21, 47
Bishop, Reg, 75
Black, H. D. 55
Body, Alf, 19
Bolte, Sir Henry, 75
Bonesteel, Charles H.,156
Boreham, Kevin, 105
Bradshaw, Barry, 147
Bradshaw, Robert, 231
Brando, Marlon, 109

Bray, John Jefferson, 17
Breen Mike, 237
Breer, Bill and Peggy, 117
Broinowski
 – Adam Richard Gracius, 46, 79, 83, 88, 116–118, 130, 132, 164, 181, 222–223
 – Alison Elizabeth, 24, 66, 106, 111, 116, 117, 124, 128, 129–130, 132, 160, 172, 176, 180, 191, 197, 199–200, 214, 218, 220
 – Anna Mariko, 44–45, 46, 47, 116–118, 130, 132, 141, 181, 223
 – Ava Rocka Thompson, 223
 – Gillis, 219
 – Mary Mona Enyd, 6, 17, 47
 – Robert Arthur, 221–222
 – Theo Philip, 6, 7, 16, 17
Brown, Denise, 209
Brown, Jeff, 179
Brown, Lady Hilda 32, 33–34
Brown, Sir Allan, 28–29, 32, 33–34

244

INDEX

Bryant, Gordon, 75
Bryson Industries, 48
Brzezinski, Zbigniew, 98
Burma, 58–79
Burmese servants, 66–68
Burmese Wars, 59–61
Burns, Creighton, 55
Bush, President George W., 98–99
Butcher, Elizabeth, 12
Butler, Richard, 217
Buttfield, Andrew, 228–233
Byroade, Henry, 64
Cairns, Jim, 75
Calderon Fournier, Rafael Angel, 212
Caldicott, Helen, 115, 118
Caldicott, William, 117, 118
Calley, Lieutenant William, 75
Campbell, Malcolm, 18
Canberra, 19, 20, 50–52, 119
Caravelle Hotel Saigon, 144–146
Cardenas, Eki, 111
Carver, Robert, 147
Casey, Richard, 64
Cars
    Austin 7 'Chummy' 1928, 11–13
    Austin 7 'New Ruby', 1936, 6
    Austin 10, 1936, 14
    BMW 1800 *Neue Klasse*, 1–2, 89–90, 95
    BMW 520i, 104, 111–113,118, 210
    Buick Roadster, 216

Chrysler, LHS, 208–210
Citroen Goddess DS, 1960, 18
Chevrolet, 1967, 50, Chevrolet Impala, 216
Daewoo Leganza, 167–168, 225
Daihatsu F-20, 127–128
Daimler V8, 124–127
Dodge, Kingsway, 216
Ford Model T, 2,12, 41
Gaz 69 command car, 142
Hillman Imp, 37–39
Hillman Minxes, 8–9, 93
Holden Calais, 179–181
FX, 1952, 14
Holden FC, 1958, 17
Holden EK, 1961, 17
Holden EH, 1964
Holden Kingswood HT, 67–68, 72, 74, 79
Holden Torana, 103–104
Holden VL, 179
Honda S 800 sports, 40, 41
Hyundai Excel, 166
Hyundai Elantra, 167
Hyundai Santa Fe, 167
Jaguar Mark 1, 48
Jaguar Mark 2, 48–50
Jaguar 'S' type, 181–183, 197–198, 219–220, 224, 240

Jaguar SS, 1937, 21, 47
Jaguar XJ6, 88, 90–94, 95–96, 124
M35 trucks (REO, Kaiser, GM), 142–143
Mercedes Benz 280E, 163–164, 165
Mercedes Benz 300, 204, 208
Mitsubishi Magna, 224–225
Morris Minor, 37
Nissan Patrol, 232–233
Nissan President, 134
Oldsmobile Super 88, 216
Peykan, 93
Portland, 164
Praga, 142
Prince, Skyline GT, 44–45
Renault 16, 102
Riley, 1.5 litre, 21, 22, 240
Rover, 50
Suburban, 210–211
Subaru Impreza RV, 225–226
Tatra, 142
Toyota Crown, 138
Toyota Hi Ace, 138, 140, 141
Toyota Land Cruiser, 106, 229–231
Toyota Lexcen, 180
Toyota Prius, 226–228
UAZ 469, 142
Ural, 142

245

Vauxhall, 1936 Light Six, 6
Volkswagen Kombiwagen, 117
Vauxhall Victor 101, 56
Zil, 142
Cars – new technology, 237–239
Carter, President Jimmy, 98
Casson, Robin, 124
Castro, Fidel, 214–215
Cavdarski, Vanco, 163
Central America
 – Australian diplomatic representation in, 217–218
Chapman, 119
Chifley, J. B. 16, 18
China – new auto engineering, 237–238
Choe-Wall, Young-hi, 155
Chou En-lai, 62
Chun Doo-hwan, 159, 163
Cirilo, 204–205, 208, 210
Clark, Christopher, 34
Clarkson, Jeremy, 40, 179, 227–228
Clarsen, Georgine, 243
Cleland, Pamela Mary, 17–18
Clendinnen, Inga, 200
Cliburn, Van, 109
Clinton, President, 206
Clune, Frank, 220
Coates, John, 171
Coffey brothers, 50

Coffey, Selwyn, 50
Coles, Philip, 171
Colosio, Luis Donaldo, 206
Commonwealth Public Service marriage bar, 100–101
Concepçion, Rosario, 106
Conroy, Paddy, 183
Consultative Committee on Relations with Japan, 121–124
Conybeare, Chris, 243
Coppola, Francis Ford, 109
Cortéz, Hernán, 200
Costa Rica, presenting credentials in, 211–212
Cotton, Bob, 198
Cowan, Sir Zelman, 55, 128
Crean, Simon, 121
Cuba, 213–216
Cuenavaca, 202–203
Cyclone Tracy, 184
Daihatsu Motors, 127
Dalton, Bruce, 243
Danabalan, 143
Darwin, 233
Dasmariñas, 103, 111
Davis, Neil, 132
Davis, Sammy Jr., 215
Democratic Socialist Party, 31
Deng Xiaoping, 120
Derian, Pat, 108
Deveraux, Bob, 136
Devine, Frank, 46
Dingle, Tony, 23
Dixon, Geoff, 234
Djambala, Marawili, 231

Don Muang Airport, Bangkok, 133, 139
Donald, William Henry, 220
Doody, Leith, 171
Downer, Alexander, 194, 218
Du, Madame, 138
Dulles, Allen, 97
Dulles, John Foster, 97, 158
Dunster, Peter and Paul, 182
Dzu, Mr, 138–139
East India Company, 59
Edwards, John, 116
Eiffel, Gustav, 135
Eisenhower, Dwight D., 158
Elliot, John, 174
Elizabeth II, 128–129
Enrile, Juan Ponce, 107
Estrada, Joseph, 114
Evans, Gareth, 214–215
'Exercise Team Spirit', 168
Fall, Bernard, 141
Farah Diba, 87
Fatima, 88, 92
Fernandez, Roy, 68
Figueras Olsen, Jose Maria, 211–213
Fischer, George, 215
Fisher, David, 147
Fitzgerald, John, 171
Flashman, Harry Paget, 59–60
Flood, Philip, 218
Forbes Park, 111
Foreign Policy magazine, 115
Forrester, Geoffrey and Rosemary, 101

INDEX

Fraser, Dawn, 46, 172
Fraser, George McDonald, 59
Fraser, Malcolm, 116, 129, 131
Friedman, Thomas, 235
Fuji, Mount, 32–33, 44
Furflex, 181, 197, 198
General Motors-Holdens, 15
Genders, Alexander Forbes, 17
George, Geoff, 122
German vehicle industry, 43
Giles, Geoffrey, 75
Gillespie, John, 147–148
Gilson, Peter, 147–148
Ginza, 35
Goldner, Viva, 221
Goldston, Peter, 106, 114
Gomez, Federico and Concepçion, 203
Gorton, John Grey, 51, 75
Gosper, Kevan, 171
Gotanda, 34
Greenwood, Trevor, 105–106
Gyngell, Allan, 68–69, 243
Hai, Mrs, 138
Hall, Barry, 83
Handmer, Wally, 68–69
Haneda Airport, 24
Hanoi, 94, 139
Harada, Masahiko, 46
Harris, Stuart, 155
Hartnett, Laurence, 15
Harvard University, 115
Hatanodai 34
Havana, 215–216

Hawke, Robert, 129, 175
Hayden, William, 129, 131, 143, 152, 159, 189, 211
Helu, Alfredo Harp, 206
Hemingway, Ernest, 215
Henderson, Peter, 122, 129–130
Herbert, Michael, 147
Hewitt, Clement Barnett, 243
Hill, David, 175–176, 183–185, 187, 189
Hino plant, 42
Ho Chi Minh, 154
Ho Chi Minh City, 141
Hodge, Errol, 55
Hodge, General John R., 157
Hoffman, Stanley, 115, 116
Hogue, Cavan, 103
Hohler, Adrian, 32
Holden, James Alexander, 14
Holden, Henry, 15
Holt, Harold, 51
Holten, Mack, 75
Howard, John, 105
Hu Jintao, 168
Hughes, Thomas, 60
Hummel, Arthur, 72
Hun Sen, 152–153, 189
Hyslop, Anthea, 202
Hyundai Heavy Industries, 164
Imperial Palace, Tokyo, 26
Inya Lake Hotel Rangoon, 65
Iran nuclear plans, 85–86

Iran Oil Industry, 84–85
Irvine, David, 124
Isuzu plant, 42
Iztaccihuatl, 203
Jackson, Gordon, 121, 122
Jamieson, Cecile, 190, 191, 222
Jamieson, Jim, 28, 160
Japan-Australia trade, 120–121
Japan – gains from Korean War, 159
Japan National Railways, 35
Japan Socialist Party, 31
Japanese bureaucracy, 53
Japanese vehicle industry, 43
Jindabyne, 126–127
Jockel, Gordon, 151
Jones, C. R. (Kim), 53
Kahlo, Frida, 207
Kamaki Satoshi, 43
Karatsu, 33
Kasumigaseki, 31
Katherine, 232–233
Keating, Paul, 192
– and bid for Security Council seat, 217–218
Ken and Yasuko Myer Fellowships, 221
Kennedy, Robert, 51
Keio University, 26
Kent, Jacqueline, 243
Khorramshah, 96
Kim Dae-jung, 159
Kim Hae-ryeung, 163
Kim Hyung-kyu, 163
Kim Il-sung, 157, 158
Kim Young-sam, 159

King Martin Luther, 51
Kinokuniya, 26
Kissinger, Henry, 94
Khomeini, Ayatollah, 97, 120
Komeito, 31
Korea: American bases, 169–171
Korean motor industry, 165–168
Korean War: origins, 156–159
  casualties: 158–159
Koreans, 161
Kortlang, Helen, 136
Kwak, Ki-song, 155
Laughlan, Ken, 68, 69
Lawton, John William Magary, 223
Lee, Mr., driver, 164, 204
Lee Myung-bak, 159
Leyden, Fleur, 221
Liberal Democratic Party, 31
Lilly, James, 169
Lincoln, Ian, 136, 243
Little, Reg, 21, 28, 39
Lollobrigida, Gina, 109
Long Bien Bridge Hanoi, 135
Long, Malcolm, 183, 191
Luhrmann, Baz, 209, 233
Lyons, William, 12
Manalo, Rosario, 106
Manila, 102
Mansfield, Bob, 193–194
Manson, David, 243
Maranouchi, 35
Marcos, Ferdinand E., 107–110, 114

Marcos, Imelda, 107–110, 115
Marcos, Sub-Comandante, 206
Matsuki san, 34
Mazda plant, 42
MacArthur, Douglas, 156, 157
McCarthy, John, 132
McCloy, John J., 156
McCormack, Gavan, 30
McDonald, Hamish, 77–79
McFarland, Lyndell, 221
McIntyre, Sir Lawrence, 28
Mackay, Malcolm, 75–76
McLean, Lyndall, 136
McMahon, William, 94, 95
Meiji period, 30
Melbourne, HMAS, 33
Melbourne Symphony Orchestra, 163
Melchor, Alexandro, 107, 111
Menzies, Sir Robert, 28, 31, 64
Mexico
  – and drugs, 206–207
  – economy, 206
  – lawlessness, 207–208
  – pollution, 204
  – road manners, 209
Mexico City, 203–204
Mike Roddy Motors, 182
Millar, Caroline, 136
Mills, Helen, 183
Mingaladon Airport, 64–65

Mitsubishi, 29, 42
Mitsui, 29
Mole poblano, 203
Morgan, Hugh, 214
Moro National Liberation Front, 107
Morrison, G. E. 'Chinese', 220
Moses, Sir Charles, 54
Mossadegh, Mohammad, 82, 97, 98
Mount Fuji, 38
Mulally, Alan, 235
Mundine, Warren, 231
Mya Aye, 70
Myer Foundation, 221
Myer, Kenneth Baillieu, 121
Myer Report, 53, 121
Napoleon, 150
Nardelli, Robert, 235
Nasser, Gamal Abdel, 62
Nehru, Jawaharlal, 62
Ne Win, 62–64, 70, 73, 77, 79
Newcombe, John, 95
Newman, Jocelyn, 188
Newton, Colonel, 68
Nichol, Charlie, 20
Ninohashi, 26
Nissan plant, 42
Nixon, Richard, 94
Nkrumah, Kwame, 62
Noi Bai Airport, Hanoi, 133–134
Nougarede, Jean François, 66
Nui Dat, 76
Nureyev, Rudolf, 109
Nutter, Gerry, 101, 106, 110, 114, 115, 243

O'Brien, Matt, 191
Ochiltree, Margaret, 22
Olympic Games, Seoul,
    171–174
Pagadian, 106, 113–114
Pahlavi, Mohammad
    Reza Shah, 81–82,
    86–87, 95, 96–97,
    98
Pahlavi, Reza Khan,
    81–82
Panmunjom, 170
Parbo, Arvi, 121, 122
Park Chung-hee, 159
Parker, Richard,
    147–148
Parkinson, Richard, 223
Patterson, Graham, 22
Pearce, Ruth, 213
Pearl, Cyril, 220
Persepolis, 81
Peters, Philip, 28
Phelps, Michael, 173
Philip, Duke of
    Edinburgh,
    128–129
Philippines, 102–115
Philippine road system,
    104
Pohang Iron and Steel,
    165
Pol Pot, 77, 120, 149,
    158, 196
Popacatépetl, 203
'Prague Spring', 51
Pritchard, Geoffrey, 230
Pueblo, 51
Pyongyang, 51
Qajah dynasty, 81
Qantas, troubles with,
    233–235
Radio Australia, 53–55,
    74, 195–196

– budget, 185
– existence, 186
– and Royal
    Australian Navy,
    188
– and Saddam
    Hussein, 188
– sale of East
    Burwood site, 193
– transmitters,
    183–184, 187

Ramirez, Raoul, 95
Ramos, Eddy, 114
Rangoon, 57, 70–71, 77
Reese, David, 83
Renouf, Alan, 62, 101,
    116
Republic of Korea, 159,
Republic of Korea-
    Australia trade,
    159–160
Revill, Stuart, 183
Reyes, Bobby, 111
Rhee, Syngman, 157,
    158,159
Richardson, Graham,
    171, 172
Riley, William, 21
Ringwood, Professor
    Ted, 238
Rivera, Diego, 207
Rivkin, René, 171–172
Rix, Alan, 122
Romulo, Carlos, P., 111
Roo Myo-hun, 159
Roo Tae-woo, 174, 175
Roosevelt, Kermit, 97
Roosevelt, Theodore, 97
Rosado, Alicia, 205, 211
Rose, Lionel, 46
Rudd, Kevin, 123, 124,
    236–237

Ruiz Massieu, Jose
    Francisco 'Pepe',
    206
Rusk, Dean, 156–157
Sachiko-san, 35
Salinas de Gortari,
    Carlos, 201, 205,
    206
Salmon, Charlie, 108
Scoble, Robert, 136
Searcy, Elizabeth, 190,
    191
Searcy, Philip, 190
Seoul, 160–162, 176
Seoul Olympics,
    171–174
Shah's military plans, 85
Shearer, David, 239
Shearer, Ivan, 243
Sheffield, HMS, 129
Sheen, Martin, 109
Shelley, Percy Bysshe, 80
Shibuya, 25, 31
Shimonoseki, 40
Shinjuku, 31
Short, Jim, 28
Shwedagon Pagoda, 68
Sicat, Jerry, 106
Sihanouk, Prince
    Norodom, 153
Sin, Cardinal Jaime,
    107
Sinatra, Frank, 215
Sirocco, 172
Smart, Peter, 66, 90
Smith, David, 128
Snowy Mountains
    Engineering
    Corporation, 70,
    106
Sokka Gakai, 31
Solomon, Barry and
    Darren, 243

Solzhenitsyn, Alexander, 116
Stalin, Joseph, 158
Standing Committee on Japan, 121–124
Stanley, Dr Fiona, 146
Stark, Koo, 129
Stephen, Sir Ninian, 128
Stoltenberg, Jason, 164
Stone, John, 122
Stonehouse, Philip, 136
Street, Tony, 129
Sukarno, 62
Sullivan, Bill, 98
Taisho, Emperor, 30
Tang, Sir Arthur, 54
Tehran, 81, 82–84
Television Australia, 191–193, 194–195
Tenoctitlán, 203–204
Termeil, 191, 222
Tet Offensive, 51, 75
Tetsuan, 34–35
Thach, Nguyen Co, 148–149
Than Shwe, General, 78
Thatcher, Margaret, 120
Tho, Le Duc, 148
Thompson, Peter, 70
Tiffin, Dr Rodney, 186
Tina the cook, 204
Tokyo, 30
Tokyo Olympics, 25, 30, 36
Tomotoshi, Kenzo, 35
Toyo Kogyo plant, 42
Toyota plant, 42, 43
Tranter, Lynn, 243
Truter, Michael, 243
Trotsky, Leon, 207
Uchiyama, Kamonosuke, 41

Ueno Bunka Kaikan, 31
U Nu, 62–63
U Saw, 61–62
U Thant, 62
Vance, Cyrus, 98
Vietcong, 51
Vietnam
– Agent Orange, 146–147
– Australians missing in action, 147–148
– driving licences, 140–141
– end of the war, 145–146
– invasion of Cambodia, 150, 151–152
– military equipment, 137
– Soviet perspective, 150–151
– strategic hamlets, 19
Vietnamese in Australia, 153–154
Vietnamese invasion of Cambodia, 119–120
Visontay, Michael, 243
Vizard, Steve, 178
Voyager, HMAS, 33
Vung Tau, 76
Vuong, Monsieu, 138
Wagoner, Rick, 235
Wakabayashi, Akiko, 39
Wall, Harold, 189
Wang Gung Wu, 121
Watson, Bruce, 121
Webb, Arlene, 126
Webb, Jeremy, 126

Weisser, Rebecca, 215
Wellesley, the Marquis, 59
Whear, Ray, 233
White Australia Policy, 69
White Derek, 191
White H. D., 83, 87, 94
Whitesell, Joe, 179
Whitlam, Gough, 95, 101, 105, 110, 116, 122, 128
Whitlam, Margaret, 110, 128
Wilenski, Peter, 176, 199
Willemsen, Gary, 119, 220
Wingnut, 181
Woodroffe, Alison, 21, 22
Woodroffe, Jack and Mavis, 47
Yamanaka, 38
Yamanote-sen, 35
Yarralumla, 128
Yellow Waters, Northern Territory, 233
Yoshida, Shintaro, 41
Young, Harold, 75
Zapatistas, 206
Zedillo, Ernesto, 206
Zhengrong Shi, 238

www.ingramcontent.com/pod-product-compliance
Lightning Source LLC
Chambersburg PA
CBHW022044290426
44109CB00014B/972